MW00911220

How to Sell Your Software

How to Sell Your Software

Robert Schenot

WILEY

John Wiley & Sons, Inc.

New York • Chichester • Brisbane • Toronto • Singapore

Publisher: Katherine Schowalter
Editor: Tim Ryan
Managing Editor: Maureen B. Drexel
Text Design & Composition: Alexander Graphics

Designations used by companies to distinguish their products are often claimed as trademarks. In all instances where John Wiley & Sons, Inc. is aware of a claim, the product names appear in Initial Capital or all CAPITAL letters. Readers, however, should contact the appropriate companies for more complete information regarding trademarks and registration.

This text is printed on acid-free paper.

Copyright © 1994 Robert Schenot
Published by John Wiley & Sons, Inc.

All rights reserved. Published simultaneously in Canada.

This publication is designed to provide accurate and authoritative information in regard to the subject matter covered. It is sold with the understanding that the publisher is not engaged in rendering legal, accounting, or other professional service. If legal advice or other expert assistance is required, the services of a competent professional person should be sought.

Reproduction or translation of any part of this work beyond that permitted by section 107 or 108 of the 1976 United States Copyright Act without the permission of the copyright owner is unlawful. Requests for permission or further information should be addressed to the Permissions Department, John Wiley & Sons, Inc.

Library of Congress Cataloging-in-Publication Data:

Schenot, Robert, 1949-
  How to sell your software / Robert Schenot.
    p.   cm.
  Includes index.
  ISBN 0-471-06399-1
  1. Selling—Computer programs. 2. Computer software—Marketing.
  I. Title.
  HF5439.C67S347 1995
  005.3'068'8—dc20
                                                          94-29851
                                                          CIP

Printed in the United States of America
10 9 8 7 6 5 4 3 2 1

Contents

Apologies and Acknowledgments

Very few of the ideas in this book are truly original. I think of myself more as a compiler of ideas than as an originator of them. I'd like to thank the many people in the software industry who really do believe in sharing. This book would have been impossible without that idea permeating the industry.

I'd like to thank my wife (and you should too) for taking most of the semicolons out. She also acted as both editor and art director for *The Shareware Book* and as first-pass editor for this edition. She has a wonderful way of applying gentle pressure to problems until I finally do the right thing.

Tim Campbell was instrumental in pointing out that there might be a market for this book. He began "Telling It Like It Is" topics on both CompuServe and GEnie that convinced me there was both a need and lots of resources for a book like this. I was privileged to be the scrivener in the right place at the right time.

I'd like to express my thanks to a number of people who have made valuable contributions to this book: Hans Salvisberg, David Hamel, Jim Samuel, Charles Schell, Bob Falk, Tom Droege, Dan Veaner, Jim Hood, Paul Munoz-Colman, Chris Bowyer, Marjolein Katsma.

Thanks go to my mother-in-law for providing the nightshirts in which this book was written (truly a classic bootstrap project).

Final personal mention goes to my father-in-law, who doesn't understand much of this, shakes his head at what he does understand, and is immensely supportive nevertheless.

Although I'm a publisher based in the United States, I've had great feedback from small software publishers in other countries that has allowed me to include more global references in this edition. If you are from outside the United States, I especially encourage you to contact me through either CompuServe or the Internet. The only way I have of knowing what isn't obvious to you is to have you ask questions. You can find my Email address on the order form for the Software Publisher's Kit at the back of this book.

Last, please ask questions and offer suggestions. If you contact me via Email, I will respond.

!ReadMe.1st

How to Sell Your Software is a revision of *The ShareWare Book*, originally published in May 1992. You may still be able to find it on bulletin boards as file ShareBk1.zip. In addition to expanding the book by about 50 percent and updating the contact information (the copyright office changed its phone number the week after publication of *The ShareWare Book*), the primary focus of the book has changed. . . .

ABOUT THIS BOOK

This is a book about bootstrapping. There aren't many nuts-and-bolts books about starting a software company, and the ones that do exist tend to tell you to start by obtaining $3 million in venture capital, then spend most of it on advertising in major computer magazines. This book is about starting with just your computer, your compiler, whatever space you can steal from your living quarters, and less than $1,000. I think this may be the best way to start your first software company for a number of reasons.

- It's pretty tough to convince someone to give you $3 million—especially if you have no experience or proven product.
- I think the money is more likely to hurt than to help you in the early phases. Money stands in the way of recognizing weaknesses in your marketing approach and allows you to put off dealing with the fundamentals.
- Most software (especially yours) shouldn't be marketed this way anyway.

I hope to save you, the aspiring software publisher, the years it took me to assemble this information. I also think this book will be useful to the small software publisher who has been in business for a while. This book is most appropriate for products that fit somewhere in the middle ground between universal, mass-market software and highly specialized, narrow-market software. This book won't be of much help to you if your product will compete head to head with the office suites offered by Microsoft, Novell, and Lotus or have a potential world market of six customers, each of whom will be willing to pay over a million dollars for it.

On the other hand, if you think you've found a solution to a problem that is shared by a substantial number of people or businesses, then this book is about finding a way to get that solution into the customers' hands and getting paid for it.

A word or two about myself, then a word or two about what I'm trying to accomplish are in order.

I began my career in data processing writing tape sorts in assembler on the third model of the Univac series. Along the way, I learned higher-level languages, earned my master's degree in business, and started my own consulting firm specializing in solving production, inventory, and quality-control problems for manufacturing companies. I also dabbled in writing niche (DOS) applications as a way of dealing with the variability of demand for my consulting services.

Hit by the recession at the end of the 1980s, New England companies experienced a dramatic decrease in their need for consulting services in production control systems. The obvious path was to take my software publishing a bit more seriously and join the ranks of the many successful shareware programmers already out there. No more cold calling; no more dealing with unhappy people; no more marketing. I'd just write a useful program, send it to a couple of the bigger disk vendors and user groups, and the magic of shareware would take care of the rest.

The vision was idyllic. I'd build a house on a lake and spend my days coding, watching the waterfowl, and taking calls from appreciative customers. Every day I'd walk down to the mailbox and pick up the checks. Then I'd enter the names into a database, do a mailmerge to print the labels, and drop off the registration packages on the way to the bank.

I started the way most shareware authors do. I took a program I had written for myself (TimeTrac) and one I had written for my existing client base (PC Canary), fixed up the interfaces a bit, put price tags on them, sent them to a few disk vendors, and waited for the money to start coming in.

It didn't.

I needed a consultant. I *was* a consultant. I got to work. Eventually I came to a number of conclusions:

- Successful software companies don't make money selling their software to new customers. *Profits come from marketing additional products* and services to customers. Acquiring a customer requires spending money to attract them to the goods/services you offer them. Their initial purchases may not offset the money you spent in mailings, phone support, or whatever to attract and acquire them in the first place.

- In general, *there are two fundamentally different ways of acquiring new customers*—direct and indirect. The nature of the market determines which method is more efficient. For most products, direct methods are more cost effective.

- *All software is shareware.* As a software publisher, the sooner you realize this, the sooner you can begin making this fact of life work for you instead of against you. If you don't know what shareware is and how it works, just keep reading.

- *Marketing is more important than programming.* There's a reason that marketing people outnumber technical people by a factor of at least seven to one in large software companies.

- *Market segmentation is critical.* Market segmentation allows you to acquire customers at a much lower cost and then "upsell" them to more sophisticated and expensive products once they have committed to your file layout and user interface.

- One key to making market segmentation work is to develop one software "engine" from which you can quickly and easily *spin off multiple software "products,"* each with a unique name, price point, marketing channel, features list, and visual presentation. The engine remains essentially the same; a configuration table determines the behavior of the software.

- Much like the saying that success is 1 percent inspiration and 99 percent perspiration, *successful software companies are positioned for serendipity.* They remain flexible and open to any new business possibility and try to be in enough places that opportunity knocks on their door.

The purpose of this book is either to dissuade you from the crazy idea that you can earn a living as a small software publisher or to save you months of time on your way to success.

THINGS TO DO RIGHT AWAY

You'll want to do some low-cost things right away that, if put off, could delay your software project later.

- Get connected. You'll never learn everything you need to know on your own. Most software publishers do not compete with you, and most are very willing to share what they know, so long as you are willing to share what you have learned too. For most markets, "getting connected" means either the Internet, CompuServe, or both. Sometimes it also will mean becoming active in a local software entrepreneur's group, if you're lucky enough to be near one. If you choose to order the Software Publisher's Kit offered at the back of the book, you'll receive a coupon that will save you $35 on an introductory subscription to CompuServe.

- Call your library to find out if it has a recent copy of *Data Sources* (a "magazine" published by Ziff-Davis). The last time I looked, *Data Sources* was published in three volumes twice a year, and a subscription cost $500 per year. If it doesn't, find out where you can locate it. Go there with a pocketful of dimes and look up the software category your product will be in. Copy those pages. This will give you a quick take on the major product features, product names already used, and an indication of pricing. If you have trouble locating a copy, the full information is:

Data Sources
Ziff-Davis Publishing Company
20 Brace Road
Cherry Hill, NJ 08034
(609) 354-5000

- Establish a federal trade name for your product. Just getting the forms takes a while. The first step is to get a copy of "Basic Facts About Trademarks" from:

U. S. Department of Commerce
Patent and Trademark Office
Washington, DC 20231
(703) 557-3341

- Request the forms with which to register your copyright (see the copyright section in Chapter 9 for a list) from:

Register of Copyrights
Library Of Congress
Washington, DC 20559
(202) 707-9100

- Start looking for a local accountant and a lawyer.
- If you don't own one already, start shopping for an old clunker computer for disk duplicating and testing of your software in the minimum supported configuration. You'll need both 3.5- (high density; 1.44Mb) and 5.25- (low density; 362Kb) inch disk drives. If you lack either (1.2Mb drives cannot reliably produce 360Kb diskettes), you can purchase reconditioned (half-height) floppy drives from:

ERM Electronic Liquidators
37 Washington Street
Melrose, MA 02176
(800) 776-5865
(617) 662-9363
fax (617) 665-4856

Included with 3.5-inch drive orders is a free faceplate for 3.5-inch drives put into 5-inch bays. The prices and stock numbers are:

Size	Stock #	Price
360Kb 5.25 hh	#FD360	$29
1.2Mb 5.25 hh	#FD1.2	$49
720Kb 3.5 hh	#FD720	$49
1.44Mb 3.5 hh	#FD1.44	$59

ELEMENTS OF SUCCESS

Successful software companies seem to have these things in common:

- They develop a range of products that all target a particular class of customers. As the customers' sophistication grows, they can grow within the product line.
- All of their products are outstanding in meeting the needs of their target users within each range.
- They are aggressive direct marketing companies that specialize in software and use every customer acquisition method that fits their overall marketing strategy.
- As is true of any successful direct marketing company, they understand that their job is to acquire and hold customers who will purchase from them repeatedly.

WHERE WE'RE GOING

The rest of this book is about planning and executing a successful software publishing bootstrap. It will cover:

- Researching your target market
- Defining a product family that will be sold to that target market
- Using diverse marketing channels, products, and price points to add to your installed base
- Planning a strategy for maintaining a mutually beneficial economic relationship with your customers
- Protecting and managing the enterprise as it grows
- Establishing international connections
- Finally, the mechanical details necessary for execution of the plan

CHAPTER 1

Researching Your Market

◆ One of the keys to success is being the first or at least one of the first with packages to fill a niche. One of the best ways to do this is to anticipate the next wave of technology—think of yourself as a surfer who has to paddle furiously to be ready for the next big wave. For instance, you might ask yourself what the impact of inexpensive, portable laptop computers might be in your target market. Or you might consider what your customers could start doing on computer that they previously did manually. If you have chosen a corporate market, start thinking about developing UNIX and networking products.

I once spoke at a user group meeting where a person talked excitedly about a wonderful product he had been developing that would create forms on a laser printer. When I asked him how it differed from FormGen, he admitted he'd never heard of the product. After we looked at the description of FormGen in the *Public Brand Software* catalog, this fellow realized he'd just spent six months duplicating someone else's efforts and would have to spend another year or so just to match the features mentioned in the catalog.

DETERMINING MARKET SIZE

The first step is to determine if there is a market of sufficient size to support a family of commercial products. For the uninitiated, here's a quick word about vertical and horizontal markets. A horizontal market is one where almost everyone could use the product. Word processors, spreadsheets, games, and income tax preparation programs come to mind immediately. A vertical (or niche) market is one where there is a highly defined group potentially interested in the product. People outside the group, by definition, probably won't be interested, no matter how good it is. An ambulance billing system, for instance, is about as vertical as you can get. A diagonal market (I think I just coined the phrase) is a horizontal vertical one; in other words, it is a collection of vertical markets.

TimeTrac, for instance, appeals to attorneys, accountants, architects, consultants, and anyone who has to produce a time or expense report—certainly not everyone, but still a large number. If you check the lists of successful software products, horizontal products lead the list, simply because of the size of the potential market. This is true in all distribution channels. Generally speaking, horizontal markets are dominated by large companies selling sophisticated products at a low price in an environment of intense competition. They can charge lower prices and deliver sophisticated products because of the tremendous volumes involved. Again, generally speaking, vertical markets are served by smaller companies selling less sophisticated products at a much higher price, again because of the difference in potential sales. Typically, there are a small number of competitors in each vertical market.

You are looking for a market large enough to support a company, yet small enough to avoid trying to compete with Quicken, with its massive distribution and its $38 street price. My research suggests that a market of between 250,000 and 5 million potential customers is large enough to support a product while small enough to avoid attracting so much competition that only the largest and most sophisticated competitors survive. As an example, if you were able to manage to gain a 3 percent share of a 250,000 market with average net of $15 per customer, your annual income would be $112,500, enough to support a two-person operation comfortably.

There are a couple of ways to estimate the size of a market. Consider the circulation of almost any magazine. This is a good starting point for guessing at the size of the potential market for a product designed for that population. If a special-interest magazine is sold at the supermarket, there are a lot of people with that common bond. I'm not quite sure what a *Cosmopolitan* or a *Biker's Brides* application might be, but you could probably convince a distributor that there were enough people with that interest to try distributing the product.

The two ways I use to find and check out a market initially are to look at the counts in mailing list catalogs and to check periodical directories that list the circulation of specialty magazines. Chapter 5 supplies names of list brokers. You'll need to confirm that magazines and lists exist for your market, since you will use them both for publicity and as you open new channels.

You'll be able to find the periodical directories and copies of the periodicals themselves at any major library. After you determine what magazines are appropriate, go through them carefully, looking both for advertisements and for the names of writers who write about computer topics. The advertisements may help you find allies or competitors. The writers may be valuable sources or (especially in trade magazines) competitors in disguise.

Reference works that list periodicals and their circulations include:

Gale Directory of Publications and Broadcast Media
Gale Research
835 Penobscot Building
Detroit, MI 48226

Ulrich's International Periodicals Directory
R.R. Bowker/Reed Publishing
121 Chanlon Road
New Providence, NJ 07974

Standard Rates & Data's Business Publications
Standard Rates & Data's Consumer Agr-media
3004 Glenview Road
Wilmette, IL 60091

Newspaper/Magazine Directory
(formerly Bacon's Publicity Checker)
Bacon's Information, Inc.
332 S. Michigan Avenue
Chicago, IL 60604

Writer's Market
Writer's Digest Books
I&W Publications
1507 Dena Avenue
Cincinnati, OH 45207

National Directory of Magazines
Standard Periodical Directory
Oxbridge Communications
(800) 955-0231
(212) 741-0231

Remember, you are not looking for *PC World*—you are looking for *Ambulance Corps Management* (or the corresponding periodical for your selected market). Another useful way to gather information is to call the advertising department of a magazine and ask for a media kit. This will include a great deal of information not only about how many people read the magazine but also something (occupation, age, income, etc.) about them. Some kits even include the percentage of households owning a computer.

RESEARCHING THE COMPETITION

It's more complicated than this, of course, but you want to be either *better* or *different* than your competition (preferably both). If you're not, your only other alternative is to be cheaper, which is almost never a successful strategy in software.

In order to do this, you need to find out all you can about your potential competition. Besides learning what you can from *Data Sources*, you'll want to check any other directories you can find (a list is included in the publicity section, Chapter 7), and review as many shareware catalogs as you can. The Software Publisher's Kit includes a catalog of products published by the members of the Association of Shareware Professionals (ASP).

"YADS" stands for "Yet Another DOS Shell." Distributors don't even bother taking them out of the package anymore. If you are planning to develop a me-too product, you'll be violating a basic rule for success in software:

> It doesn't matter how good your program is if the field is already crowded. On any one platform, software vendors rarely earn market share; they take advantage of a situation where another publisher has thrown it away.

Request demo copies and brochures for the shelfware products that serve your market. (Shelfware is software that sits on a shelf until it is sold, a product designed for indirect channels.) Buy copies of the better ones if you can afford it. Next, get copies of all the shareware products that serve your market. If PsL (see the shareware section in Chapter 4 to learn about PsL) publishes a megadisk collection, that's probably both a great way to get copies of everything cheaply and a warning that this niche is already saturated. You may be able to spot some products sold through both shelfware and direct channels, under either the same name or totally different names.

You are attempting to *survey the market* at this time, not evaluate products. Put together a simple matrix, listing products with their attributes. A reasonable attribute list might include:

- Company name. It would seem simple, but this is sometimes complicated. 4DOS, a very popular shareware product of JP Software, is also marketed by Symatec (Norton) as NDOS.
- Product name. Again, spotting duplicates and derivative works may be difficult.
- Street price. The price a customer will probably actually pay. For shelfware, this is likely to be somewhere around 65 percent or less of the listed price.
- Target market. To whom is this product sold? While Visual Basic and assembler are both programming languages, they hardly compete with each other.
- Distribution channels. These might include any combination of shareware, mail order, trade catalogs, outside salespeople, value-added resellers (VARS; people who assemble hardware and software components into systems), specialty stores, large software stores, and general computer stores.
- Differentiation. The major points of differentiation are the unique attributes that might cause a buyer to choose one product

over another. Being a Windows application is an obvious one; others might be special features not ordinarily found in this class of software. For instance, TimeTrac offers the ability to track nested interruptions. If you want this particular feature, only TimeTrac offers it. Differentiation features are almost always advertised in bold print or at the beginning of the features list.

Now it's time to *define your niche.* If you can't express in a slogan how you are going to be different from the existing products, you don't have a unique product idea. If you can connect a slogan, a mailing list, and a periodical, you have a good beginning.

If you've discovered the Holy Grail of software marketing, a niche that isn't currently served, go for it! More likely, you're going to have to find some cracks in the market between existing products and fight to hold your territory.

Follow the MAP philosophy—MAP stands for *m*oney, *a*uthority, and *p*ain. When I first started out as a consultant, I naively assumed that people and companies took actions because it was in their best interests—that they bought benefits. After having very little success in marketing, I read a couple of books and took the basic sales course IBM offered to its business partners. It was there I learned the truth—people respond much more quickly to pain than they do to any possible future benefit. If they don't have the authority to make a decision, they have to inflict pain on the decision maker in order for action to be taken. (Secondhand pain is much less effective than firsthand pain.) Finally, if there's no money available, nothing will happen.

The educational market is a good example of this phenomenon. While teachers may be very enthusiastic about software, classroom-oriented software is rarely purchased, simply because teachers almost never have the authority to spend the school department's money. The school board, on the other hand, doesn't purchase one copy per machine as the license requires, even when a teacher requests that they do, because the consequences of not paying for software are perceived as being much less painful than not paying for other things, say new team jackets.

If you don't have MAP, you don't have a market. Include a concise and vivid description of the pain and the cure, the target decision maker and the financial resources of your typical buyer as a starting point of your product description and your marketing literature.

If your product idea has survived this far, do a thorough analysis of each of your competitors, starting with a definition of their target markets. There is no such thing as a "best" program. Each product will be best at solving a different problem and will have a different target market.

At this point you'll need to start *making contacts* in your target market. Most beginning publishers already have some. A way to get more is by becoming active in the trade groups specializing in that market. You'll find many of them in the:

Encyclopedia of Associations
Gale Research
835 Penobscot Building
Detroit, MI 48226

Decide if your goals eventually will include international sales. Even publishers who offer only English language versions report a quarter of their sales come from overseas. Decide if your product will be designed for eventual translation. If you do want to hold open the possibility of eventual foreign distribution, be sure to read Chapter 12 before writing any code.

Finally, plan a follow-on family of products appealing to the same market. Strength and profits in the software market come from follow-on sales, either as upgrades to existing products or new products needed by existing customers. If you can't define a family, think twice before you start on the first product.

WHAT'S HOT

• *Sex.* Sex is very hot. Just ask any BBS sysop bulletin board operator. I'm not quite sure what to do with this information, but I suspect that if someone were to produce a series of games a little raunchier than Leisure Suit Larry, he'd have a runaway hit. Another possibility might be a fantasy role-playing game. Just think of the possibilities for additional products!

• *Windows* is hot. Whatever the reason, a large proportion of new users are being brought in via Windows. Since the market is so new, sales are high (people who have had a computer for a couple of years rarely buy new software), and the competition is low. Producing a Windows version of an existing DOS product before the original developer does can be a successful strategy.

• *Local Area Networks* are proliferating. A LAN version of a program may be chosen simply because it is the only product in its category that can work on a company's LAN.

• *Graphical games.* Games are one of the few categories where people generally want more than one product and "wear out" software. Good games take a great deal of time and skill to write, and are a bear to debug. Games are a truly horizontal product where the market can never be thoroughly saturated. On the other hand, games have shorter lives than many other products.

• *Educational software.* There's always lots of talk about software for educational settings, especially as more schools and families acquire computers. But the unfortunate fact remains that teachers don't have the authority to buy, and they can't afford to take the money out of their own pockets. Most parents are unwilling to spend serious money on software for the kids. I have not yet heard of a satisfactory solution to the getting-paid problem for this market. Now, if you can find a way to reach the grandparents, you have a shot at making a sale. (They'll probably buy for the wrong platform, and then you'll have support problems.)

WHAT'S NOT

• *Amiga, Apple II, Macintosh.* They're all fine machines, but there simply aren't enough of them. By and large, these markets tend to be dominated by products that have been ported from other (Windows) platforms.

• *OS/2.* Software developers love it. No one else seems to use it. With the possible exception of software development tool sets, you're probably better off developing for Windows. If you can get an OS/2 version out simply by running another compile, go ahead and do it; otherwise, the market is spread too thin.

• *Text-only adventure games.* People have come to expect graphics and mouse support. If you can't approach Sierra's level of quality, you'll never compete with its low street price.

- *New competition* for entrenched products. It is almost impossible to get a distributor to change products, even if yours really is better.

There is an enormous amount of inertia in most marketplaces. Software is especially prone to this. Most of us can think of major software packages with tremendous market share even though there are better and cheaper products available. Being the first with a credible package in a specific market segment seems to be the key. After that, market share is yours to lose. The desire to be the first is part of the reason why large software companies were aggressively developing Windows applications early, even when the Windows installed-and-used base was less than 10 percent of all PCs.

The Software Publisher's Association reports that the 1993 market was split 51 percent for Windows products, 28 percent for DOS products, 16 percent for Macintosh products, and 3 percent for all other platforms combined.

DOS appears to be dying quickly. The Association also reports that while the Windows market in 1993 grew by 80 percent, the DOS marketplace shrank by 26 percent. Only in entertainment and home education did the DOS market grow at all, while in the Windows marketplace, database, home education, finance, productivity, and integrated applications each had over 100 percent growth for the year.

Therefore, given a choice of products to develop, you should choose the one that doesn't exist yet on your platform but still has a broad potential market. One way to find new product ideas is to watch for emerging new technology. The year the PC/XT was introduced, I was involved in producing a tax package. This package needed 6Mb of disk storage in order to run. Needless to say, I was among the first to solve that particular problem on a DOS platform, since the technology necessary for the application was just becoming available.

More recently, I noted that laptop computers were dropping in price and gaining in popularity. Part of the reason I developed TimeTrac was because the laptop computer made a time and expense logging system for professionals truly feasible for a large market for the first time.

To summarize, the more successful software packages are:

- The *first* (or nearly so) program to address the problem in the software market. Subsequent products will have to be much better in order to displace them.
- Horizontal (or at least *mainstream*) products that appeal to a very large proportion of all potential users.
- *Comprehensive*. If a feature table of all programs of the same type were produced, this family of programs would have covered the most features.
- *Intuitive*. The program has been tested with many new users, their false keystrokes have been recorded and then alias keys or help messages developed, then the program has been retested. The developer knows through testing that both a novice and an experienced computer user new to this package can use the program successfully without reading the manual.
- Part of a *family* of products. When customers register a product, more products are available for sale to them.
- *Updated* constantly. It has been proven statistically that more than two-thirds of the user base sends in money for updates about once a year.
- *Flexible* in their resource requirements. They will generally run on the minimum configuration for their platform.

CHAPTER 2

Product Development

◆◆ Once you've figured out to whom you're going to sell this
product and how you're going to segment your market,
it's time to begin getting more specific about what your
product is actually going to do and how it's going to do it. This
book is not meant to be any kind of primer on systems
development. All I'll try to contribute here are a couple of pointers
I discovered in developing mass market (as opposed to semi-
custom) software.

DOCUMENTATION

In this book, I discuss documentation before design because I
believe that documentation bridges the research and the development phases of overall product development. To some extent, you
want to produce the user's manual and then code, using the
manual as your specifications. Doing so will result in a program
that is closer to the vision developed in the research phase and that
presents itself to the user in a way that makes sense.

If you are new to the business of creating your own documentation, try studying the formats of manuals you consider well
designed and easy to follow. Make a list of the characteristics you
think contribute to their successful presentation. Consider the
practical aspects of layout and design as well as the style and
substance of the writing. Try to apply these positive attributes to
your own work.

Before you write your first word, consider who will be reading
it. He may be an absolute beginner; she may be a computer

professional. You must document your program so it is understandable to the novice without being condescending to the sophisticated user. This applies to help messages and other on-screen information as well as the user's manual.

If you know someone with a superb sense of punctuation, spelling, and grammar, with communication skills to match, do what you must to engage this person as your editor. The less this person knows about computers in general and your program in particular, the better. Then write your manual in the friendliest, most straightforward way you know how. Give your editor a hard copy and a red pencil. Promise you will not weep audibly when you see your participles undangled, your most brilliant passages rewritten, and entire paragraphs deleted.

If you can, structure your documentation so each subject or chapter flows from an extreme novice level on to the expert. This lets experts skip the things they already know ("what is a batch file?") and go on to the information they need ("command line switches"), while at the same time providing novices with the information they need in order to solve their problems You might even consider using some kind of notation so people know where to start reading. (Occasionally I have fantasies of using green dots, blue squares, and black diamonds, the symbols used to label easy, intermediate, and expert ski trails. For now I'll stick to character-based monochrome manuals.) Do go into excruciating detail about the basics: For novice users, you are giving them what they really need; for experienced users, the size of your manual alone may turn out to be the determining factor in making the sale.

Everybody has his or her own idea of what should be in the documentation, and in what order. My list includes:

Benefits must be clearly cited. If I have to search to find out what this thing does and how it will make my life better, I'm unlikely to continue.

Even the least experienced user wants to start up the program and hit a few keys before getting too far into the manual. Describe the *installation* procedure in simple, sequential terms. Remember: If they can't run it, they won't buy it. A nice touch is to offer an install program that does everything interactively, or to offer to print out the instructions if your program discovers it has not been installed properly.

Deinstallation may be as important to sophisticated users, especially if you are selling through the shareware channel. Given a choice, I heavily favor those products that I know I can remove when I no longer need them. This ability to truly remove a product from the hard disk (as opposed to removing just the Windows icon) may be especially important in shareware, demo copies, low-cost software, and software that solves temporary problems.

Program your software to start the first dozen times with a Welcome screen. Besides setting the tone, this screen can offer to print out a *Quick Start* for new users. Ideally confined to a single piece of paper, a Quick Start should outline in clear, nontechnical language the basic operations and associated keystrokes a person needs to run the program at its most rudimentary level.

Include *introductory material* for new users at the beginning of the manual. More experienced users should be able to pass over this material without missing anything essential. Again, keep your language clear and nontechnical. Present a general overview of what your product is and can do. Go on to describe the program's basic operations. If you choose to write your introductory chapters like a tutorial, set up a series of problems to be solved and provide sample data and/or templates where appropriate. New users will learn your program more successfully if they can be "walked through" basic operations in a step-by-step manner, each step building on learning gained in the previous step.

Save references to DOS commands for later chapters, where you can at least direct new users to a DOS manual should the need arise.

Next comes the *essential information* section, which contains exactly that. It is a collection of the few facts essential to running the application properly. For instance, in a communications package, you might list the equipment needed and the default settings and give an overview of a typical session.

The *main functions* section is where the bulk of the information about using the program is presented. I include information most users will need at one time or another.

Configuration information comes next. Here I give information about navigating the configuration menus and discuss the implications of selecting one option over another.

The *license* and warranty come next.

I include a section on *support*. Besides answering the question of how to get support, I also try to help users be prepared with the information I'll need in order to help them.

Next I present a list of *system files.* I include a table with a short description and columns showing size, which ones are shipped with the package, which ones are created by the application, and which ones are required for execution.

For Windows products, your customers will appreciate a *list of files and the subdirectories* they normally appear in as well as any changes to system files (such as Win.ini). They also may be much more likely to try a program if they know that they have the information necessary to deinstall it if they need to.

Technical notes come next. Here I put in all the details most people won't need—such things as compatibility with other software, network setup, memory and operating system requirements, and so on.

Consider adding a *glossary.* To assemble it, use a small spell checker with no personal dictionary attached. Go through the documentation and try to replace anything the spell checker doesn't recognize with a word or phrase that it does know. If you can't reasonably do this, the word in question belongs in a glossary.

When I hear the same question a couple of times, I consider adding an entry to my *Frequently Asked Questions* section.

On the back cover of the manual, and on a tear-off card (the back cover is wider than the front and is folded back into the book), I put a *command summary.* People like the convenience of the card, but they always lose it. When that happens, they can photocopy the back cover to make a new one. You also might put on a menu the option of printing out a Quick Reference sheet listing a terse command summary.

Here is my personal checklist of dos and don'ts for documentation:

• *Consistency is important.* Try to use the same style and tense. Be consistent in how you use different paragraph types; the same shape should always mean approximately the same thing. A sloppily laid-out manual is confusing as well as unattractive.

- *Create examples* to illustrate hard-to-describe concepts. Sample data and tutorials are extremely useful. Offer plenty of "for instances."

- *Use an active*, not passive *voice*. "Press the F1 key" is much more understandable and authoritative than "The F1 key should be pressed."

- Consider your customer's level of proficiency, and *break things into the smallest steps possible.* For instance, if beginners are likely to use your software, don't simply write "insert the diskette." Say something like:

> Remove the paper envelope covering the diskette, if there is one.
> Hold the diskette by the side opposite from the oval opening and so that your thumb is on the label.
> Find the diskette slot in the front of your computer. If the little flipper is turned so it blocks the slot, flip it parallel to the slot. Some computers have a button at the diskette slot instead of a flipper. Push the button to eject any diskette already in the slot.
> If a diskette is already in the slot, remove it.
> Slide the diskette into the slot so the label faces the flipper.

... And so on. (It's incredibly tedious, I know, but wouldn't you rather write it once than say it over and over on the phone?)

- Do a global edit to *remove every occurrence of the word "that,"* then proof again. You'll replace only half of them.

- *Keep logical blocks short.* It's amazing how programmers who really believe in structure for their programming throw those concepts away when they write documentation. You can use the same principles in organizing and writing documentation.

- Use writer's software to *check spelling, grammar, and reading level.* Write at a sixth-grade level, if possible. Then put a good editor to work. Nothing beats human intelligence for picking up on stuff that slips through writer's software.

- The layout and design of your hard-copy manual should not resemble a novel, one solid block of text following another. Plan your pages in an outline format, with ample white space between and to the sides of your paragraphs. Contrary to being a waste of paper, white space lets you scan material for headings and key words, and leaves room for handwritten notes in the margins. *Indenting paragraphs* is an effective way to create white space on a page. This list is an example: The paragraphs are indented from the main body of text and bulleted, creating a margin of white space on the left.

- Use **bold type,** underlining, and *italics* sparingly—think of them as seasonings. If you fill a page with these special characters, they'll undermine their own usefulness through sheer clutter. The same rule applies to the use of fonts and typefaces.

- Allowing the user to access documentation from inside the program has been well received. *Give the user a string search capability*—it really empowers them and cuts down on support calls.

- *Consistency in your language is also essential* for novice users. Spell out any acronym you use the first time and pair it with the acronym itself—that is, "CRT, or cathode ray tube"—so a string search will reveal the definition to a questioning user. String searches are not successful if you merely bold initial caps ("Cathode **R**ay **T**ube") when you define the term. Where synonyms abound, decide which word you are going to use. Is it the "manual," "user guide," "program reference," "documen-tation," or "book"? Being absolutely consistent will help in string searches and also limit the new vocabulary customers must learn in order to use your product.

- *Update and test your documentation* with each release. You'll be amazed at your own assumptions. Watch people try to use the documentation, then fix the weak spots. Ask for feedback on your registration form.

One company will write the user documentation for shareware packages without charge to you. It earns its money by selling its manuals about your program to your users. For information, contact:

McBride Technical Services
31 Longa Road
Merrimack, NH 03054
(603) 424-5823

SOFTWARE DESIGN

If you have never written widely distributed PC software before, I will warn you that the "PC standard" isn't. Things as simple as screen colors sometimes become gnarly problems. The vast majority of bugs I've had to correct dealt with specific hardware/software configurations. Since I generally didn't own or have access to these configurations, debugging occasionally has been very difficult. In your programming, keep it simple if at all possible, and don't assume anything.

Mimic the interface of the software your potential users already know. If your customers are likely to be users of Microsoft applications products, they'll be familiar with pull-down menus. If you are marketing a WordPerfect add-on package, make sure that your function keys match WordPerfect's. This is especially important when selling software to corporations, which are very concerned about training costs and getting people productive quickly. You might even consider offering a choice of interface types in your configuration menu.

Control of color and sound belong in the configuration menu. I prefer three levels of sound: all, emergency only, and none.

Installation

I use LHA as my DOS installation program—it's free and it provides a self-extractor from a very compressed form. A copy of LHA is included in the Software Publisher's Kit advertised in the back of the book. LHA will self-extract to a specific directory (creating it if necessary) or to the current directory. While it can be used as a Windows installer, there are better products available for this task. A good way to approach the problem of installation is to look at many install routines, especially in products designed for novices, then copy the ideas that are appropriate to your product.

For DOS:

Whatever you do, don't change config.sys or autoexec.bat (or anything else, for that matter) without asking permission and backing up the old files. By the way, according to software publisher George Abbot (ProDev), some Tandy machines don't even look at config.sys on disk; they work from a copy in EProm and require a proprietary program to modify it. If you can, program so your application will run on a machine with no autoexec.bat or config.sys. Close and open files as necessary to avoid the need for files or buffers statements. In the long run, doing so will be much less work and will result in more people being able to use your product.

For Windows:

Be very consistent in using the first four characters of your product's name in any file names or variables. In this way users can hope to find the changes you made to the Windows files you changed.

Put everything you can in a separate subdirectory so that things can be deleted as necessary.

Advertise the fact that the product can be cleanly deinstalled. Deinstallation is beginning to become a real issue for people who have been using Windows for a while.

Show benefits (not features) as a part of the de-archiver's introductory screen (also in the read.me or .doc file and the Welcome screen). Have the de-archiver display your product name and key differentiation points.

First Impressions

Your product's initial screens should be both attractive and professional-looking while providing critical information.

Consider a bright yellow or white on blue or black color setting as your default. These color combinations are visible on color, LED, and monochrome displays. Make the ability to change the screen color easy to find so that if the screen is not very readable, users can change it without switching computers. You're supposed to be able to tell what kind of monitor is being used by interrogating memory, but in my experience most laptop LCD displays say they are color VGA monitors.

Test your product for user-friendliness. Your market will probably include confused first-timers as well as experienced users. While most programmers consider their products' operation intuitive, the fact remains that "user-friendly" is a term referring to whether you guessed right about someone else's intuition. Only by watching many people try to install and use your program without any help from you (try setting up a video camera and walking away) can you make those first critical minutes more likely to be successful.

Make many keys invisible aliases (that is, tab and return complete a record; page down, down arrow, and the + key all go "forward"). If you don't employ numbers in the program, the 3 key could perform a page down no matter what the setting of the number lock. If somebody wants to hit the Enter key to page down, that's fine.

Depending on the nature of your program, sample data and/or templates can go a long way in helping prospective customers see how your application can help them with their problem. You may choose to preload the program with this data, offer it in a tutorial or walk-through, or offer it as a separate data file that can be loaded at will.

Product Complexity

Complexity is a double-edged sword. It is good in that you may gain sales if you offer many features.

On the other hand, every additional feature adds to the confusion a new potential customer experiences, possibly resulting in lost sales. Every option also adds to your support costs and potential bug list as well as to the complexity of testing.

The best solution seems to be to design your program so that any possibly confusing features are turned off when the application is first installed. Hide your configuration options behind a menu or function key so as not to confront customers with options right away. Allow customers to turn on options as they discover the need for them.

Make your first release relatively spartan. Doing so will help you find out if there really is a market and what features your market really wants. Once released, a feature is almost impossible to discontinue in future releases.

If you can, design your application so users never need to know a file name. If you can't avoid that (for example, if your product is a word processor), provide default names and give users access to the disk directory.

Don't abort. Trap error messages and allow users to decide. If you have to abort, save the data first. If in doubt about its integrity, save it in an alternate file name. Do data saves automatically at critical points. When users lose data (even if they did do a global delete), it's your fault, not theirs.

Conventions and Standards

Absolutely, positively, and at *any* time:

• **The** Enter **key (or** Return **key) should always do something,** even if it has to say "Leave me alone, I'm working."

• **The** F1 **key should always give some form of context-sensitive help,** even if it has to admit it's confused.

• Any time you are doing something other than listening for the next keystroke, **display what you are doing** and your progress on-screen so users know the system isn't "frozen." Doing so also will be helpful to you in debugging. Without this feature, users might report that your word processing program "just locked up" while they were reading the screen. If you were doing background pagination, automatic save to disk, or reorganization of memory at the time and had discreetly indicated that in a corner of the screen, you'd have a better idea of what to look for.

• **If the same key is used in error repeatedly, give a context-sensitive help message** rather than a beep. For example, if an operator hits the PageDown key more than once when this key is not valid, show a screen with the valid keys listed and perhaps a reason why that key isn't valid at that time. Even better, make the key do something, even if some other key is the primary key defined as performing that function.

• **The** Esc **key should always "pop up" one level**, and perhaps exit from the top level. If it doesn't, it should pop a window that shows clear directions to return.

• **In Windows, the** Alt+F4 **key combination should pop up one level**; you might even want to have the Esc key do the same thing for those of us who grew up with DOS. Be sure that you don't disable Alt+Tab switching (as a product I evaluated last week did).

If you don't do these things, people will say your program locked up, even if the "correct" key combinations were staring them in the face.

Other rules:

• Function **key and** Alt **key combinations should always mean the same thing**; that is, if F3 means recalc, don't use any F3 derivative in any submodule for anything else.

• **Use the** Shift **key to mean "super"**; that is, if F3 means recalc, then S/F3 should mean global recalc.

• **Don't use** F11 **and** F12. There are too many XT and foreign keyboards out there.

• **Allow users to toggle between insert and overlay mode using the Insert key**. Use cursor size to provide a visual clue as to which mode they're in.

• **Be consistent**. If possible, be consistent with the Microsoft applications software user interface (it is becoming a de facto standard) or the market leader program most likely to be used by your customers. In any case, be internally consistent. Never change meaning for a function key. Decide, for instance, if the Esc key will or won't ask "Are you sure?" and stick to it.

• **Always provide feedback**. As soon as users hit a key, do something on the screen so they know you're working on it.

• **Provide an easy and consistent way to back out of anything**. If you can't back out of changes, save a snapshot as the application boots and allow users to return to their status at the beginning of the session.

• **Help should be context-sensitive**. Ideally, the manual should be available from inside the application; I use a second hit of the help key. In TimeTrac, a first hit of F1 gives context-sensitive help, a second brings up the manual at the place customers last looked at it, and the next hit brings them back to the application screen they left. This allows toggling with a single key to compare the input screen, help message, and manual. The ultimate would be to know what page is associated with which input—that is, to take users right to the correct page immediately. If you do make the manual available from inside the application, remember your place: Don't force multiple page-downs each time users toggle between the application and the manual.

Pull-down menus are more popular than hint bars, even in those situations where they are less effective. For those of us who tire quickly of multiple key combinations for frequently used functions, please do include "shortcut" keys in both the pull-down menu and in the command summary.

If you use normal menus, you might want to give users a choice of using numbers, letters, cursor keys, or a mouse. Using this method, the accountant who is most comfortable with a number pad can use it to press the 5 for inventory, while the clerk who likes the keyboard can press the I key. The manager can use the mouse, and the consultant can use the arrow keys to place the cursor and select an option.

Don't allow your menus to be too busy, but at the same time try to avoid going more than three deep.

While we're on the subject of menus, many users simply don't know how to copy a file to diskette, much less figure out which files comprise a system. If you want your happy customers to pass a copy on, have "make a copy of this program for a friend" a part of your menu. Allow them to select the drive, then check to see if there is a blank, formatted diskette before they begin.

You will probably want to have an exit screen ("Thank you for ..."). If your program encounters a fatal error, the last screen may be an abort message. In my early releases, I forgot that many people use DOS shells. The exit screen and abort screens just flashed before the customers' eyes before being erased by their

DOS shells. I found out when a customer called for support and it became obvious that he couldn't see the abort message. If your exit screen message is important, either hold for "any key" or wait a couple of seconds before returning to DOS.

• If you do develop for DOS/Windows, ask for a free subscription to the *Microsoft Developer Network News*:

Microsoft Developer Network
P.O. Box 10296
Des Moines, IA 50336
Internet: msdn@microsoft.com
CompuServe: >INTERNET:msdn@microsoft.com
voice: (800) 759-5474

Intellectual Property

Be sure to display intellectual property messages (see the legal section, Chapter 9) every time the program is run. Equally important, hide the text of this message within your executable to discourage hacking. You might want to use a simple algorithm to decode the text from an encrypted string to displayable text, or hold the text in a numeric table that translates to your message. Secondarily, to add one more layer and to make the executable smaller, use LZEXE or PKLite to compress the executable; a copy of LZEXE comes with the Software Publisher's Kit.

Integrity

As a first defense against hacking, and as a partial defense against virus infection, it makes sense to build some rudimentary integrity checking into your program. I use a module that tells me the name of the program (in case someone renamed it), its location (drive and subdirectory), size, and creation date and time. Briefly, here's the logic for DOS:

• Use interrupt 21/62 to get the program segment prefix (PSP).
• Using the PSP, get the drive, path and name of the program.
• Use interrupt 21/4e to get the file length and date/time.

In addition, you may want to open the program as a file and check its contents against a known result. This is not the place to describe the theory of checksums; you may wish to use a checksum or a simple algorithm. You are looking for two possibilities—a hack job (altering your intellectual property notices, inserting a Trojan, or similar things) or a virus.

In essence, a virus has to intercept a jump, insert some code, then jump back to where the program logic was going in the first place. Most viruses are not smart enough to parse a whole program; they grab the first jump they can see. They may insert their code at the back, but the smart ones insert it in "empty" space. (Some exists in almost all compiled programs.) The easy way to do some basic integrity checking for viral infections is just to examine the first thousand bytes (either a checksum or an actual byte-by-byte compare) to look for the jump. If you want to be complete, you will have to compare length and byte-for-byte for the whole program. This method will not protect against a stealth virus. You'll have to manipulate the hardware directly for that, if you feel it's appropriate.

A hack job is generally harder to protect against, since the person doing the work has a chance to test against your defenses. Mostly, you want to find a way to detect changes but delay showing that the changes have been detected. This helps extend the test cycle for hackers and makes their job much more difficult.

Whatever you do, don't document any of your protective measures. First, it makes you a target. Second, it may create a legal liability: If you say your program is protected against viruses and hack jobs, a person who relied on that information might come after you legally if your defenses fail. In general, it's better just to show the message "Program damaged, do not use" or "Error 4905; aborting; call support" if you detect changes.

Testing

I do much of my DOS testing on a PC XT clone running a monochrome monitor, DOS 2.2, and no config.sys or autoexec.bat at 4.77 Mhz. You might want to pick up a similar machine and run it the same way. A used XT can be had for under $400 and offers a couple of advantages:

- It is slow. This isn't a bug, it's a feature. Watching your program run at this speed, you'll notice all the little places where loops can be tightened up and file access can be improved.

- It's the machine a significant portion of your customer base will be using. If your application won't run on this kind of machine, you want to know this before you ship it to vendors.

- It's a great machine to use for communications. I get up in the morning, have the slow machine call up CompuServe, and pretty much ignore it while it runs. Meanwhile, on the development machine, I can get some work done.

- It's a good virus buffer. While I do scan things prior to allowing them onto the XT, my serious security starts when something moves from the XT to the development machine.

- That early monochrome screen will give you an idea of what your program will really look like to many people using it. I "tune" my video defaults to make the program look decent on both screens. As I mentioned earlier, interrogating memory about the type of video monitor is not reliable. Many people have after-market boards installed that lie, and many laptops will report a color screen, even though it isn't attached.

- Disk formats and copies work at the same speed on either machine. Again, you can get some work done while performing these tasks.

If you don't have a low-end machine in your attic and can't find one locally, you can call a broker of used equipment. The one I use is:

The Boston Computer Exchange
55 Temple Place
P.O. Box 1177
Boston, MA 02103
(617) 542-4414
(800) 262-6399

I teach part time at a couple of local colleges, so I know the instructors who teach the data processing courses. When they get to a part of their course involving testing, I'll often get a call asking if I've got anything their students can bang on. This is a great deal for all of us: The students get a real sense of what testing and systems development is all about, and I get to read their papers—which frequently reveal bugs that have been in the software for three releases. I recommend contacting data processing instructors near you to offer them a similar arrangement for alpha testing.

Beta testing really is necessary, even though it feels like a mandatory delay between you and cash flow. Once distributors have rejected you because they found bugs, or pull your program because of customer complaints, getting a second chance is extraordinarily difficult. I prefer to use a base of about twelve testers and try to have a mix of user experience, machine type, and DOS level. With smaller numbers, the nonperforming testers will leave you with an inadequate test. I find that half the new testers don't produce useful and reliable information. Testers I've used happily in the past tend to stay good. A number much higher than twelve yields more work without much more information.

Many authors have only an informal agreement with their beta testers. "Give me some feedback, and I'll give you a licensed copy when I'm done." I use a semiformal "letter of understanding" with my beta testers because it helps avoid misunderstandings and greatly increases the quality and quantity of feedback I get.

There's a copy of a letter I used on pages 28 and 29.

Don'ts:

• Don't assume that people will read documentation. Test your program with people who are not familiar with it and who have no documentation. If customers can't figure out how to do the basic functions without reading the documentation, they'll never become users.

• Don't use graphics unless you are designing for a graphics environment. If you are planning on international distribution, graphics include the ASCII "box characters": They display differently in different countries.

• Don't use coprocessor code. Most people don't have coprocessors, and don't know they don't have them. Write DOS products for the 8088, and test on an 8088. Buy one if you have to.

- Don't restrict yourself to a single type of printer unless you're writing a printer utility.

- Don't require a hard disk or a disk greater than 362Kb if you can help it. It's amazing how many people still have floppy-based systems. If possible, don't even assume two drives.

- Don't make any assumptions about drive lettering, especially about the existence of a drive A, or that drive C is the primary hard drive.

- Don't hard-code a directory name into the program.

- Don't allow your program to create files all over the disk unless you're writing something like a word processor. For normal business programs, have the program use the PSP to determine the "home" directory and create your configuration file and data files in that directory.

- Don't assume your users know anything about DOS. Many programs are installed by a "guru" but run by a novice. Many new Windows users have never seen a DOS prompt.

- Avoid writing printer drivers. There are just too many different printers and new ones are being introduced constantly. For most applications, it's even a good idea to avoid sending "standard" printer control codes. Many printers do not support the basic IBM control code set. At the same time, minimum printer support probably includes the following:

   Allow user selection of printing to Lpt1 through 4, Com1 and 2, and a disk file.

   Assume there are a maximum of 80 characters per line and 55 lines per page unless the customer selects other values.

   Use an ASCII 12 to form feed (rather than counting lines). End each line with both a carriage return (10) and a line feed (13).

   Allow your customers to select a default left-hand margin (assuming their printers are capable of printing more than 80 characters per line), page length (this varies by both type of printer and country), and number of lines for the top margin.

   Allow your customers to specify a set of control codes to be sent to the printer both before and after a report is printed. If you choose to support the more popular printers, have customers pick printers from a menu but be sure to let them

>>date<<

>>inside address<<

Thank you for agreeing to help beta test 1040Trac. Enclosed you will find a second copy of this letter, a single page of preliminary documentation, and a diskette containing a self-extracting archive of 1040Trac (1T92b07.exe) as well as an evaluation copy of TimeTrac (there was room on the disk, so I thought I'd send along a sample of completed work). If you agree to the conditions in the following paragraphs, please sign one copy of this letter and return it in the enclosed envelope.

You (your firm) agree to use 1040Trac and report your experience with the product in your own practice in exchange for the right to use the executable program that is the outcome of this test period.

You will promptly notify Compass/New England of any anomalies (bugs) that you find in the operation of the program; you (and your firm) recognize that the product has not been extensively field tested, and that regular data backups in multiple generations are essential to recovery, should that become necessary.

From time to time, you may offer suggestions for improvement of the product. Compass/New England may or may not choose to incorporate these suggestions into the product; this will not affect the ownership of the product.

You agree to take reasonable steps to keep copies of the beta test versions of this product confidential and also agree that you will keep your experiences with the beta test versions confidential.

It is not our intent to form any business arrangement except for a simple exchange of a license to use this software in

type in the actual ASCII values to be sent. This will allow them to use compressed print for your application's reports and then return to normal mode after printing.

exchange for the work and risk that you take in assisting Compass/New England in field testing it. This is not an exclusive agreement.

Compass/New England will retain all intellectual property rights.

It may become necessary to use copies of your data files in re-creating program error conditions. It is understood and acknowledged that this information is your property and that disclosure of this information could potentially harm your business. You agree that you will supply Compass/New England with a copy of your data file at our request. Compass/New England will keep this information strictly confidential and will destroy all copies of the file as soon as the program is corrected.

Compass/New England acknowledges that prompt correction of errors in the software will be important and pledges to correct, test, and forward program corrections in a timely manner.

Disputes under this agreement will be subject to binding arbitration by a mutually agreed to arbitrator or, lacking agreement, by an arbitrator furnished by the American Arbitration Association.

If this letter fairly states our agreement, please sign and return one copy.

Sincerely,

Robert Schenot

Agreed	date

Allow for printers that require pages to be fed individually. They still exist. You may want to have an option on the print menu to pause between pages.

There is disagreement over the issue of whether you should send no form feeds, one form feed, or two form feeds after printing a report. I suggest adding that to the menu as well, using one as the default.

One (out-of-print) source for printer control codes is:

The Printer Bible
Que Corporation
11711 N. College Avenue
Carmel, IN 46032
(800) 428-5331

CHAPTER 3

Acquiring Customers

Another key to a successful software venture is to have effective distribution. Because no one channel is effective in reaching all types of customers or selling all types of software, most successful software companies use more than one marketing channel. One of the jobs of the marketing manager (you) is to choose the most effective channels for the product being sold.

One way to visualize the software marketplace is to view the audience for the software as one dimension and the support requirements as another dimension. It might look something like Figure 3.1.

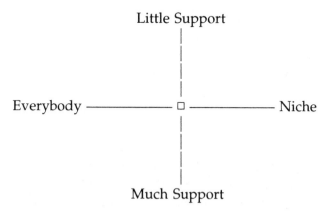

Figure 3.1 A software product's audience and support levels.

Using this model, an application such as word processing would generally belong in the upper left quadrant, while a comprehensive veterinary practice management system would belong in the lower right quadrant. A program helping collectors to keep track of their collections might belong in the upper right quadrant.

Different software marketing channels work best in different places in this matrix as well. In general:

- Retail computer stores serve the upper left quadrant. Some stores in large cities have decided to specialize in serving specific industries, serving the upper right quadrant.
- Consulting firms that specialize in training do a reasonable job of selling, installing, and supporting packages in the lower left and lower central areas.
- VARs (value-added resellers) generally have the lower right quadrant to themselves.
- The shareware marketing channel belongs mostly in the upper left and central areas of this grid.
- Direct mail covers an area farther to the right and maybe a little farther down than the shareware market.
- Low-cost retail (LCR) occupies the extreme upper left corner; no support is offered, and the product must appeal to a very high percentage of shoppers cruising the computer software department of a mass retailer.

This concept is important, because the area in the grid the distribution channel occupies *must match* reasonably well with that of the product being sold. Trying to sell a comprehensive veterinary management practice package through a retail store simply wouldn't work. Few veterinarians wander through retail stores looking for a package that would take a salesperson several months of training to understand well enough to sell. Conversely, if you were to send highly trained salespeople to perform on-site demonstrations of a word processing program, the sales call would cost more than the price of the product.

If your package will require much support for installation or training of users, shareware is not going to be an effective channel for you, no matter how hard you try. If you have a product that is easy to install and support but appeals to a very well defined target audience, direct mail probably will be your most effective marketing channel. It won't hurt to try shareware, but you really shouldn't expect much from it.

On the other hand, if your product would appeal to a large percentage of the population, is easy to install, and requires very little support or training, shareware may be a very effective initial marketing channel for your product and retail sales might be a reasonable ultimate goal.

Usually, the price of software is lowest in the upper left quadrant and highest in the lower right. There are two main reasons for this. First, as the audience grows larger, the costs of development can be spread over a larger number of people and more efficient delivery mechanisms can be used. Second, support costs money—whether included in the price or billed separately later.

Software distribution channels include shareware, direct mail, bundling, catalogs, advertising, retail, and VARs.

Shareware's main advantage to the publisher is the low cost of entry. This channel is not appropriate for high-priced, high-support products. It is appropriate to horizontal and very large vertical markets. It does not reach small niche markets effectively. Shareware reaches a very small proportion of the total base of PC users (I'd estimate under 5 percent) and tends to reach these users when they are at an intermediate or higher level of skill, after they have purchased "base" or first applications. These generalizations are changing rapidly, however. With the growth of rackware and certain catalog operations, shareware is reaching a much broader base and much less experienced users.

Many software publishers start their marketing by using *direct mail*. Because the marketing effort can be targeted so effectively, this channel is excellent at reaching niche markets, especially with low-priced (under $100) products.

For low-priced horizontal products, *bundling* offers the opportunity to have an instant installed base of thousands with virtually no marketing costs. Bundling reaches a market only as large as the product you are bundled with.

For low-priced products that can be explained in a headline but have a narrow market niche, *catalog* sales can reach well-defined markets at a low price.

Either as a reinforcement to other marketing methods or as part of a two-step sales process, *advertising* can reach large numbers of people at a superficial level. Few software products can be sold successfully through advertising alone. Successful advertising campaigns generally require large outlays of capital.

There was a time when you could work from the bottom up in entering the *retail* channel. It used to be possible to leave a few copies of your product with selected stores on consignment, and they would pay you when and if the product sold. This is no longer true. In general, the retail market is now reserved for medium-price horizontal products with very sophisticated, well-financed, and professionally run mass-merchandising organizations.

For niche markets with high support needs (and correspondingly high prices), an outbound sales force actively selling a small number of products to a well-defined local market is essential. *VARs* meet that need. Many software houses start out as consulting/custom programming organizations, find themselves selling to the same kind of client, put together a standard application, and finally end up using VARs as their primary marketing channel.

SEGMENTATION

Earlier I wrote "Successful software companies don't make money selling software." While this is certainly an overstatement and subject to exceptions, consider:

- Computer Associates has been handing out products for "free" (a small "handling charge" is involved); you have to wonder why they'd do this.
- The majority of products are selling for under $100 and the software publisher typically only gets 45 percent of the list price from wholesalers.
- A full-page four-color ad in a major computer or business magazine costs over $30,000.
- Even the major bread-and-butter applications such as word processing, database, and spreadsheet are being bundled and sold at very deep discounts.

I conclude that it is becoming more and more difficult to make a profit selling new software products to new users.

The profits have to come from somewhere else; if you do have a long-term goal of building a company, this is the time to start thinking about your strategy. I suggest you start by planning to pursue a single market with a minimum of three products:

- A "lite" or "student" product that will sell for a nominal price or even be given away. This product will be very easy to learn, be uncomplicated in its features, and will be the most attractive and unthreatening alternative to a person just starting out. Most people who have a serious need for this function will find that they need more power after using it for about a year.
- A "regular" product that will meet all the needs of 85 percent of the population needing this particular application.
- A "professional" version that will be sold through direct mail to existing customers, an outbound sales force, VARs, and specialty computer retailers.

Additionally, you'll need to be prepared to create clones of your products with different names and screens that are visually different. This will allow you to pursue different marketing channels with different price points without the appearance of conflict.

Many people have a hard time visualizing how to segment a market. They seem to try to limit the number of records, which is entirely missing the point. What is important is to protect your entry-level buyers from the issues that your sophisticated users will find essential. I have found that giving some examples helps a lot in understanding this.

In financial applications:

Entry level: Something that can make balancing a checkbook easy.

Intermediate level: Add mortgage and IRA functions. Perhaps a schedule C business function. Offer (or have a relationship with) a basic tax package.

Advanced level: Portfolio tracking, accrual and double-entry accounting, multicorporation accounting, electronic banking and currency conversion.

For a general database:

Entry level: Target market is the casual user who wants to keep track of information that won't be shared. Start with basic tables (flat file) and a report generator.

Intermediate level: Target market is an advanced or corporate user. Assume that this person is a sophisticated nonprogrammer who needs to share the information, perhaps over a local area network, with locking at a file level. Add hierarchical relationships. Perhaps provide a compiler that requires a runtime system.

Advanced level: Target market is the MIS department of a corporation. Only a site license is offered. Add record locking, true multiuser, and networking capabilities. The ability to distribute protected applications will be important here.

For a vertical business application:

Entry level: Target the smaller firms in the industry; probably mostly sole proprietorships. Cash accounting only for a single location.

Intermediate level: Add multilocation accrual accounting, perhaps (depending on the industry) add inventory, partnership accounting, and scheduling modules at this level.

Advanced level: Target specific niches within the industry; add multicorporation accounting and communication links between locations. Offer source code and consulting at this level.

Architectural design:

Entry level: Able to put together a basic floor plan. Primary market is the person planning a new home, office, or renovation. Does not provide the level of detail necessary for obtaining a building permit.

Intermediate level: Changes on one floor automatically make changes on other floors (moving a chimney, stairs, or supporting wall). Does roof design. Includes functions for design of plumbing and electrical systems. Appropriate for a builder but not an architectural firm. Provides the documentation necessary for a building permit.

Advanced level: Allows work groups to work together on the same project. Includes ability to maintain a library of previous work and cut and paste into new designs. Adds structural analysis. Primary market is architectural firms.

Before you begin working on the first product, develop a description of your target market, functional specification, and feature list for all three products.

Develop the regular product first. Reserve development of the professional features for the professional product since taking features out of an existing product is very difficult. Once you have a mature and stable product with support and marketing under control, you can begin penetrating new channels. You'll probably want to start with bundling, direct mail, and catalogs. (See "Working with Software Publishers," Chapter 6.)

By the time the regular version is a mature product, you will have a waiting and eager market for the more sophisticated product and you will have the experience to do the job well.

Finally, introduce a third, "lite" product, a bannerware product designed for very elementary or student use. (See "Bannerware," p. 40). The idea is to get people started as students or as very small businesses (before they become profitable) so that when they are actually ready to buy software, they will be familiar with your product and very likely to purchase it. If you offer some incentive for registration (even though the product may be free), you will have a way to stay in touch with these people and continue to offer them upgrades to your more sophisticated products. A nominal charge for a bound manual is a good way to do this.

Again, this student version is not a crippled product, but a product that meets all the needs of a different audience. The BASIC shipped by Microsoft with DOS 5 is a good example of this technique. It is entirely adequate for hobby programmers or students who want to learn programming and develop things for themselves, but will not produce a stand-alone executable. To do this, users must step up to the next product (QuickBasic). In turn, QuickBasic has limitations (such as not being able to handle overlays) that encourage a professional programmer to buy the high-end (PDS) product.

Part of the reason for thinking about this now is that you'll want to pick a common name for the product family, with derivations for the individual products. Eventually, you may have nine products: bannerware, regular, and pro in DOS, Windows, and UNIX versions. They will need names that tie them together but also make it obvious they are different.

This strategy also will give you the flexibility to pursue different channels effectively. The bannerware product will feed you prospects for a direct mail campaign of the regular product, and the regular product will provide leads for the professional-level product. Even if your retail and wholesale dealers force the regular product out of the shareware channel, you will still have the bannerware product out there recruiting new customers.

In the next several chapters, I'll discuss different distribution and marketing methods for getting your software product into the hands of paying customers.

CHAPTER 4

Marketing Your Product as Shareware

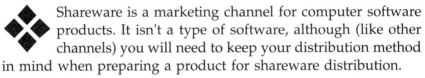 Shareware is a marketing channel for computer software products. It isn't a type of software, although (like other channels) you will need to keep your distribution method in mind when preparing a product for shareware distribution.

The primary advantages of shareware to buyers is that it lets them try the product before buying it and generally has a different price point from products available through more orthodox channels. The shareware channel contrasts with the "shelfware" channel, which pulls buyers with advertising and requires customers to pay first. The primary advantage of the shareware channel to software developers is that it allows them to substitute patience for cash up front.

Shareware is often confused with other electronic methods of software distribution:

• *Public domain* software is software to which authors have given up all intellectual property rights and their right to control the use of the product. Since 1989, authors must explicitly make that declaration. Lack of a copyright message does not make material that could be copyrighted public domain. Public domain software is emphatically different from a shareware product for which the author has decided to selectively suspend some of his or her rights for a limited term under specific conditions.

• *Freeware* has come to mean software where the author has not given up intellectual property rights but does not demand payment for specific uses. It is sometimes called "$0 shareware."

• *Bannerware* is a form of freeware, used primarily for advertising purposes. It can be very effective in promoting other software products or services.

• *Demoware* comes in two flavors: (1) Slide shows (programs displaying one screen after another; not a "working copy"); and (2) crippled products ("working copies" that lack essential features; these are frequently confused with shareware).

• *Crippleware* is type-two demoware that calls itself shareware.

• *Olderware* is a marketing strategy frequently used by shelf-ware companies to boost sales of their current product. The company releases an earlier version of the product as freeware or shareware in the hopes that people eventually will purchase the newer version.

• *Nagware* is shareware with excessive registration reminder screens. Typically they are excessive in number, inconvenient in where they appear, or lock the system for an excessive amount of time.

Shareware originally was envisioned as being distributed primarily through user groups. What the vision didn't account for was the amount of work required to collect, test, catalog, and distribute the constant stream of shareware. Generally, even the largest user group libraries are composed of a few hundred titles and tend to be rather dated. User groups can be effective at distributing well-known shareware products to beginning users. Shareware is distributed through four primary subchannels:

• *Catalog vendors* who mail catalogs to prospective customers, allowing them to order trial disks from the catalog.
• *Bulletin boards* that allow customers to phone in using their modems and download compressed files containing shareware distribution packages.
• *Rack vendors* who place shareware disks in retail racks, from which customers select titles they'd like to try.
• *CD manufacturers* who sell either to end users or to other distributors. Some CDs are designed to be "BBS-ready," which means that they can be mounted on a drive connected to a bulletin board without further work.

None of these subchannels serves vertical markets well (there are a couple of exceptions), and generally they won't handle a product that only a small percentage of their customers might want. Take a look in *Data Sources*—you'll find over a hundred pages devoted to applications software for the financial services industry. Next take a look at the catalogs of the major disk vendors. At best, you'll find one or two products specifically aimed at that same industry.

The simple truth is that disk vendors can't (currently) sell vertical products, so they don't carry them. If you try to launch a truly vertical product exclusively through shareware, you are likely to fail today simply because you won't get distribution, no matter how good the product is. There are exceptions. Church management software sells because there are 400,000 churches in the United States, and almost every church has at least one member who knows about shareware.

The theoretical foundation of how shareware works is twofold:

First, the assumption is made that most people prefer to be honest and that, if they are trusted, they will honor that trust.

Second, as copyright holder, the author may voluntarily suspend some of his or her rights for a limited period of time. After the specified period, someone who continues to use the software is in violation of domestic and international copyright laws.

While this is all true, experience shows that a little "grease" makes a vast improvement in helping these gears of honesty turn; we'll get to that later.

Consumers can obtain shareware from a variety of sources, usually from one of the subchannels just mentioned, less frequently from a user group or a friend. In theory, after they are satisfied that the software is what they need, they pay the author. If not, they stop using the product. When the author receives the payment, he or she issues a license allowing the consumers to continue to use the software. All of this is, of course, based on the theory that enough people are law-abiding and/or honest.

The concept of shareware goes back to the dawn of the PC era. Credit for the concept generally is given to Andrew Fluegelman, who trademarked the term "freeware." Since the term was trademarked, other words were frequently used in its stead. Eventually,

Bob Wallace used the word that *InfoWorld* had coined—"shareware"—to describe the marketing method for his product (PC-Write). PC-Write was one of the first shareware hits, so the name stuck.

Most authors enter the shareware marketplace by polishing an existing internal product a bit, then uploading it to a couple of computer services to test the water. Since it is a test, almost no market research or beta testing is done. Typically, the documentation is sparse at best, since the software is "completely intuitive." When money doesn't start pouring in, the author concludes that thousands of people are using the product without paying, and the companies that have prospered by offering a product through shareware did it during a dimly remembered period in history when all the rules were different.

The easiest way to approach the essential elements of success in shareware is to list the three reasons for failure:

1. The product isn't distributed.
2. The product isn't used.
3. Users don't pay for the product.

I see successful shareware marketing as having five steps:

1. Get widely *distributed*.
2. Get the program *ordered*.
3. *Hold customers* once you get the program into their hands.
4. Convince customers to *send you money*.
5. Continue to provide services and products desired by customers, resulting in *repeat sales*.

Most unsuccessful authors assume their problem is that there are many users who aren't paying for the product. This is almost never the case. It is much more likely these authors never got that far—people aren't using their software at all.

THINGS TO DO RIGHT AWAY

Call Public Brand Software and ask for a copy of "Guidelines for Shareware Authors." As of this writing, it's free. Ask also for a copy of the catalog and to be put on the mailing list for the Summer Shareware Seminar. Contact the company at:

Public Brand Software
3750 Kentucky Avenue
Indianapolis, IN 46241
(317) 856-2085

The original Summer Shareware Seminar was run as a three-day weekend event in Indianapolis by Bob Ostrander and friends for the first three years under the Public Brand (Ziff) banner. When Bob O. left Public Brand, Ziff claimed the tradename for the seminar, moved it to Atlanta, and raised the price to $325. BobO & friends are now running the Shareware Industry Conference at the time, place, and price ($75) that the Summer Shareware Seminar used to be held. To be put on the mailing list for next year's conference, contact:

Bob Ostrander
Software Co-op National Product Referral
5437 Honey Manor Drive
Indianapolis, IN 46221
CompuServe: 76635,1670
Internet: 76635.1670@compuserve.com
voice:(317) 856-6052
fax: (317) 856-2086

Just about every significant shareware product appears on Public (software) Library's (PsL) Reviews disk; your market research begins here. You want disk number 7000:

Public (software) Library
P.O. Box 35705
Houston, TX 77235-5705
(713) 524-6394
(800) 242-4775

GETTING STARTED IN SHAREWARE

The shareware idea is not a substitute for intelligent market selection, product design, or anything else except cash. It is a way of dealing with the fact that wholesalers will carry only those products with demonstrated "pull," retailers will carry only those products with "pull" that wholesalers carry, and "pull" costs a great deal of money.

Shareware doesn't work for mediocre products. It won't work for products aimed at very narrow markets. It rarely works with products used only occasionally, such as small utilities. It won't work without a well-thought-out strategy. In developing a successful software product, marketing is more important than programming. Using the shareware channel does not change this.

Shareware is a marketing channel that should be used in conjunction with other channels because:

- It is a way of conducting very cheap market research.
- It is an excellent way of road-testing a completed product before manufacturing thousands of copies and putting them out on retail shelves, where they are very expensive to retrieve.
- It is an excellent way to reach thousands of sophisticated computer users quickly and cheaply with your message.
- It is an excellent way of introducing people to an entry-level product with the hope of eventually upselling them to a more sophisticated, nonshareware product.
- It is an excellent way of reaching foreign markets, where you can then attract distributors.
- It can be used to display that you do in fact have a market and a marketable product to distributors in other channels.
- It is the cheapest and fastest way to get a crash course in software publishing that I know of.

This is and isn't a book about shareware. It's a book about bootstrapping a software company from a spare bedroom to whatever you want the company to become. This book is about shareware only because shareware is one of the few ways to get into the packaged software business without a team of people and a lot of money. It is not about using the shareware marketing channel exclusively. No software company should plan on using any single marketing channel exclusively.

As your market and your products change, you will need an array of tools to deliver your product to the public profitably. If you reach the multimillion-dollar mark, your distributors probably will force you out of the shareware channel, as they have with other successful companies. Personally, I'd like to have that problem.

During my college days, I visited a local auction house to buy household items. It was a way to drastically reduce the cost of a "new" washer or toaster. One expression I frequently heard from the auctioneer as he presented some machine of dubious history was "It runs if you run with it." Shareware is a little like that.

Shareware program structure and function is not inherently different from other widely distributed microcomputer programs, with these exceptions:

• The first impression must be a strong one. Shelfware products have already been paid for, so the user has a commitment to making the program work. Your job in shareware is to get potential customers to give you a few minutes to convince them your solution will work for them.

• Shareware programs must be extremely user-friendly and self-supporting. This is not always the case with the more complex, expensive shelfware packages, since their prices can include extensive telephone support and dealers willing to run local classes to help customers learn how to use the programs.

• Shareware typically has built-in differences between "registered" and "evaluation" operation, primarily in the area of registration reminder techniques.

Bulletin Board Systems (BBSs)

User groups often set up bulletin board systems (BBSs) for electronic collection and distribution of their libraries. Hobbyists frequently set up bulletin boards as well. Since most bulletin boards are one-person operations, they tend to be idiosyncratic, spotty in their quality, and short-lived. Some bulletin boards are very large and run as profitable businesses; they tend to be better run and live longer. Because of their diversity and the cost of communications, bulletin boards are especially effective in distributing smaller products appealing to special interests.

The largest online systems are called *information services*. These firms (usually subsidiaries of large corporations) were established initially to provide worldwide electronic access to the various parts of the parent company. H&R Block owns CompuServe; General Electric, not surprisingly, owns GEnie. Almost as an afterthought these companies began offering access during off-hours to the public. These services attract people who need access to electronic information on a regular basis. Information services can be effective at distributing shareware for specific professions or interests and are an excellent place for seeding distribution to the other shareware channels.

Shareware Vendors

Shareware vending and many shareware vendors started out as *fleamarket operators* who rent booths at computer shows and sell disks out of bins. Mostly because these tend to be people who are new to the business, the professionalism and quality control of many is spotty. For this reason, some authors prohibit this method of distribution. On the other hand, this channel reaches many small business and retail customers who otherwise would not be reached at all.

Selling shareware disks by direct mail allows *catalog vendors* to expand business without having to travel and hire weekend help, although it requires much more capital. Most catalogs are evolving toward serving specialized markets. Some firms have very limited catalogs and service users who are new to computing and shareware, while others offer extensive libraries and serve more sophisticated buyers. If you request catalogs from the largest catalog vendors and analyze who they are attempting to reach, I think you'll find that they have completely different target audiences. Just as *Sports Illustrated* doesn't compete with *Cosmopolitan*, Public Brand and PsL are reaching entirely different classes of buyers. We are just beginning to see catalogs seriously specializing in niche markets such as games, specific hobbies, or professions.

Shareware has finally entered the retail marketplace. *Rack vendors* prepackage shareware and distribute the product to retail establishments for resale. This venue is exciting because of the opportunity to reach customers who never would have been exposed to shareware before. It is dangerous because typically these venders are selling to a much less sophisticated user who may require more support, and because there is more opportunity for customers to misunderstand what they are buying with their $5.

DISTRIBUTING YOUR PRODUCT

A word about protecting your reputation is in order. Distributing a product with a virus will ruin your reputation. I use a minimum of two virus scanners, both of which are kept religiously up-to-date, and I scan every disk sent to me or file I download, no matter what the source. A certain disreputable maker of virus scanners (whose product I don't use) has given shareware a reputation for spreading viruses. Distributors are very sensitive about this issue and will spread the word if you get careless and spread a virus.

There are many ways to get into the shareware business. These range from uploading a single .exe to a couple of bulletin boards with nothing but a registration screen ("It's intuitive; you don't need documentation") through quitting your job, forming a corporation, going through all the phases of development that large software companies do, then sending/uploading the product to every warm computer in the universe.

I advocate a *middle road*. Without polish and planning, your product (almost) can't possibly succeed. Unless you are an experienced software company CEO, you will lose control and crash if you are successful in pursuing a fast-track strategy. A basic distribution plan might consist of the following:

• Recruit some *beta sites* on the basis of what you developed in planning your publicity. If you are already active in your target market, doing so should not be difficult. I recommend using a dozen beta sites, for reasons I discuss under "Testing" in Chapter 2. Keep in mind that you need a reasonable cross-section of your potential customer base (especially after the inevitable dropouts). Be sure you include Tandy and Toshiba machines in this group if you are ever going to support them.

• Once you are completely through with beta testing, and your beta sites are willing to give testimonials for your product and act as references, it's time to *distribute your product to a few local distributors and bulletin boards*. A list of bulletin boards is included in the Software Publisher's Kit. You are beta testing your distribution vehicles, your support mechanisms, your installation procedure, and looking for any bugs that weren't found in beta testing. Keeping your customers local in the beginning makes it easier to drive to a site if a user reports a problem that you cannot duplicate. After I released my first packaged software, I was surprised to learn how nonstandard DOS machines really are. Depending on the hardware and other software being run, most bugs reported to me have been ones that I could not duplicate on my machine.

• *Wait* at least three months. It will take that long for the program to begin circulating and for users to try it. If you have a personal relationship with your local distributors, ask them how many downloads/orders they've received, especially in comparison to similar products. Most of the time, you will discover flaws in your original distribution vehicles here. Rework them and retest.

• If you plan to *join the ASP* (see Chapter 11), apply now.

• When you are convinced there are no big surprises left, *upload the product to the big information services*. It's really handy to have an account on these services so you can promote the product and respond to customers' questions; a deep discount on an initial CompuServe membership is included in the Software Publisher's Kit. If you choose not to upload the product yourself, there are upload services listed in the "Distribution Services" section of this book (page 74) that will do it for you.

• Send out press releases and *try to get reviews*. Wait some more.

• When you are convinced that you've done everything you can to make your distribution vehicle effective, *send copies of your product to the top disk distributors*. If you've managed to get a review, mention it. (Send a copy if you can get the magazine's permission.) Pareto's law is in effect here: Authors who are widely distributed report that 80 percent of their registrations come through the very big disk distributors. You've held off because you want to make an outstanding first impression. Most authors send to the top distributors first, then fall prey to the "We don't need to look at this; it was junk before, it'll still be junk now" syndrome.

• Once you have had at least one mention in the press, get ready to *start massive distribution*. If you're an ASP member, use its distribution service. In addition, consider using a purchased list and using an upload service. Begin building your own list.

• Once your product is established, *put out new releases* no closer than six months or farther apart than a year. Any earlier and vendors won't take your product seriously. Any later and people may look at the date and assume your product has been discontinued.

If you're thinking that all this takes a lot of time, you're right. Personally I'm convinced it's the fastest route in the long run. I do hope it's obvious that you shouldn't plan (even with a real hit) to see significant cash flow in the first year. Successful authors often tell of some watershed event in their second or third year that suddenly increased their distribution and pull once the product and the company were mature enough to withstand the sudden customer interest.

Shareware Distribution

The primary reason software products fail is because they don't get wide distribution. The primary reason for not getting wide distribution is because the product doesn't fit well in the distribution channel the publisher has chosen. The second reason is because the product duplicates an existing offering. In order to displace another product in a catalog, it has to both be demonstrably better and customers have to call the vendor requesting the product.

Before distributors will carry a product, they have to be convinced that a significant proportion of their existing customer base might be interested in it. That's why you can't buy shrink-wrap machines in your local office supply store. The principle is the same for disk vendors and bulletin boards: They carry only shareware appealing to broad markets.

If you can, visit a vendor before you begin general distribution. I think you'll be surprised at how many disks vendors receive daily, the extraordinarily high proportion of unacceptable material, how few diskettes even get into a disk drive, and how little time the typical package is given before it is rejected.

At a minimum, the package you send to distributors should consist of:

- A 5.25-inch 360Kb *diskette* for DOS products, a 3.5-inch diskette for Windows products.
- A laser-printed *label* with your name and phone number, the product's name and release number.
- Your *program*, taking up no more than 350Kb. (Vendors will need 10Kb for their stuff.)
- A diskette *sleeve*, preferably either blank or with your company logo on it.
- A *flyer* folded into the sleeve, the disk inside of both.
- A 6 × 9-inch white *booklet envelope*, addressed with a laser printer, with DO NOT FOLD in the biggest font or rubber stamp you've got.
- A first-class *stamp*.

Besides making sure the program arrives, the most important thing is that you hit your potential distributor between the eyes with the answer to the question "So what?"

A reviewer performs the initial screening of disks arriving in the mail at a rate of approximately one per minute. A disk deemed worthy of a review must first be scanned, then installed, and finally reviewed. Given that a reviewer is expected to process about four disks per working hour, and that a review sufficient to place a disk in a catalog takes about four hours, this means that for every twenty disks submitted, sixteen will never make it into the drive, three will be installed and quickly rejected, and one will be given an in-depth analysis.

Your first job is *to be in the 20 percent of disks getting into the drive.* You can do this by having a serious appearance and providing a sheet of paper (the flyer) telling the reviewer why this disk stands a chance of being more popular than the disks already in the company's catalog. To do this, your product description must tell the reviewer who the target audience is and why these people will be eager to order this disk.

Who is the market? How big is it? Why will these people be eager to order this disk? Include this information in your flyer. Give the reviewer the copy that will appear in the catalog.

Compare your product to existing products (it's the reviewer's job to know who they are) by examining all significant features, including the ones your product doesn't offer. Include shelfware products in this comparison.

Your flyer and your press releases will have many words in common. You want the flyer to:

- Immediately convince the reviewer that the flyer is *worth reading*. As with a press release, he or she may never get past the headline.
- Convince the reviewer that the enclosed product fits the *distributor's existing market* and may sell more disks than some of the products already carried. (Almost all vendors have limited catalog, rack, or disk space.)
- Convince the reviewer that it is *worth his or her time* to scan your disk for viruses, install your program, and test it. If you send hand-labeled diskettes without flyers, they probably won't make it into the drive.
- *Provide the copy* you hope the distributor will use in selling your product.
- Provide a *summary* of the information the distributor needs in deciding whether to carry your product—distribution terms, minimum configuration, target audience, and so on.
- Provide the information the reviewer needs to properly *install* your product.
- Point the vendor to your vendor.doc file for *detailed information*, such as in which category your program belongs and technical requirements.
- *Highlight* favorable reviews, after getting the publisher's permission.

Have someone with advertising experience review your package before you send it out.

The size of your product on disk may affect your distribution. I did some research on the information services where download counts are available, and found that anything over 200Kb has tough sledding on bulletin boards—presumably because of the long download times. One way to stay under the 200Kb limit is to archive your program and documentation files separately.

On the other hand, an archive size of less than 250Kb may result in delay in being distributed by disk vendors, since they prefer to ship a "full disk" to their customers. They may wait for a complementary product to fill out the disk. Whatever you do, always keep your archives under 350Kb so they can be shipped on low density 5.25-inch diskettes with the vendor's files. You can say what you want about the older technology, but most catalogs still list a price for both 5.25- and 3.5-inch disks. If your product can't be shipped the way it's advertised, most distributors won't carry you in their catalog at all.

If you use an archiving program, you are much more likely to keep your files together. If you distribute only a single .exe file that is essential to the application and creates the other essential files the first time the program is run, you are even more likely to keep the files together.

In general, your main program name should be six characters or less. This will accommodate CompuServe and lets you name your archive with those same six characters plus the version number; for example, CA$H.exe is the program file and CA$H1.exe is the self-extracting archive. CA$H1.zip or CA$H1.lzh is the archive file sent to bulletin boards.

Vendor.doc

I include a file named vendor.doc on all distribution diskettes. This file is your primary way of communicating with vendors. Unlike the flyer, it is likely to be passed along to other vendors. I frequently get calls from secondhand vendors who have found one program and are impressed enough that they want to look at the others. Besides containing a reprint of your flyer, vendor.doc might contain:

- Short, medium, and long descriptions of your product for a catalog
- A suggested archive name for bulletin boards, together with a 40-character description
- A description of hardware and software requirements
- A summary of major releases and the reasons for them
- A comparison (perhaps a table) of your product and the shareware and shelfware competition

- A list of differences between shareware and registered versions
- A features and benefits list
- A detailed list of your registration incentives
- Your distribution policy in detail
- A statement of ASP membership, if you are a member
- Information about all of your other shareware products

I put a copy of vendor.doc in every archive and also put a plain text version on the disk outside the archives. This allows a vendor or bulletin board sysop to scan the file quickly without having to extract it and to use the file for building a description.

For an example of good copywriting, take a look at the product descriptions in the flyers of the mail order software companies. Note both the length of their copy and their techniques. Look closely at the product descriptions in the catalogs in which you want to appear. Estimate how many words they are likely to allow you. Try to pare down your description so it could fit in these catalogs. If you don't, the vendors will, and they don't know your package and market as well as you do.

Some authors have tried to charge vendors for the "privilege" of carrying their products. I don't know of any vendor with significant distribution who will pay authors either for disks or for distribution royalties. To the best of my knowledge, all authors who have tried this have failed to collect any money and also have ruined whatever relationships they had built up. On the other hand, some vendors have tried to get authors to "advertise" in their catalogs or "chip in" for card mailings featuring the authors' products. I have yet to find a situation where money passing hands in either direction actually worked to the advantage of the author.

Remember that the disk librarian's job is to keep your product out of the catalog. One of the best ways to hit the bit bucket quickly is by forcing the vendor to fill out and sign a permission form—especially a complicated one or one that your lawyer designed. If you feel you must insist upon a written agreement before granting permission to vendors to distribute your product, make the agreement short, and to the point, and don't include any onerous penalty clauses. The vendors who are worth doing business with are not likely to spend $200 to have a lawyer review your agreement. They are much more likely simply to refuse your submission instead.

I use a *negative notice clause* in my vendor.doc file that lets any vendor distribute my products with very few provisions until I ask for the distribution to stop. In my experience, the ones you don't want distributing your product won't cooperate anyway. If you are uncomfortable with this wide-open approach, consider at least giving blanket permission to all ASP vendors. ASP has an active compliance program that keeps abuses to a minimum.

Distribution Policy

You should include an *explicit distribution policy* in your vendor.doc file. Without a statement giving the vendor the right to distribute your shareware, he or she will be violating the copyright law by distributing it prior to getting permission. (My distribution policy is shown in Figure 4.1.)

Some authors refuse permission to vendors if the vendor charges buyers more than a specific arbitrary amount. Their reasoning is that if the disk was purchased for more than that amount, buyers might reasonably feel they had paid for the program. I prefer to deal with this type of problem as it occurs. If I receive an irate call from a customer, I investigate to find out why he or she believes the program was paid for. While the price the customer pays sometimes contributes to the problem, I find it is usually a communications problem. Generally I call the vendor to discuss the problem. If a second customer calls and it appears that this vendor has not taken appropriate action, I send a registered letter, return receipt, informing the vendor that I withdraw my permission for him or her to distribute any of my products. I enclose a photocopy of my copyright registration. This does not happen often.

User Groups

User groups are a great source of publicity if you speak at one of their meetings. On the other hand, I generally have little respect for their libraries and have given up sending disks to them. If you think about it, maintaining a shareware library is at least a full-time job; the more successful vendors have a couple of librarians each. A volunteer group can't possibly do the same job.

For example, I'm a member of the Boston Computer Society. I sent the society six disks during one eighteen-month period. During this time, I never heard a word from it or saw a listing in its new arrivals section. Finally I sent a nice letter, another disk, a self-addressed stamped postcard, and a $5 bill to the personal attention of the librarian, asking him to confirm the arrival of the disk into the proper hands and to check off a couple of boxes to tell me if the disk would be placed in the library. I'm still waiting to get my postcard back.

I do think it is worth your while to cultivate the specialty user groups. If your product market includes lawyers and there is a lawyer's user group that maintains a disk library, the chances are pretty good that your program will be distributed.

The Association of PC User Groups (APCUG) is an umbrella group for the vast majority of PC user groups. It maintains a shareware library that is available to all member user groups. Adding APCUG to your list makes sense, since through it your program will be made available to virtually every PC user group. You can upload directly by calling the APCUG bulletin board at (408) 439- 9367. Or mail a disk to:

Paul Curtis, sysop
Association of PC User Groups BBS
Suite 700
1730 M Street NW
Washington, DC 20036

Computer Shopper magazine lists user groups about once every three months. See the next section for its address.

Bulletin Board Systems (BBSs)

BBSs can be a powerful distribution medium, but they are very difficult to work with. All sysops have their own idea of what the world ought to be like and feel free to do almost anything they want with anything on their board. In general, many if not most

Dear Shareware Vendor:

This file contains our distribution policy and information on all products.

Compass/New England has a simple distribution policy: You have permission to distribute our shareware in its original form as long as you:

• identify it as shareware (with an appropriate definition)

• leave all intellectual property (copyright) notices in place

... and as long as we do not request that you stop.

That's it.

You may archive our programs, unarchive them, include/exclude optional files (like this one), include them with other programs on the same diskette, and do essentially anything you want as long as you follow these simple rules. We want the widest possible distribution, and don't want to stand in your way so long as you are honest with our mutual customer.

We suggest that you include all files with the same name (TimeTrac.exe, TimeTrac.doc, TimeTrac.rev) in your distribution together with the file register.doc. You may choose to include all or a part of this file with your distribution at your option.

Our normal distribution sequence is:

1. New versions are offered to our registered users and are automatically shipped to new registrants.

2. New versions are posted on CompuServe (use IBMFF on ID 70511,720)

3. All ASP distribution members are included in the regular ASP CD. This saves both of us both money and effort; if you are not an ASP vendor or bulletin board member, please consider joining.

4. Then we send copies of major revisions of software to non-ASP vendors who have notified us of their interest. If you are a catalog house, send us a copy of the catalog in which the program appears, together with a copy of the diskette(s) containing the program(s) you wish to distribute;

Figure 4.1   My shareware distribution policy.

we will send you a copy of any major updates to our software. If you run a bulletin board, send us a diskette(s) containing the program(s) you wish to distribute and your mailing address, and we will update the diskette and mail it back to you. Since all program copies are serialized by to whom they were originally sent, we are able to track registrations by vendor. As long as we receive registrations containing your number for any product, we will continue to provide you with updates for all products.

If you have any questions, concerns, or complaints, please contact me:

Bob Schenot
Compass/New England
Post Office Box 117
Portsmouth, New Hampshire 03802-0117
Voice: (603) 431 8030
CIS: 70511,720

International: If you are a publisher interested in translating and supporting our products in another language, please contact us to discuss an exclusive agreement for your language and country. If you are interested in providing registration and support services outside of North America in English, we are interested in working with you on a nonexclusive basis.

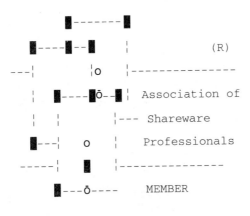

Figure 4.1 My shareware distribution policy (continued).

diskettes mailed to sysops are never posted, simply because it is drudgery to uncompress files, figure out what to say in the description field, then rearchive them in the BBS's preferred format—compared to watching someone else do the work through an upload. I certainly haven't found the key, but I do think you will have more success if you do the uploads yourself or use an upload service.

To locate BBSs, check the list of service providers included on page 74, use the BBS list that is provided in the Software Publisher's Kit, or refer to *Computer Shopper*:

> **Computer Shopper**
> **Ziff-Davis Publishing Company**
> P.O. Box 52567
> Boulder, CO 80321-2567

Many bulletin boards use a standard file that will both help the sysop and increase the chances that a decent description is associated with your shareware. If you wish to have your description automatically posted with your archive, create a file called File_ID.diz as a text file of up to ten lines, each up to forty-five characters long. The bulletin board software will automatically search within the archive and extract the default maximum number of description lines for the board.

Different boards have different defaults; one, four, eight, ten, and twelve lines are common, so you will want to put the most important things first. If there is a reasonable chance that your archive name will become garbled along the way, your product name should be on the first line. Some of the software that is supposed to do this extraction works only with .zip files, so you may be well advised to use this type of archive. High ASCII (box) characters are allowed but are probably not a good idea since some bulletin boards will concatenate lines to their own preferred line length.

The advantage in including a File_ID.diz file is that you are more likely to have your product described the way you would like it to be—otherwise, the description will typically be a couple of words written on the fly by the person uploading the file.

While you can do pretty much whatever you want with this file, there is a recommended structure. The first line should contain the complete name of the product, the version number, the <ASP> designation if appropriate, and whatever description you can fit in the space left over. Each of these elements is separated from each other by a single space, and the description is set off by a dash. As you might imagine, this is quite a task to fit into forty-five characters. *The ShareWare Book*'s File_ID.diz was:

> *The ShareWare Book* 1st Ed -Bob Schenot <ASP>
> 190 page How-to manual for making money with
> shareware. Hard to find tips, tools and tech-
> niques for shareware marketing & development.
> Includes marketing, publicity, getting paid,
> distribution, resources, product protection,
> registration encouragement, trademarks, copy-
> rights, manuals, shipping, international.
>   "Trophy Rating"- - Public Brand Software
> "Absolutely essential" -$hareware Mktg $ystem

As you can see, I gave up on including a description in the first line, thinking that including my name would be more effective for me. (I think I was right.)

Do try to avoid hyphenation. On many bulletin boards, the preceding description gets automatically concatenated so that it reads ". . . Hard to find techniques for . . . ."

The archive file name should reflect the program name and its version. For example, you might use CA$H.exe as the program file and CA$H01.exe as the self-extracting archive. CA$H01.zip or CA$H01.lzh would be the archive files sent to bulletin boards. If your program runs on different systems (DOS, Windows, OS/2, Macintosh), use a unique name for both the program and the associated files—perhaps CA$HW, CA$HO, and CA$HM.

To the extent possible, file names should have the same root and different extensions; for example:

program.exe	The actual program
program.doc	Documentation file
program.rev	Revision history
program.dat	Main data file
program.cfg	Configuration file
program.ix1	Index 1

| program.fil | List of files shipped with the shareware package |
| program.man | Manual, if you decide to have a short doc/long doc strategy |

If you have multiple files that must have the same extension (such as .exe, .com or .bat files), use the same first characters: pro_main.exe, pro_rpt.exe, pro_updt.exe, and so forth.

I break this rule myself, by the way. I have register.doc and vendor.doc files that are common to and included with all my shareware products. They contain all shareware information for each of the products. When I need to send a shelfware copy of a product, I simply remove those two files.

The convention of using a single date and time for all files in the distribution archive (and the archive itself) is a useful one. This allows a customer who has loaded your product into a directory with other applications to guess which files belong to which packages without wading through each package's documentation. You might also want to follow the convention of setting the time as the release; for example, a time of 2:41 would be release 2.41.

To sign up for CompuServe (CIS)

Purchase the Software Publisher's Kit offered at the back of this book. Really. This kit comes with a coupon good for a $35 credit on your introductory subscription to CompuServe.

Drop by the Shareware forum (Go Share) and introduce yourself.

To upload to CompuServe

Assuming that you are using a navigator, this script will perform an upload once you have logged on to the proper forum. You will, of course, have to use an editor to change the forum, library, and file names.

```
* Be sure to do global edit on version;
* Alt t, then script = tt.scr
* Ctl d returns to ato
**
* IBMapp lib 0 (gets moved after a month)
**
sendline 'lib 0'
```

```
match 'LIB 0'
upl TimeTr.exe/proto:b/type:bin|d:\ato\TimeTr.exe
match '/EXIT'
pause 2
* MAX 465 char (6-7 lines)
send 'This is the first line of description'^M
send 'This is the second line of description'^M
send 'You can have up to 465 characters of description'^M
send 'Generally, the limit is between 6 & 7 lines'^M
send 'On the last line, you need the ''exit'' as shown'^M/EXIT^M
match 'Keywords'
* limit seems to be about 80 char
send 'Time Log Lawyer CPA Consultant ASP Shareware'^M
match 'Title'
* limit is 49 char
send 'TimeTrac time & expense log ver 91i <ASP>'^M
match 'okay'
send 'y'^M
```

Please note that CompuServe file names are limited to six characters, with a three-character extension.

To sign up for GEnie: You can use its automated sign-up procedure. Be sure to have your credit card handy.

1. Set your communications software for half duplex (local echo) at 300, 1,200, or 2,400 baud.

2. Dial (toll-free) 1-800-638-8369. Upon connection, enter HHH.

3. At the U#= prompt, enter XJM11718,ALADDIN and press return.

4. As soon as your account is activated, go to the Aladdin forum and download Aladdin, the free navigator program. It will make GEnie easier to use and will save you a lot of money on the extra-charge forums.

There is no initial fee to join the GEnie network. At the end of the online registration, a personal User Number and temporary password will be displayed on your screen. Both are required for logon, so be sure to make a note of them.

To upload to GEnie:

Assuming that you are using Aladdin, the process is pretty easy:

1. Invoke Aladdin from a DOS prompt.

2. Select the appropriate roundtable from the main menu. Depending on which you've joined, you'll be using keys a through k.

3. Use the down arrow key to select the library section.

4. Press the letter u, for uploads.

5. Fill out the form. (You are offline, so there's no need to hurry.) You'll need to know the filename for the file on your computer, the filename for GEnie, the library number to upload to, any keywords that people can search on to find your product, a short (one-line) description, and a long (about eight-line) description.

6. When you're done, just do an automatic pass 1 or 2. Your program will be uploaded as a part of the automatic pass.

Bulletin boards are picky about the compression method used as well as self-extracting files. If you're serious about using bulletin boards as a primary distribution method, you'll have to contact each one to find out what its policy is. If you want to use the same format for bulletin boards, the best advice is probably to use the old .zip (prior to 2.0) format and not use self-extractors. If you are wedded to your self-extracting installation program, you can zip the entire thing (at zero compression, of course). Many sysops will accept this.

If a compressed file will exceed either 360Kb uncompressed or about 200Kb compressed, split it into two or more files, preferably one with the executables and minimal documentation, the other with the full documentation. This is to accommodate both 360Kb floppy disk users and the fact that telecommunications breaks are common. A 400Kb download has a 50 percent chance of failing in some areas.

If you are going to mail a disk to a BBS, include a flyer telling the sysop immediately (1) why this will be a popular file for his board and (2) that he can easily get the needed descriptive text from the uncompressed vendor.doc file on the diskette—that is, the vendor.doc file is in text form on the disk as well as inside each archive.

The most common reasons for a sysop not loading a program mailed on disk to him seem to be:

• No program descriptions could be found in the .doc files.

- Archive type was not the one the BBS uses. The disk was put on hold until the sysop could get around to it (which he never did).
- The product didn't sound interesting to him.
- The programs were sent as unarchived files, and no recommended BBS archive filename was mentioned in the literature or .doc files.
- The product was distributed as a self-extracting archive and no instructions for BBS distribution in ZIP, LZH, or ARJ format could be found.

I include CompuServe, GEnie, America OnLine, and Delphi in the general category of bulletin boards, but they are clearly special cases.

Heated discussions can get going in the online communications medium because it lacks the body language and tonal inflections a normal conversation provides—one person can't tell when the other is joking. To deal with this problem, shorthand expressions and emoticons were invented. Judicious use of these will help express what you're really trying to say. Some of the more frequently used shorthand expressions and emoticons used in online communications are:

<g>	grin (I'm smiling when I say that)
<G>	big grin
:-)	smile
8-)	smile with glasses
:-}	confused or worried, closed-mouth smile
;-)	wink; we share the joke
P-)	big wink
<rofl>	rolling on the floor laughing
<g,d&r>	grinning, ducking, and running
IANAL	I am not a lawyer
CI$	CompuServe
RTFM	Read the * manual

Catalog Vendors

Opinions about disk vendors vary tremendously. Like any other business, there are good and bad, competent and incompetent people in the disk vending business. I think part of the reason there is often friction between authors and vendors is because the personality types tending to go into the two fields are very different. Most vendors are very extroverted, not detail oriented, and enjoy sales. If they weren't selling shareware, they'd be selling something else.

Vendors add value by cataloging, advertising, and market segmentation. Understanding some of the dynamics of the shareware catalog business will help you a great deal both in working with vendors and in making the most effective use of this channel. Some truths about the catalog business in general:

The *costs* involved in the shareware catalog business are mostly in the areas of printing, mailing, and list management. The costs of library maintenance and order fulfillment are small by comparison. The size of the catalog is determined by these costs. Product selection is largely a matter of ranking the most productive sellers for this particular catalog, then adding them until the catalog is filled. The cutoff point is, therefore, rather arbitrary.

The *profit* on each individual sale is extraordinarily small. The moment a customer calls a vendor with a problem, that sale has become a loss. If your product generates this kind of call, the catalog is losing money on your product and it will be dropped.

Catalogs are like magazines. *LIFE* magazine is still kicking around, but more *specialized* magazines are constantly nibbling away at its readership. The catalogs that have survived and will survive understand this and no longer try to be all things to all potential customers. The ones that do are forced to be very superficial in their coverage. Even a ubiquitous product such as the As-Easy-As spreadsheet can't get into an arcade game catalog. You won't get into all catalogs either. Your job is to know which audiences different catalogs cater to and explain to these vendors how your program also reaches their audience.

Catalog vendors don't want their *product mix to change* quickly. They know it usually takes a number of impressions before the customer is moved to act and order a disk. The first three to six times a product appears in a catalog, it will not pull enough orders to be profitable, while orders for the product that was bumped will stop immediately. Many sales come from people who read or heard about a product a year ago and finally need it. It doesn't matter that it's been replaced by something better. If the customer can't find that particular product, the order is gone. For an author, this means that you have to be first into new catalogs and have enough "pull" through reviews and such that older catalogs will bump a poor seller to take the chance on your new product.

Ultimately, the decision to try a new product in a catalog is a gut decision by the person responsible for marketing. Usually this is not the person with the title librarian, although the librarian will be consulted. It is probably worthwhile to *cultivate the decision makers* at the major vendors—a personal relationship sometimes helps in getting listed.

Rack Vendors

Shareware is now being sold in retail establishments. Typically, it is packaged in colorful plastic packages (with a hole at one end to hang from a rack) and sold from racks in office supply stores, bookstores, airport stores, and even some general merchandise stores.

The good news is that shareware is now reaching a market that it never would have otherwise. The bad news is that, first, the shareware concept frequently is not communicated effectively to the customer; and, second, some real novices are now buying shareware, resulting in a serious support problem.

The vast majority of rack vendors sell the same mix of shareware on every rack and maintain very small libraries, typically about 120 different products. As this market matures and the vendors discover that different types of products sell in different types of stores, more products will have a chance at this kind of exposure.

CDs

This medium is new enough that it is still suffering from teething problems. Early CDs were prone to hold very old versions, duplicates, hacked versions, and incomplete archives.

The main current problem with CDs is that they can't be erased; once your software is pressed on a CD, it's there forever. Since CDs are rarely thrown out, you run the risk of having people use very old versions of your software.

The sheer size of a CD works both for you and against you. It is much more difficult for the editor of a CD to check each product carefully for permissions and completeness. The chances are good that on any one copy of a CD, your product may never even be looked at; the buyer may have bought the CD for the games or because a particular product was on it. Alternatively, if the buyer is interested in your product, there's a good chance that competitive products will be there right beside you. For Windows applications, a deinstallation feature becomes very important. Given a choice of half a dozen products that might meet the need, potential customers are likely to install first the products that sound most likely to work best for them and are most likely to be easy to get rid of if they don't.

Even though you are battling with competing products on a CD, the numbers work for you in terms of the sheer size of the market; the current projection is that 10 million CD drives will be shipped in 1994. I always said that I'd take CDs seriously when Montgomery Ward was offering a CD-equipped system for under $1,000. That happened in early 1994.

The advent of CDs also will open up a new universe of possibilities for content-based products. It is now possible to consider developing a product that requires 200Mb of space—so long as it can remain on the CD itself.

Manufacturers of shareware CDs who are members of the ASP include:

Bud Jay
JCS Marketing, Inc
P.O. Box 1216
Lakeville, MN 55044
Bud supplies a free copy of the CD to authors on it.

Rick Olson
Advantage Plus Distributors
7113 Halifax Court
Tampa, FL 33615
This company currently has the ASP distribution contract.

Nelson Ford
Public (software) Library
P.O. Box 35705
Houston, TX 77235-5705
PsL is a supplier to many other shareware distributors.

Alex Hahn
Bureau of Electronic Publishing
141 New Road
Parsippany, NJ 07054
Another supplier to distributors.

Garnet Brown
Pearl Agency
3946 SW Ida Street
Seattle, WA 98136
Best bet for northern Europe (German distributor).

Nicolas V. Kelemen
DP Tool Club
99 Rue Parmentier
Villeneuve D'Ascq F-59493
France
This is the best bet for southern Europe.

Terry L. Bryer
Top 40+ $oftware, Inc.
P.O. Box 520
Storrs, CT 06268

Dixon Yee
Micro Technology
21 Vintage Drive
E. Windsor, NJ 08520

Robert L. Pierce
Shareware Systems
72 Cascade Drive
#36 Building 2 Level 2
Rochester, NY 14614

Richard Graham
Night Owl's Publisher Inc.
1611 Falconer Stillwater Road
Jamestown, NY 14701

Lawrence Delaney
$ave On $oftware
P.O. Box 1312
Wilkes Barre, PA 18703-1312

Rob Mosley
Shareware To Go
P.O. Box 10
Bostic, NC 28018

Frank Stokes
Fasco Software 'N' Stuff
2748 NW 9th Terrace
Wilton Manors, FL 33311

James Boyette
LiRoPS
P.O. Box 151808
Tampa, FL 33684

Elizabeth A. Colontonio
DataMicro, Inc.
P.O. Box 3527
Port Charlotte, FL 33949-3527

Anthony Saliba
Most Significant Bits
15508 Madison Avenue
Lakewood, OH 44107

Ted Balog
Compustuff
P.O. Box 58317
Medina, OH 44258

George Croft
Printers Shareware
5019-5021 West Lovers Lane
Dallas, TX 75209

Ronald A. Ames
Key Systems, Inc.
575 Caldwell Boulevard
Niampa, ID 83651

Christian C. & Patty Lee
Wonderful F1 Shareware
650 Pantera Drive
Diamond Bar, CA 91765

Edna Scomph
Walnut Creek CDROM
4041 Pike Lane, Suite E
Concord, CA 94520

Michael/Jonas Plumecocq
Domainsoft
8 Bonus Court
Werribee, Victoria 3030
Australia

Pierre Dumont
Info-Soft Inc.
825 Belvedere sud Bureau 100
Sherbrooke, PQ J1H 4B9
Canada

Peter Ellis
Encode Business Systems Inc
434 West Street North
Orillia, ON L3V 5E8
Canada

Marius Miller
MilData
Centre Commercial Gatines
Plaisir F-78370
France

Herrn Wolfgang Gabler
CDV—NEWSOFT
Ettlinger Str. 5
7500 Karlsruhe 1
Germany

Sonda Scheffel
S.+W. Scheffel
Schillerstrasse 95
Berlin - 12 D-1000
Germany

F. van den Berg
Hillsoft
P.O. Box 16
Vriezenveen 7670 AA
Holland

Massimiliano Baldazzi
Masled Informatica
Via Dei Pioppi,9-04011 Aprilia (LT)
Aprilia Latina 04011
Italy

Eric van den Broek
BroCo Software
P.O. Box 446
Soest Utrecht 3765 AK
Netherlands

Bill Strauss
Computer Library of New Zealand Ltd.
P.O. Box 162
Timaru 8615
New Zealand

Wolfgang Willaredt
Prime Soft, W. Willaredt
Dorfstrasse 548
Schneisingen AG CH-5425
Switzerland

Daniel Valls
SMS Shareware
19 Carshalton Road
Camberley, Surrey GU15 4AQ
U.K.

Larry Rozmaryn
North London Shareware
188 Osidge Lane
Southgate, London N14 5DR
U.K.

M. J. Gearing
Softville Computer Supplies
35 Market Parade
Havant, Hampshire P09 1PY
U.K.

Neil Blaber
P. D. (&Shareware)Software Library
Winscombe House, Beacon Road
Crowborough, Sussex TN6 1UL
U.K.

Torsten Droste
Totronik
Rotebuehlstrasse 85
D-70178 Stuttgart 7000
West Germany

Building in an Expiration Date

Once you launch a product into shareware distribution, there is no calling it back. A"stale message" is very simple: When run, the program checks the system date. If the system date is beyond a preset value (I set it to three years after release), the program shows a message something like:

> This is an old version of this program; you are probably about five releases behind. We can no longer support this version of the program. Please obtain a current copy of this program. This program will continue to work as designed, but you are missing out on new features and support for modern hardware.

The program does not stop running. After displaying the message, it runs normally. The purpose of the message is to let the customer know it is time to upgrade and to encourage vendors and bulletin boards to carry current versions of the product.

In addition to using a stale message, you may wish to put a subject-to-price-increases message on your registration screen once the stale date is passed.

I believe in including a stale message in shareware products for a number of reasons:

- You may move. A stale message will help limit the length of time you will have to deal with mail forwarding.
- You will probably adjust the price of your product. Unless you have some way of getting the channel to carry recent releases, you will have to honor an old price for a long time to come.
- It is likely you will need to change registration services or that they will move. By including a stale message, you limit the amount of time you spend redirecting registrations sent to these services.
- An old copy doesn't show your product at its best. You want to compete against similar programs using your most recent releases. Especially if disaster strikes and you ship a product with a bug, a stale message will limit the amount of time you will have to deal with it.
- It's a good way to encourage registered customers to upgrade to new revisions. Especially if you include a data conversion utility (from one release to another) only in registered versions, many unregistered users will register at this time.
- You may become so successful that your distributors pressure you to leave shareware distribution. Stale messages limit the amount of time that old shareware copies float around interfering with your new strategy.

- It helps in forcing vendors to notify you that they are carrying your product. You can be sure they will contact you when they ship products displaying this message to their customers.

Protecting Your Product

Once your product is out in the distribution channel, you really lose control of it. Your documentation may require vendors to contact you before distributing your product, or at least send you a copy of their catalog. Only the ones you would approve automatically will bother to comply with your license terms. The sleazy/lazy ones will do what they want with your program without bothering to look. The cost of suing someone (once you find out) halfway across the continent or globe to stop such practices is prohibitive. In addition, computer vandals are always with us. If you have a popular product, someone will hack it, either for the thrill or out of simple greed.

Your primary ally in defending against these problems is time. Utilize any natural forces that will cause your product to expire. *The ShareWare Book*, for instance, had a couple years' life span at best. Much of what made it useful and valuable was the current information it contained about various players in the industry. A tax return preparation program needs to be updated annually. Using such natural forces of expiration, you can limit the length of the distribution chain and thus limit the amount of time a hacked version of your product is in circulation.

Have the executable spin off any required files when it is run in a new directory. There's no reason that you can't check for your essential .doc files and re-create them if they aren't in the current directory. Doing so will cost a bit in terms of product size, but it is much more likely that the product will move in registerable fashion from computer to computer. No matter what your documentation says, most people will copy only the .exe file when they are making a copy for a friend. Be sure that the things essential to running the program and registering it are in the .exe.

Encouraging Customers to Try Your Product

I do everything I can to encourage my users and customers to share copies of my program. One way I do this is by including a menu option to make a copy. Many, if not most, users don't know enough about computers to copy the necessary files for a friend. If you can do this for them, you may increase your distribution. If you publish a newsletter, this is another place you can encourage people to share copies with friends.

Distribution Services

The ASP offers a distribution service from its author members to its vendor and bulletin board members monthly.

Information on ASP membership is given in the trade association section of "Running a Business," Chapter 11. An author application form is included in the Software Publisher's Kit.

SDN (Shareware Distribution Network) is a North American network of over one hundred bulletin board systems that will quickly transmit your product to all participating boards. You will need an SDN kit (included in the Software Publisher's Kit) to prepare your product for the service. Author participation is free but SDN asks for a $35 donation for setup.

Megapost is a shareware uploading service that seeds the major bulletin boards. A large number of potential customers can be reached quickly and easily, and authors can avoid the hassles and expense of doing it themselves. Megapost includes compression by PKZIP (with authenticity verification) at no extra charge. Download counts for Exec-PC, GEnie, Delphi, and CompuServe are available. A discount coupon for this service is included in the Software Publisher's Kit. For more information, contact:

Andrew M. Saucci, Jr.
641 Koelbel Court
Baldwin, NY 11510-3915

An excellent guide to marketing through shareware is:

Make Money Selling Your Shareware
by **Steven Hudgik**
Windcrest/McGraw-Hill
ISBN 0-07-030865-9
$29.95

The List Shootout

I have long advocated using SDN and the ASP mailing service as an author's primary distribution method, mainly because my early experience in using Jim Hood's method of sending a disk to every possible distribution point in the universe didn't work very well. Then I tried the mass-mailing approach again, using an already successful shareware product to see if my early lack of results was due to the product or to a fundamental problem with using large mailing lists of distributors.

In order to do this, I used the ASP mailing service as a kind of control and tested the effectiveness of Unicorn's (Charles Schell) CompUser, Jim Hood's $hareware Marketing $ystem, and Steve Hudgik's list.

I have one criticism of all the lists: None of them comes with ZIP+4 coding. This fact also tells me that none of them has been "cleaned" by one of the address/ZIP verification programs. If you are going to mail one copy of your shareware to every possible distribution point, being able to use the post office's discounts for clean, sorted, and ZIP+4 coded lists can make a real difference in the cost.

Additionally, only the ASP list has a field for "country." As a result, countries for non-U.S. distributors typically are in the "state" field, and mailing only to U.S. addresses becomes a bit more complicated.

One of the things I did for this test was to take a look at how each list dealt with my own little corner of New Hampshire and Maine. I extracted all records for ZIP codes starting with "03" and compared them with my actual knowledge of the area. If I were to publish a list for my area, it would pretty much mimic the current ASP list. The only addition that I might make would be in the notes area, remarking that The Simple Series is a small distributor with a fairly restricted list of products and that the GEnie Home Office/Small Business bulletin board accepts software relating to small businesses only. The ASP lists two bulletin boards and a single vendor for the area in question.

The mailing itself was composed of 150 identical pieces (except for the "branding" for registrations) sent to names on each list. Since both the M and CompUser lists are rated, only names with an "A" rating were used. Steve Hudgik's list is much shorter and is not rated, so no distinction was made in that case.

The first step was to eliminate ASP vendors and bulletin boards, because they had already been mailed to and they were to serve as the baseline. In order to break out the lists randomly, each list was given a preference series based on the last two digits of the ZIP code; this resulted in approximately 150 names for each list. Where more or less than 150 names were chosen., I used my judgment to select the best names to swap in or out in order to make the number of distributors equal for each list. Duplicates (within the same list source, or because the ZIP codes differed) also were eliminated.

ASP

The ASP list is really three lists, of which I used two: vendor.dbf and bbs.dbf. (An author.dbf comes in the same archive.) You may use the list for free, and ASP membership is not required. A current list of ASP distributors is included in the Software Publisher's Kit.

Vendor.dbf is a dBASE III file. The fields in each record include:

Name	40	Character
Company	40	Character
Address1	35	Character
Address2	35	Character
City	20	Character
State	12	Character
Zipcode	12	Character
Country	12	Character
Country_co	3	Character
Phone	22	Character
Fax_number	20	Character
Vendornum	4	Character
Cis_ppn	11	Character
Rack_vend	1	Character
Royalty	1	Character
Joined	8	Date
Changed	1	Character

BBS.dbf is a dBASE III file. The fields in each record include:

Field	Length	Type
Last_name	30	Character
First_name	20	Character
Company	30	Character
Street	30	Character
Street_2	30	Character
City	20	Character
State	5	Character
Zipcode	12	Character
Country	12	Character
Country_co	3	Character
Low_high	1	Character
Bbs_phone	17	Character
Bbs_number	4	Character
Cis_ppn	12	Character
Joined	8	Date
Changed	1	Character

Both files are updated monthly; since these organizations are ASP members who pay dues to belong, and the ASP mails both disks and newsletters to them regularly, the mailing addresses are extremely accurate, and there are very few inactive addresses on these lists. The ASP listed the following bulletin boards and distributors for my own little test area:

Bulletin Boards:

GARDINER JONES III
THE NOR'EASTER PREMIMUM BBS
67 BAYBERRY LANE
LONDONDERRY, NH 03053-4606

SCHENOT ROBERT
GENIE HOME OFF/SMALL BUS
PO BOX 117
PORTSMOUTH, NH 03802-0117

Distributors:

MR. JAMES C. RICHARDS   Simple Series
PO BOX 1167
PLAISTOW, NH 03865

The ASP would have had an author send three disks to reach three actual distribution points, for a score of 3 and an accuracy rating of 1.0. The ASP database is included the Software Publisher's Kit.

Correcting for the size of the lists, the ASP list (vendors and bulletin boards) generated twenty-one registrations.

Unicorn's CompUser

CompUser calls itself a "rated cyclopedia for Computer Users" and comes on two disks, a program disk and a data disk. The archived files unfold on your disk into almost 1.2Mb of space. The documentation files are stored in justified format, so they are a bit difficult to read, given the variable number of spaces between words. Registration is $30. The documentation states that new data files are distributed three times a year.

The data file, Dist.dat, is a dBASE III file with 1,559 records. The fields in each record include:

Attn	40	Character
Company	45	Character
Address	45	Character
City	30	Character
State	29	Character
Zip	11	Character
Day	15	Character
Dit	1	Character
Bbs	15	Character
Fax	15	Character
Free	15	Character
Updated	8	Date
Assoc	3	Character
Type	1	Character

Rate	1	Character
Rm1	76	Character
Rm2	76	Character
Flag	1	Character

Two fields are worth special mention:

In Assoc, the compiler, Charles Schell, breaks out members of the Association of Shareware Professionals, Independent Shareware Dealer's Association, and Shareware Data Network.

In Type, Schell separates out Authors, BBSs, Computer Clubs, Distributors (vendors), Foreign Distributors, Hardware Dealers, Magazines, Newsletters, Commercial Software Vendors, and Peripheral and Other Supply Vendors.

While this is useful, the length of the fields involved makes it impossible to use a single record for a company that does more than one thing—for example, a club with a newsletter or a distributor with a bulletin board.

Schell has gone to some pains to be sure that the data file is useful only when used with the Clipper access program he has written for it. The data file is called "Dist.dat," meaning that some users won't know to rename it to a .dbf extension in order to use the file with other dBASE software.

When you do bring the data file up with other software, you discover that every field except "company" is encrypted in a crude fashion: All of the characters are raised by the value of 99, and selected fields have the characters in the field in reverse order.

Unless you are willing to do some programming, this limits the utility of the database to the functions included in the associated program. Since I wanted to select a number of records (based on Schell's rating and the type of company), tag those records with a flag that told me that the source was the CompUser database, then merge this file with the other files to eliminate the duplicates, programming to unencrypt the data was necessary.

Unless your printer is hooked to Lpt1, you can't print using this program. This fact also had the effect of preventing (without special measures) export of the database. The menu allows you to print postcards or a list of vendors (without the Attention field).

There was no way to print envelopes for submission of disks, nor any way that I could find to bring a selected list over to a mailmerge to word processing.

I was doing my own programming to get the dBASE format files into a format my word processor could handle anyway, so I simply added a couple of lines to the part of the program exporting CompUser data to deal with these. It took an extra 15 minutes or so.

The format of the CompUser program also makes it difficult to spot duplicates, which may be the reason there were so many of them. In my own little test area, CompUser listed the following bulletin boards and distributors:

Bulletin Boards:

GARDINER JONES
THE NOR'EASTER PREMIUM
67 BAYBERRY LANE
LONDONDERRY, NH 03053

JANET ATTARD
GENIE HOME OFF/SMALL BUS
C/O ROBERT SCHENOT
PORTSMOUTH, NH 03802-0117

Distributors:

JAMES C RICHARDS, PARTNER
SIMPLE SERIES
PO BOX 1167
PALISTOW, NH 03865

JIM RICHARDS, LIBRARIAN
THE SIMPLE SERIES
P.O. BOX 1167
PALISTOW, NH 03865

AUTHOR SUBMISSIONS & UPDATES
THE SOFTWARE KINGDOM
168 PLAISTOW ROAD
PALISTOW, NH 03865

AUTHOR SUBMISSIONS & UPDATES
THE SOFTWARE PRESCRIPTIONS CO.
168 PLAISTOW ROAD
PALISTOW, NH 03865

AUTHOR SUBMISSIONS & UPDATES
THE SOFTWARE SHOPPE
168 PLAISTOW ROAD
PALISTOW, NH 03865

Portsmouth is a small town, but I doubt that mail would be delivered to me (GEnie HOSB) without the post office box number (although the ZIP+4 code does make that a possibility).

The original street address of The Simple Series is 168 Plaistow Road. When I called Jim Richards to ask him about the listings for Plaistow, he told me that the other distributors listed (besides The Simple Series) simply don't exist or were once suppliers to him.

CompUser would have had an author send seven disks to reach two actual distribution points, for a score of 2 and an accuracy rating of .286. Of the 150 disks mailed first class using this list, 22 were returned by the Postal Service as undeliverable (15 percent).

The mailing to this list generated no registrations at all.

$hareware Marketing $ystem

Jim Hood's $hareware Marketing $ystem is both a newsletter and a database. Outside of the ASP lists (which are not well known, and are hard to find), M is probably the industry standard, and deserves the trophy award given it by Public Brand.

The newsletter portion is extensive in its reach, is well written, and full of useful information for authors. On the other hand, Jim Hood doesn't seem to check his data all that well. In the edition being evaluated, he listed seven sysop associations that he suggested authors mail disks to. I did. Of the seven, two came back marked "no such address."

Jim calls M "shareware," but isn't completely "try before you buy" (more like "look before you buy"); the screen used to unpack the database makes it very clear that you must license the use of the database *before* doing any mailing to it, that it contains decoy addresses, and that you agree to pay extra penalties if you are caught using the database without a license.

The entire package requires over 3.5Mb of disk space. Registration for a single issue is $49.95; an annual (quarterly updates) subscription is $175. I wish that Jim would split registration of his database from that of his newsletter; I am not likely to mail to the list quarterly, but I sure would like to read the newsletter. On the other hand, I'm not sure that the newsletter alone is worth $175 a year.

There are two data files; Databas2.dbf is a corrections file to the main database. The main data file, Database.dbf, is a dBASE III file with 4,302 records. The fields in each record include:

Company	44	Character
Address	50	Character
City	30	Character
State	43	Character
Zip	12	Character
Date_revis	8	Date
Type	6	Character
Rating	2	Character
Labeltop	40	Character
Firstname	20	Character
Lastname	20	Character
Position	30	Character
Day_tel	28	Character
Bbs_tel	19	Character
Fax_tel	16	Character
Tollfree_o	13	Character
Affiliatio	13	Character
Print_	1	Character
Remarks1	80	Character
Remarks2	80	Character

The TYPE field is worth special mention: It may contain one or more codes indicating that a name is a Disk vendor, Foreign, Club, BBS, Magazine (or newspaper), Corporate user, and Key shareware contact; for example, a foreign club that ran a bulletin board would have the code "F,C,B."

The fact that M is a simple dBASE file makes it reasonably easy to spot duplicates, which may be part of the reason there were so few of them. In my own little test area, M listed the following bulletin boards and distributors:

Bulletin Boards:

THE SHOP
EXETER, NH 603/772-7803

GARDINER JONES
THE NOR'EASTER PREMIUM
61 BAYBERRY LANE
LONDONDERRY, NH 03053
603/432-6711

HOBBIT HOLE
SANFORD, ME 207/490-2159

ROBERT SCHENOT
COMPASS, NEW ENGLAND
POB 117
PORTSMOUTH, NH 03802
603/431-8030

Clubs:

F SCHULZ
MS DOS USERS GROUP
POB 153
BARRINGTON, NH 03824

JEFF WADE
PORTSMOUT PC USRS GROUP
5 THORNTON LANE
ELIOT, ME 03903

JOHN RALEIGH
DBASE ACADEMY
TT&T CORP 387 LAFAYETTE RD BX 180
HAMPTON, NH 03842

C HARRIMAN
PORTSMOUTH IBM PC USERS GROUP
57 SOUTH
PORTSMOUTH, NH 03801

Distributors:

JIM RICHARDS
THE SIMPLE SERIES
POB 1167
PALISTOW, NH 03865 603/372-3344

As with the other lists, I did some checking. For the bulletin boards, one of the numbers was no longer correct—but the number had been changed recently enough that the telephone company gave out the new number. Jim Hood did less well with the clubs. Cynthia Harriman, John Raleigh, and Jeff Wade are all known to me personally, both through the Boston Computer Society and through local professional associations.

I spoke to Cynthia first. I asked her: "What's likely to happen to an MS-DOS shareware diskette sent to this (above) address?" Cynthia was very forthright and didn't hesitate a moment. She told me that, since 1988, all mail addressed to the IBM PC group at her address has been thrown away unopened. I had kind of guessed that that might be the answer, since I knew that she had committed to the Mac universe at about that time.

I then spoke to John Raleigh, and asked him when he had last held a "dBASE Academy" meeting. The answer was about two years ago. When I asked what would happen to a disk addressed as per the list, he said that he'd probably look at it out of curiosity if it was a subject that interested him. Then it would be recycled into his scratch bin.

The last time the Portsmouth chapter of the Boston Computer Society had a meeting that was announced in the society's calendar was about 18 months ago, and the chapter had never maintained a library, so I thought I knew what Jeff Wade would say when I called. Jeff wasn't sure if the group was still meeting, but confirmed that it had never maintained a formal library. When asked what would happen to a disk sent to him, he gave essentially the same answer as John Raleigh.

F SCHULZ of the MS DOS USERS GROUP of Barrington, NH, doesn't reply to letters with self-addressed stamped envelopes enclosed and is not listed in the telephone book. Since I've never seen an announcement of a users group meeting in the local paper, I have to assume that it doesn't exist.

Since I'm assuming that authors will be much more likely to mail diskettes than to call small boards in New Hampshire, I scored M only on the mailing addresses listed. M would have had an author send seven disks to reach three actual distribution points, for a score of 3 and an accuracy rating of .429. Of the 150 disks mailed first class using this list, 2 were returned by the Postal Service as undeliverable (1 percent).

Mailing to this list generated two registrations.

Homecraft

Steve Hudgik is a shareware author who specializes in software for collectors. His lists are not offered as shareware; they are strictly buy, then try. On the other hand, he offers a good deal of information at a modest price: four lists, with unlimited usage for $24.95. The lists he offers are:

Vendor.dbf (which includes bulletin boards)
Usergrp.dbf
Non-USA.dbf
Editors.dbf
Newspap.dbf

The publicity lists are not rated here, but appear to be worthwhile on their own. Since foreign addresses were not a part of this test, the Non-USA file was not evaluated, but appeared to be reasonably accurate and up-to-date.

The vendor file, Vendor.dbf, is a dBASE III file with 676 records. The fields in each record include:

Updated	20	Character
Response	15	Character

Contact	40	Character
Company	40	Character
Street	40	Character
City	22	Character
State	5	Character
Zip	10	Character
Note	15	Character
Voice	14	Character
Bbsphone	14	Character
Faxphone	14	Character
Cis	12	Character
Genie	12	Character
Royalty	2	Character
Racks	2	Character
Bbs	2	Character
Catalog	2	Character
Fleamarket	2	Character
Storefront	2	Character

The computer club file, UserGrp.dbf is a dBASE III file with 82 records. The fields in each record include:

Zip	10	Character
Name	40	Character
Address1	40	Character
Address2	40	Character
City	40	Character
State	4	Character
Note	40	Character

Like M, these are dBASE files, making spotting duplicates fairly easy. Few were found. In my own little test area, Homecraft listed the following bulletin boards and distributors:

Bulletin Boards:

Gardiner Jones
Nor'Easter Premium
67 Bayberry Lane
Londonderry, NH 03053

Distributors:

Software Connection, Inc.
P.O. Box 188
Auburn, NH 03032

Michelle Menard
Software Kingdom
P.O. Box 555
Auburn, NH 03032

James C. Richards
Simple Series
P.O. Box 1167
Plaistow, NH 03865

As with the other lists, I did some checking. Neither Software Connection nor Software Kingdom is known to the telephone company. I sent each a diskette, with a letter and a self-addressed stamped envelope enclosed, explaining what I was doing, and asking them to let me know if they were in business. Neither one responded, so I assume that these vendors are not useful distribution points.

Homecraft would have had an author send four disks to reach two actual distribution points, for a score of 2 and an accuracy rating of .5. Of the 150 disks mailed first class using this list, 20 were returned by the Postal Service as undeliverable (13 percent).

Mailing to this list generated two registrations.

List Conclusions

The ASP list was the only list worth mailing to, and even it was only marginally useful when compared to direct marketing. While it generated 21 registrations based on a mailing of 150 diskettes mailed to shareware vendors and bulletin boards, when I mailed the same number of diskettes to shareware authors, I received 16 registrations. Clearly, even the best shareware distribution is only marginally better than simply mailing shareware to prospective end users, at least for a narrowly focused product.

To put this into perspective, a single upload to CompuServe's Share Lib 4 has generated over 100 registrations and one upload to a single Internet site has generated 35.

The Distribution Package

The mailing itself was designed to be as inexpensive as possible, given the intermittent nature and low volumes a typical author is doing. For this reason, the mailing was restricted to the United States, and the pieces were designed to be sent out nonsorted first-class mail (just under one ounce). I mailed 150 disks to each of the three lists (a total of 450 disks) for just under $200.

Diskette Cost

The actual (cash) cost per diskette was: $.07264. That's right, just over 7 cents a diskette! I purchased 500 diskettes from ERM for $30 + $6.32 s/h. They are 5.25-inch DS/DD factory seconds, but less than 1 percent failed to format to at least 300Kb. I bought them in two batches; the first lot was full of overlabels (diskettes duped and labeled for software houses, but never shipped), some notch-less diskettes, and some DS/HD diskettes. The second batch was all new, unformatted 5.25-inch notched DS/DD diskettes. The person I spoke to said that shipments vary, but that most shipments are more like my second experience than my first. Given the price, I'd buy these disks for distribution even if their typical batch was primarily overlabels. I ended up not removing the labels from the overlabeled diskettes, but instead added an extra small label of my own (see Figure 4.2).

Recycled

This floppy disk guaranteed as recycled from
previously distributed software diskettes.
Disk reformatted for your protection.
All bytes remanufactured in the USA from
new, premium quality electrons.

Figure 4.2. Recycled label.

ERM's contact information is given at the beginning of the
book; they will send a flyer and ship outside the United States.
Other suppliers of very cheap diskettes include:

Media Factory
1930 Junction Ave
San Jose, CA 95131
toll free: (800) 886-6833
fax: (408) 456-9298
voice: (408) 456-9182

Publishers Network, Inc.
Box 500
Vista, CA 92085
voice: (619) 941-4100

Surplus Software International
489 North 8th Street
Hood River, OR 97031
toll free: (800) 753-7877
voice: (503) 386-1375
fax: (503) 386-4227

Disk Contents

On the disk, there were a number of files:

```
Volume in drive A is SHAREBOOK1
Directory of A:\
SHAREBK1 ZIP 293178 5-12-92 1:00a
FILE_ID DIZ 636 10-15-92 8:38a
SYSOP DOC 15704 10-14-92 9:38a
```

```
VENDOR DOC 15704 10-14-92 9:38a
SHAREBK DOC 771 5-12-92 1:00a
REGISTER DOC 2759 5-12-92 1:00a
UNZIP EXE 11644 11-07-92 2:06p
 7 File(s) 18432 bytes free
```

ShareBk1.zip is in turn composed of:

Length	Size	Ratio	Date	Time	Name
636	508	21%	10-15-92	08:38	FILE_ID.DIZ
771	563	27%	05-12-92	01:00	SHAREBK.DOC
15704	5968	62%	10-14-92	09:38	VENDOR.DOC
3108	1412	55%	08-06-92	16:04	REGISTER.DOC
771888	284215	64%	05-12-92	01:00	SHAREBK.EXE
792107	292666	64%			5

As you may have noticed, there is duplication inside and outside the .zip. First off, the Sysop.doc and Vendor.doc files are identical; they differ only in name. The reason for this is simple; many sysops won't look at a vendor.doc and many vendors ignore sysop.doc files. Since there's ample room on the disk, it made sense simply to duplicate the file under different names rather than deal with people who couldn't find what they were looking for.

There is duplication inside and outside the .zip file as well. The .doc and .diz files outside of the .zip are a convenience to recipients, so that they won't have to unzip the archive to find out what the program is about.

The reason that all those .doc and .diz files are also included in the .zip archive is because the .zip archive is the only shareware product that will be passed on by the vendor or bulletin board. For this reason, you want to have those files inside the .zip as well; the distributor is very unlikely to rezip things to include them for the convenience of the next person in line.

The product itself (ShareBk.exe) was branded with a different "sales code" for each of the three mailing lists so that I could report registration performance.

Finally, a freeware unzip program is included. This program is under 12Kb and also is included as a convenience. There actually are people out there (especially reviewers) who don't have a registered unzip program. This allows them to unarchive the .zip without hunting around for someone with the right tool. If I bottled wine, I'd send a corkscrew with any bottle I sent to a reviewer too.

A copy of an updated freeware unzipper is included in the bonus files provided in the Software Publisher's Kit.

Sleeve/Flyer Cost

The cost per sleeve/flyer was $.05. I don't use mass-produced sleeves anymore because they cost money and add weight to the package, while taking up most of the space you could be using for getting the sysop or librarian excited about your product.

When I was the gatekeeper for the Home Office/Small Business library on GEnie, I received many packages for upload from authors. Many come with flyers, but these flyers are usually not very effective, since they have to be unfolded to be seen. In doing a quick review to decide what to upload next, the only thing visible is generally the disk label, which usually tells me very little. In reaction to this, I invented my own way of making my diskette stand out.

Instead of the usual sleeve with flyer and disk inside, I have prepared a flyer that also acts as the sleeve for the diskette. It is photocopied onto 60 pound (very heavy; almost like construction paper) fluorescent lime-green paper that is very close to the color chosen for the cover of *The ShareWare Book* itself. The flyer is laid out horizontally (8.5 inches high by 11 inches wide) in three panels; the center panel is 5.5 inches wide and carries an image of the front cover of the book. The two columns to either side are 2.75 inches wide. One carries a full column of quotes from my best reviews, the other carries a features list.

The flyer is first folded almost in half lengthwise, then the two "wings" are folded in, resulting in a pocket the size of a diskette sleeve. (The words on the cover of the book are now hidden inside; the front panel of the sleeve shows only the graphic from the cover of the book.) The labeled diskette is then inserted, and the rear label attached to hold the diskette in the envelope and the wings down.

The words on the wings were spaced so that the fold will occur in the middle of paragraphs; this helps to encourage the recipient to unfold the flyer to see the full cover of the book and the remaining promotional text.

My local Staples outlet will reproduce these flyers for $.05 each in quantity 50. I could save a penny by using lightweight colored paper and could bring the cost down to 3 cents each by using standard white paper. I think that the color and weight add to the punch, so I'll continue to use the more expensive paper for now.

Label Cost

The cost per primary label was $.0096. I buy my laser disk labels from Quill (1.5 x 4 inches; 14 to a sheet, 100 sheets to a box) for $13.49 a box. If you order enough stuff in a single order (and buying just one toner cartridge does this), the shipping is free within the United States. The contact information for Quill is:

Quill Corporation
P.O. Box 94080
Palatine, IL 60094-4080
(708) 634-4800
fax: (708) 634-5708

Quill will not ship outside the United States.

The label looks like the one in Figure 4.3.

The ShareWare Book <ASP>

"By far the most comprehensive work for shareware authors
I've seen; a trophy rating"--Public Brand Software
"Complete coverage of developing for the shareware market
from someone who has been there"--Midnight Engineering

Contains Copyrighted Material
See .doc & File_ID.DIZ files for description and distribution requirements
.ZIP edition; For more information, please contact:
Robert Schenot (603) 431 8030; CIS:70511,720; GEnie:R.Schenot
POBox 117, Portsmouth, NH 03802-0117, USA

Figure 4.3   Primary label.

Only the top half of the label shows above the sleeve; the line of dashes on the label approximately lines up with the top of the sleeve. I put the information that I hope will get the sysop interested on the top half, and reserve the necessary but dull information for the bottom half of the label.

I do include the <ASP> next to the product name; I am finding that more and more vendors and sysops will look at ASP member shareware first.

The contact information on the bottom of the label is essential if the diskette itself becomes damaged. Since I never trust a sleeve to stay with its diskette, I try to get essential product identification, marketing, and author contact information on the diskette label itself. I have had people call for a copy based on just the label, after the diskette itself was reused and passed on.

Back Label

The cost per back label was $.0045. These are 2.625 x 1 inch laser labels from Quill; a box of 3,000 sells for $13.49. This label is the only place that I ask someone to *do* something (see Figure 4.4).

Please share this Shareware!

Upload to your favorite bulletin board—
Mail to a vendor that doesn't list it—
Donate to your user group library—
Give it to a friend!

Figure 4.4   Back label.

The cost of postage is $.232 per disk. Yes, I said that I'm sending the disks out first class, unsorted. I buy my postage at a 20 percent discount (80 percent of face value) from Henry Gitner Philatelists. For large mailings, I use their United Nations stamps, and mail through the UN Postmaster. (Parcel post a box full of mail there.) The stamps are old, colorful, and of various denominations that will add up to the $.29 the Postal Service wants. I'm convinced that the envelope gets noticed due to the strange stamps while saving me money. Details on discount postage are in Chapter 14.

Envelope Cost

The cost per envelope was $.0287. This is a 6x9-inch catalog envelope, sold 500 to the box for $14.34. No special mailer or stiffener.

Obviously, there is going to be some fallout sending diskettes out without any protection. It took me about two months to save up 200 diskettes that had made a "round trip"; the Postal Service had attempted to deliver the envelope, had some trouble with the address, and returned it to me. I'm not sure if this is a commentary on the number of diskettes I'm mailing out or the generally poor quality of the lists available. I tested each of the 200 diskettes by doing a Norton disk test on the files and by testing the integrity of the archive. Of the 200, three disks presented a problem. Of the three, I was able to "repair" two by simply gently flexing the diskette and rubbing the edges against a hard surface. (These are tricks I expect most sysops and vendors to be familiar with.) Only one disk of the 200 was truly beyond repair.

Quite honestly, given the number of mangled mailers I receive regularly, I was surprised at this low count. I have to assume that, given 200 round-trip tests, the dropout rate for one-way diskettes is about 1 percent. The envelope itself (see Figure 4.5) is an advertisement for the product inside.

It takes no more time and just a little more toner to print some interesting things on the outside to induce recipients to open the envelope. Since the object is to get the envelope opened, I purposely chose to tease with quotes that left the impression that this was something wonderful without necessarily telling what the heck it is. The extra-large "Please Don't Fold!" across the bottom does seem to help protect the diskette a little.

The [code] (printed very small) at the bottom simply tells me which list this address is from. It helps both in making sure that the correct branded diskettes get into the correct envelopes and will allow me to sort the undeliverables (and report them to you) and return them to the list author for correction.

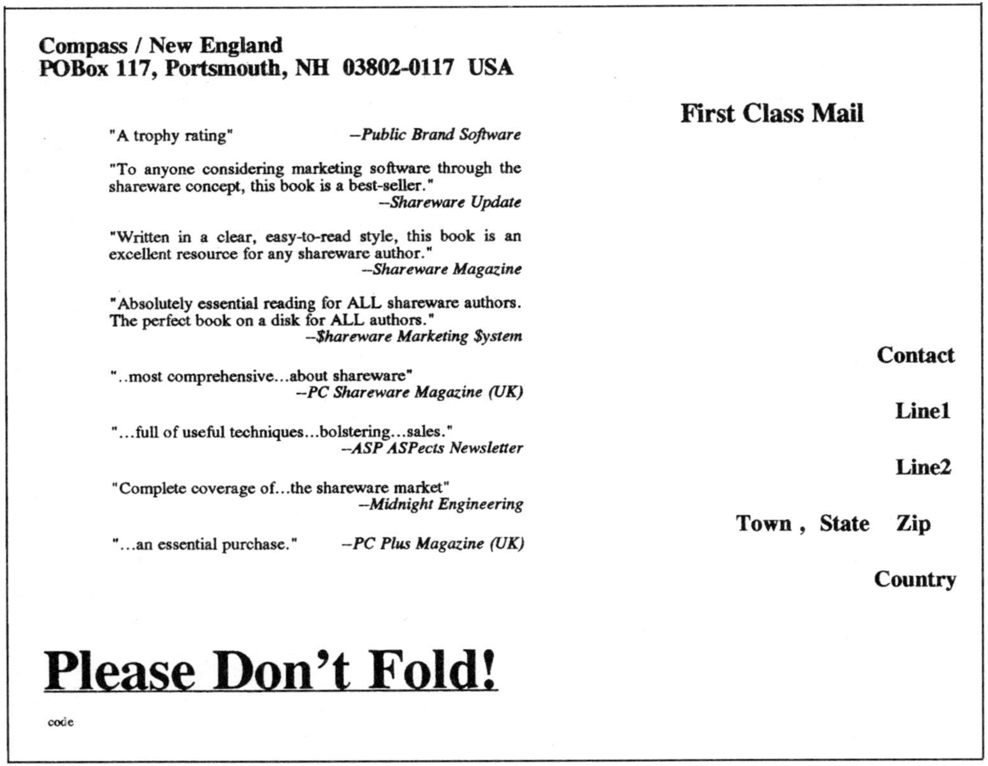

Compass / New England
POBox 117, Portsmouth, NH 03802-0117 USA

First Class Mail

"A trophy rating" —*Public Brand Software*

"To anyone considering marketing software through the
shareware concept, this book is a best-seller."
—*Shareware Update*

"Written in a clear, easy-to-read style, this book is an
excellent resource for any shareware author."
—*Shareware Magazine*

"Absolutely essential reading for ALL shareware authors.
The perfect book on a disk for ALL authors."
—*Shareware Marketing System*

"...most comprehensive...about shareware"
—*PC Shareware Magazine (UK)*

"...full of useful techniques...bolstering...sales."
—*ASP ASPects Newsletter*

"Complete coverage of...the shareware market"
—*Midnight Engineering*

"...an essential purchase." —*PC Plus Magazine (UK)*

Please Don't Fold!

code

Contact

Line1

Line2

Town , State Zip

Country

Figure 4.5   The envelope.

Registration Encouragement Techniques

The most effective registration encouragement technique is to pick your target market wisely and design your product carefully in the first place. A program used daily by many people in a business will be registered. A $50 arcade game sold to eleven-year-olds won't.

One of the best ways to approach this topic is to think about why some people don't register, even though they're supposed to. When users don't register shareware, it may be due to one or more of these reasons:

- It is an *act of omission*, not commission. To actively copy commercial software is a conscious act. To let a deadline slip by doesn't require much thinking.
- It is a *solitary act*. People think they won't be seen by others and therefore won't be caught and shamed. Besides. . . .
- *"Everyone else does it*—so it must not be so bad." This rationalization helps alleviate any guilt resulting from "solitary act."
- They *didn't take anything*—nothing physical has been stolen from the author. Like people who tie into cable TV without paying, they don't feel that you have been hurt or deprived by their actions.
- *"I gave at the office."* "Didn't I buy this program once already (from the vendor)? Somebody wants more money from me now?"
- Like a *stray cat*, a shareware program just seems to belong to its adopted owner after a while. Any sense of obligation about doing right by the true owner fades with time.
- The author is *anonymous*. People won't take a pen that obviously belongs to someone, even if that person is not in the room, but many people think nothing of taking one from work or a bank, or one that isn't attached to somebody.
- *"Poor me.* The guy who wrote this program is sitting out there just raking in big bucks, while I struggle to get by. Those fat cats won't miss my twenty bucks."
- They aren't sure you're real, and they're afraid they'll get a *fish in the face* rather than a good feeling after registering. Either they once sent a check to an author and never got a response, or they fear that result. You hear about people getting taken by bogus businesses all the time.

- *"I didn't know* I was supposed to. My friend put it in a batch file for me, and it's worked fine ever since. You say I'm supposed to send money to somebody? For what?"
- "This program *isn't perfect.* When I export an odd number of records that are exactly half of the database in .txt format, it gives me a spurious error message. If it were a shelfware product I'd complain. I just won't register this one."
- Many people *don't know how* to register. Some authors provide a text file on disk and expect the user to read it, then print a registration form. This is beyond the abilities of a significant portion of the population using computers, who never see a DOS prompt and have no idea what to do with instructions that require the use of DOS commands.

By addressing these issues in our shareware, we can gently nudge the customer to see things the way we do. The first job of registration encouragement techniques is to address the reasons for not registering. It is the author's job to remind potential customers gently that they are using the program for a trial period and that payment will be expected. Adding some humor to the documentation helps to make you a "real" person. Testing and retesting your software will help to avoid the "imperfection" reason for nonregistration. Making the program easy to register will remove many of the other excuses. I am absolutely convinced that yelling "thief" at potential customers may make the publisher feel better, but rarely brings in registrations.

Purposely limiting the software distributed on the disk—or crippling the program—is a natural (if counterproductive) reaction to an author's perception that large numbers of people are not paying their way. My personal definition of crippling is that it is a negative registration encouragement technique that depresses the distribution of the product.

Vendors won't carry your product if people complain about it. Crippling doesn't work because, ultimately, registrations are a function of distribution. Successful registration encouragement techniques do not depress distribution but offer something that customers perceive to have value in addition to the package they already have. In this sense, shareware is really advertising the real product—what customers get for registering. In this way, the shareware may in fact create demand. For example, note the way the Commander Keen games leave customers hungering for the two last games.

Crippling seems to work when you have the *only* program that performs a function. As soon as you have competition, however, a couple of things happen. First, most vendors have limited catalog space and carry only one product for each function. Given a choice between crippled and noncrippled programs, they will generally carry the noncrippled program. Because of lower distribution, registrations for the crippled program go down. To a lesser extent, word about crippled products gets around the BBSs, with the same result. People rarely respond positively to crippling. Instead, they get mad and find another solution to their problem.

There is another factor to consider as well. Many shareware registrations come from people giving copies to other people. People are more likely to keep a program on their hard disks and use it if it works, and thus are more likely to share it. The idea is that, while you might lose some registrations because of noncrippling, you gain distribution, which eventually overcomes the lower registration rate.

No matter how you distribute your software, there will always be people who keep it on their drives without paying. I'm a great believer in "what goes around comes around." If someone really is using your program without paying, that's on his karma, not yours. Try to think of him as an unpaid salesman. Since your shareware version is your advertising, he may ultimately end up providing you a free service by giving a copy to someone who does register. Having marketed software through more traditional channels as well, I'd say you may be better off without these people's money. They are the ones most likely to take up support time, complain, and stir up other trouble.

People ordinarily register shareware because of positive incentives. While feeling good about themselves (honesty) is a legitimate incentive, it seems to work rather slowly. The more incentives you can offer, the higher and faster your registration rate.

Please keep in mind that a higher distribution rate feeds on itself. As more people order disks with your product, vendors are more likely to push it. As more people use the product (whether they pay or not), the more word-of-mouth referrals you'll get. My own personal guess is that a 1 percent increase in distribution is worth a 5 percent increase in my registration rate. The implication of this is that you will be better served to concentrate on your distribution rate. If something is likely to increase registrations but decrease distribution, it isn't worth it in the long run.

I suggest you try an experiment before you consider any of the techniques mentioned in this book. Get copies of a couple dozen shareware programs. Select programs in categories that you might need in the near future—or any other category you're interested in—including the category in which your product will compete, and select both popular and little-known packages. Use the programs. Evaluate them as a typical prospective customer would. Which ones never even got installed? Which ones got only a couple of minutes of use before you knew that they weren't right for you? Which ones got deleted after a day or two because of bugs, bad documentation, or crippling? Take notes. Learn from your experience.

Now you have the proper perspective to think about registration encouragement techniques!

Depending on your product and market, you can use a variety of techniques to encourage registrations. Listed and described in the following sections, in approximate order of effectiveness, are all of the registration encouragement techniques I've found. Included are some not available to ASP members under current rules.

If you've ever taken a sales course, you know that much of your time is spent on learning closing techniques. I won't get into that here, but I do suggest that people are unlikely to buy if you never ask for the order. Remember to close the sale.

Trust

Honesty is the time-honored registration incentive. By providing your prospective customers with a fully functional product and asking them to reciprocate that trust, you are using this technique. This technique seems to be most effective when used with programs that are used frequently by affluent adults. As your target market moves toward a less affluent audience and toward education or recreation, this incentive seems to become less effective. It has mixed results in business. Many managers and accounting departments won't pay just because "it is the right thing to do."

In government, doing the right thing may even be illegal: Civil servants paying for something the government is not obligated to pay for may be fired or jailed for their efforts. Setting a legal time limit on your shareware product's evaluation period creates the legal obligation a government employee needs to send you money.

FBI Warning

Legality is the second time-honored registration incentive. Simply by putting your prospective customers on notice that they have a time-limited trial period and are obligated to pay in order to continue use, you are using this technique. This notice seems to be most effective for programs that are used frequently in businesses. In situations where "doing the right thing" isn't sufficient, displaying the following sometimes brings results:

> Continued use is a violation of 17 United States Code, sections 101 through 810. This carries severe personal and corporate penalties.

The next time you rent a video, take a good look at its FBI WARNING for ideas.

Registration Reminder Screens

The registration reminder screen method of notifying/reminding your potential customers that they are expected to pay is to have the shareware version of the program display a screen or two explaining the shareware concept, pointing them to a registration file that can be printed out, then waiting for an "any key" press. These screens usually are displayed at the beginning and/or end of the program's execution. Registration generally brings some instructions on how to turn off the display of these screens.

If you don't do anything else, do this. I hope you'll also use some additional techniques that will make this basic idea more effective. A registration reminder screen or two seems to be the most effective in reinforcing your honest user's inclination to register. Additional screens seem to work against it because of a perceived lack of trust.

This technique is very effective with businesses, since using a product that hasn't been paid for (and is vocal about it) is hardly the example a business wants to set for its employees.

Randomness

If people know that a registration reminder screen appears every time the program is used, they quickly stop "seeing" it. They expect it and blast by, usually hitting the "any key" before the screen is even written. By making the occurrence of the screen random (both the likelihood of its appearing and just when it appears), program users will notice it each time. This actually allows you to use fewer registration reminders, since the ones you do use become more effective.

Another way to use randomness to your advantage is to have a number of registration reminder screens, each one emphasizing a different single benefit of registration. While you may show only a couple in any one session, the change and different reasons will get noticed.

Good Vibrations

Why do people really register? In many cases, it's because they like you. You have done something for them and they feel that the appropriate thing is to reciprocate. Anything you can do to let them know you trust them and want to help them (such as taking their support calls during the evaluation period) will reinforce this feeling. Excessive reminder screens and threatening language tend to destroy this rapport.

By injecting your personality into your product, you also make it difficult for your potential customers to feel that failing to register hurts "nobody."

Be Real

Many people pick up the phone before registering. They may say it's a support call, but many of them are trying to be sure that you are really there—they don't want to send a check and never get a response. Some of the things you can do to be more "real" to potential customers include the following:

- Provide a professional look—both in the program and in the documentation.
- Publish your phone number and offer free installation help prior to registration. Even if you'll take calls only during restricted hours, this allows people to confirm your existence to their own satisfaction.
- Send out new releases on a regular basis.
- Be visible. If you are talking, or people are talking about you, you must still be around.
- Guarantee that you'll send a registration package before depositing their check.

Ramping

Different people respond to different registration incentives. Some will be impressed with a program that is unobtrusive in very occasionally suggesting registration. Some won't respond unless reminded repeatedly. Others won't register until and unless they are faced with an FBI WARNING and continuing to use the product becomes inconvenient. By changing your registration encouragement messages and techniques slowly, you can appeal to the different reasons for registering.

I begin with no registration reminders at all. The first dozen times the program is used, I'm doing all that I can to hold customers, not turn them off. After that initial period, I begin offering very gentle reminders that appeal to the customers' sense of honesty and trust. If honesty and trust turn out to be ineffective, I try to sell registration based on the additional incentives that registration offers. Finally, I inform the users in no uncertain terms that their trial period has expired and that they are violating the law.

If you are going to use any kind of a counter, it is critical that it be reset whenever the program is passed on. One of the techniques for doing this is discussed on page 107 under "automatic unregistration." Unregistered copies also have all counters reset to zero, and the program reverts to its "default" state. You also might consider resetting the counter when the unregistered program has not been used for some period of time.

Times Square

I call this technique "Times Square" because it resembles the sign made up of lights in Times Square (New York) that displays a moving message. It combines the random and good vibrations techniques. If you have a line on your display screen that is normally blank or is filled with graphic characters, you may choose occasionally to have a pleasant registration reminder travel slowly across that row (at a rate of about four columns per second) and then return to normal. No user keypress is used. This technique should be coded so it does not interrupt any ongoing work. (You may want to wait for a short time with no input; you want your potential customer reading and thinking when this occurs.) Most users are amused and respond favorably.

Branding

Especially for business programs, "branding" is a simple and effective way to encourage registrations. Using this technique, an unregistered program shows "Evaluation copy; your name here" on the header of the main screen and, perhaps, on reports produced by the program. When a customer pays the registration fee, you send a registration key file along with the current copy of the program. The existence of the registration key file turns off the registration reminder screens and inserts the customer's name in the headings.

When used on a printed output that is given to others—as on invoices payable to "Evaluation Copy," tax returns prepared by "Evaluation Copy," or an environmental compliance report submitted by "Evaluation Copy," this technique is called "watermarking."

Branding requires additional work and makes direct shipping from your distributors impossible.

Convenience

I am constantly amazed at how difficult some authors make registering their products. I believe the registration rate is directly related to how easy it is. For that reason I go through a fair amount of work to let potential customers register from inside the program.

Doing so also gives me a chance to gather some very interesting and useful statistics. By having customers print out and send to me an invoice generated from a "Register" option inside the program, I can accomplish a number of things:

- I get them to print out an acceptance certificate and license acknowledgment. If a situation developed where we found ourselves in court, this would be a very useful piece of paper to have.
- I can obtain a signature for a credit card order. Without a signature, any credit card charge can be reversed. With both a signature and a certificate of acceptance, you have a reasonable chance of keeping your money (if you choose to fight).
- I make it easy for business customers to have accounts payable cut a check. Without an invoice, this can be next to impossible. With the invoice I print out a second page, a "Customer Comment Form," that I use for gathering information. I find this especially helpful in learning about why users chose to evaluate my particular package and what problems they had in installing and learning to use it.
- I gather some statistics and bury them in a "sales code" that is printed on the invoice. This may actually be the best reason for letting customers register from inside the program, by the way. My sales code reveals which distribution channel delivered the program to the customers, when they first installed the program, when the invoice was printed out, which version of the program they were using, how many times they used the program, what generation the shareware copy is (how many times has it passed from hand to hand?), and the size of the database. Since I also use the ramping technique, this gives me some indication of which registration encouragement technique actually worked with a particular user.

Some shareware authors put their registration information in a text file, under a name such as "register.me" or "orderfm.txt." Many users don't have the expertise to look at text files on disk (assuming they find them in the first place), much less print them. I am honestly amazed that authors using this technique get paid as often as they do.

Handwriting is a problem. When I used handwritten forms, a significant portion of my registration packages came back as undeliverable, since I couldn't transcribe the address. Using an on-screen form that is then printed makes transcription much more accurate.

Data entry is a problem; I certainly make mistakes. If you use in-program data entry, you can use an internal validation code (part of the sales code) that should match your data entry validation code. If the codes don't match, the customer's keystrokes don't match yours, and you need to find the problem.

Finally, make it easy to get paid. I accept almost any form of payment. These issues are discussed in "Payment Methods" (page 264) in Chapter 13.

Offering a Manual as an Incentive

When surveys are taken of people who register shareware, the most frequent response is "to get a manual." Even if this wouldn't motivate you, remember that it does motivate a significant segment of your potential customer base.

A manual is an effective incentive when:

- The manual itself is long.
- The program is complex.
- Some functions are used infrequently (accounting end-of-the-year closeout, for instance).
- The person using the program tends to change (as in business use).

Volatility

Software that goes out of date can result in sales via a subscription method. Tax and other government compliance programs are an obvious example of this. Virus scanners and shareware books also can use this technique.

For software that is at least partially data-based and where timeliness is important, sell subscriptions. The normal time lag in shareware distribution is about six months. Promising to send out new version notices to people and upgrade them promptly might help in gaining an ongoing revenue stream.

The underlying data also may require a subscription. A good example of this is selling mailing lists through shareware.

Contests

Animated Software (Adventure Game Toolkit) runs an annual contest for the best game developed with its product. The contest generates a great deal of publicity that helps distribution. As you might expect, very few people enter the contest without registering first.

Fruit Basket

I call this the fruit basket technique because it is similar to a method sometimes used to sell baskets of fruit—a free sample of fruit is given out to help customers imagine what the entire basket must taste like.

This technique can be used for any collection of stand-alone programs that target a common customer base. It can be used for utilities but also can be used for a collection of statistical tools for actuaries or analysis tools for investors. It works like this:

• Establish a registration price for the entire collection that is dramatically lower than the total registration fee charged for the products if registered individually.

• Distribute each program as a separate shareware product. Each must make sense on its own, be fully functional, and be able to be registered on its own.

• Create a single documentation file that is common to all the utilities. Incorporate this file into each of the packages. The idea here is that each product carries the advertising for all of the other products.

• Distribute the products separately. Upload a single product to bulletin boards. Mail half the collection to distributors. Your aim is to get very wide distribution, while at the same time making it improbable that any one source has the entire collection. If the collection takes up more than 362Kb compressed, so much the better.

- Update or add one product every two months, so that the entire collection is updated once a year, but, again, it is improbable that any one source has a current copy of the entire collection.

- Registration brings the entire basket for, say, $19.95. If someone insists on registering just one product, it's $9.95.

Each piece of fruit will take on a life of its own. If the pieces are small enough, they'll travel widely, especially on the BBS circuit. Each piece is an appetizer for the whole basket.

If your collection is a good one and offers tools aimed at a single market, chances are good that customers will like the utilities they have, notice utilities in the documentation that they need and don't have, and pay the registration fee to get the rest of the collection.

Potato Chips

Remember the television commercial that used the line "Bet ya can't eat just one"?

The conventional wisdom is that games don't get registered. Apogee Software has turned that "truth" on its head. Apogee's primary registration incentive is to release game trilogies. The first game delivers you to the portal of the second, the second delivers you to the portal of the third. Only the first game is shareware, however. The other two have strict prohibitions against distribution. While it is possible to register the first game, almost no·one does. Almost invariably they order the trilogy at a higher price in order to play the last two games.

Registration Key

It doesn't make sense to brand some programs with the registered user's name. *The ShareWare Book* is a good example, since it is designed to be used in private by an individual; branding is unlikely to have much effect on its registrations. When customers register your program, you can provide a registration key to let them "self-brand" the program and turn off the registration reminders. Many authors simply have customers add an environment variable or a switch to the command line. *The ShareWare Book* program has you reset the date to my daughter's birthday, run the program, then set the date back again. The program then stops showing reminder screens until it is automatically unregistered. (See the next section.)

Automatic Unregistration

You do want people to share unregistered copies of your program; you don't want them sharing registered copies. Unregistration of your program has to be automatic—people don't read the manual before copying a shareware program from their hard disk to a floppy for a friend. I use a simple way to have a program "unregister" itself when it is moved. Each time the program is run, it checks the date and time of the host subdirectory and compares that to the date and time of the subdirectory previously stored in the configuration file. If the dates don't agree, I assume that this copy of the program has been passed on, and I return to the "factory defaults, unregistered" state.

If registered customers wish to move a copy of the program to another location, all they have to do is "reregister" using the registration key provided in the registration package.

To avoid having people pass on configuration and data files, I use the same technique. If the date/time changes, I ask if this is a new installation where I should return to standard defaults. If it is, I can delete the prior user's data and return to the "new user" mode that provides sample data and constant help messages.

Enhanced Retail Versions

Microsoft and Borland publish "lite" versions of their software. These are emphatically not crippled versions, but versions simplified for easy use by novices. A lite version of an accounting program might do cash accounting but not accrual, while a lite version of word processing might lack things such as a style checker. By entering the market with an easy-to-use lite version, the companies hope to capture these same customers when they need additional power, since they will already be familiar with how to use the product.

A similar strategy uses shareware for distribution of the lite version, while reserving the "heavy" version for shelfware. A good example of this strategy is FormGen Corporation, with its Form-Gen product in shareware and FormGen Gold available only in shelfware. Enhanced retail versions have the added advantage of avoiding channel conflict. The wholesalers can't complain that customers can get the same thing for free, while the shareware version actually brings people into the stores.

Advertising

Ross Greenberg's virus scanner (VireX) is bannerware that does an excellent job of scanning for and spotting, but not curing, viruses. It contains an advertisement for his shelfware product, which does remove viruses. When a potential customer catches a viral infection, what product do you think he's likely to buy?

You can sell advertising that is delivered by your product. Imagine a laser utility that displayed "Call **(800) Go Laser** when you need more toner" each time the program was used.

Shareware also can be used to build a mailing list for a particular market. By publishing a utility with a very low registration fee, you can build a list of equipment owners that can be useful in selling other products.

Support

Most support is required before registration. Do not deny support to unregistered customers who are trying to get your package running. On the other hand, help in closing out the year for an accounting package is something that can reasonably be reserved to paying customers.

A support call from an unregistered user is an excellent opportunity to ask for the sale—especially if you take credit cards.

Gamus Interruptus

Much of the satisfaction in playing computer games comes from the feeling of completion when a player has finally "beaten" the game. If a game has a couple of sections that are likely to be difficult enough to induce player frustration (preferably about three-quarters of the way through the game), you can afford to give away the game in order to sell hint books or cheat codes that allow users to continue. This technique is especially effective if the hint book has something that can't easily be retyped or photocopied, such as a magic wheel or decoder ring.

You also might consider using a 900 number to give out hints.

Notification

Tax programs, scientific programs, and programmer's libraries are all subject to arcane bugs that may or may not be important to a particular customer. Offering to notify every registered customer of bugs as they are found can be a powerful registration incentive for these types of product.

Newsletters

People generally want to hear news about products they use, and respond favorably to opportunities to upgrade the product and buy additional products. Once you have a reputation for honesty and value, your mailing list may begin to have more value than your product.

Offering Even More Goodies

You can offer quite a few extras to registered users. The products mentioned here are primarily of interest to serious shareware users and authors. You'll find, however, that many companies serving the same market you've targeted will be interested in offering discounts to your customers in order to increase their market share. Do some creative thinking, then approach the marketing department of these companies with the idea. They may even be willing to tell their customers about your product.

CompuServe offers a credit to new users brought to them by way of a shareware registration.

Authors of other shareware products aimed at your market may be willing to supply you with evaluation copies to be mailed to your registered users. The idea is that if these users registered one shareware product, they are likely to register more.

Source Code

Personally, I don't trust anybody this much. Authors who write products for large corporations often find that this is a real incentive. MIS departments often want the security of knowing that they can take over support and maintenance if it becomes necessary. Offering source code is probably essential for programmer's toolkits. With many languages, you can offer just the object libraries as shareware, then supply the actual source code only to people who pay the registration fee and sign a non-disclosure agreement.

Data Conversion

If your product manages your customer's data, unregistered users eventually will want the features that new versions offer. Since you have no obligation to ship the data conversion program with your shareware package, these people frequently will register because they don't want to give up their old data but do want the new features.

This technique also can work when you have very complex configuration options. If it will take over half an hour to reconfigure the program to get a new version, but the registered version will accept the old configuration file, you may be able to sell registrations on that basis.

Delay Screens

A variation on reminder screens is the delay screen. Invented because potential customers blew by the "any key" typically used with reminder screens, it locks the machine for a period of time. Most people find these screens very irritating, which is, of course, the point. Many find them irritating enough to discontinue evaluation of the product.

When I started a CompuServe account and got my first bill, I realized that something had to change, and fast. Other authors recommended strongly that I use an offline navigator. Most recommended TapCIS, a shareware program. TapCIS (at that time) had a twenty-one-day evaluation period, after which it used a delay screen to "encourage" the user to register. I was logging on to

CompuServe once a week at that time, in an effort to save money. I downloaded TapCIS on a Saturday and installed it during the week, which started the clock. On the fourth use of TapCIS (I ran it every Saturday), the system froze—or so I thought—with a message that my evaluation period was over. I did a Ctrl/Alt/Delete, a Del *.*, downloaded a competitor (ATO), and have been satisfied since. As a result, I have recommended ATO to many new authors.

There are, I think, three morals to this story:

- Think about the evaluation period you give your users. You may wish to count the unique days used as well as the calendar period. For a CompuServe navigator, once a week usage is not unusual.
- If you do use delay screens, be sure to display a countdown clock. The TapCIS delay (I found out later) was ten seconds. I probably waited five before I concluded that the machine was locked up, and rebooted.
- If you feel you must use negative techniques with nonpaying users, think about the marketing implications. If I had continued to use and never paid for the program, I probably would have recommended it to others.

Public Exposure

Is it possible to buy a car without getting that little plate advertising the dealership on the trunk? The "public exposure" technique is especially effective with utilities used in connection with bulletin boards, but it can be adapted to any product producing a public message. The concept is to generate a message in a small percentage of the items handled so that the technique is not too annoying. In the nonregistered version, the add-on message might read:

Serial and modem support provided by the MODEM utility, currently under evaluation prior to registration for 565 days. For more information about MODEM, call Pinnacle Software at 514-345-9578. (Free 24-hr/day files BBS at 514-345-8654)

For the registered version, the message might read:

Another honest shareware user!
Serial and modem support provided by the MODEM utility, registered to John Doe
For more information about MODEM, call Pinnacle Software at 514-345-9578.
(Free 24-hr/day files BBS at 514-345-8654)

In order to cut down on excessive additional message size, you'll want to make the use of the message infrequent and random.

Unregistered users are likely to be reminded when they receive a message that 565 days for evaluation is a bit excessive, and the posting of the author's telephone number helps to keep evaluators honest.

People who see the ad are likely to ask the source what the program does, does the user like it, and so on. In addition, the telephone number is right there to get a copy immediately.

Stool Pigeon

This is a variation on the public exposure technique. If your product sends many things out in the mail (a mailing list or a mailing list manager, for instance), include yourself occasionally in the output, with some kind of code showing how long the product has been evaluated.

You can use this information to send a newsletter or offer a "sale price" on registrations. If nothing else, this technique may give you some indication of what the ratio of registered to unregistered users is.

What's That Number?

This technique is sometimes used after the evaluation period is over. Typically, the FBI WARNING is shown, and then users are told to type in the nth letter of the nth word on the nth line to acknowledge their legal responsibility. Sometimes a random number is used instead.

Bounties

A number of authors have experimented with paying a commission to customers who pass the program on to others who then register. Those who have tried it almost universally report that it wasn't an effective incentive in the first place and quickly became an administrative problem.

Arthritis

As time stretches beyond the end of the evaluation period, critical functions of the program become slower and slower. One program using this technique actually made a kind of a creaking sound through the speaker. An essential part of this technique is to make clear that the program is slowing down because of nonregistration rather than a capacity problem. It is useful to combine this technique with randomness, so users can see how much more wonderful life could be after registration.

Short Sheeting

If you've ever gone to summer camp, you've probably been "short sheeted": When you try to get into bed, you can get only halfway in because the sheet goes only halfway down the bed before it returns. The same technique has been used in shareware on occasion. The documentation supplied with the shareware version might give enough information to set up an accounting system, but then leave out essential details for closing out an accounting period, referring you instead to "Chapter 13" of the registered version's manual.

Short sheeting generally makes people angry enough to both delete the program from the disk and complain loudly, effectively reducing distribution. To the best of my knowledge, it has never been used successfully.

Nagging

Nagging is excessive registration reminders. It usually doesn't work because it displays a lack of trust and irritates potential customers.

Scareware

This technique has been used but never successfully. No legitimate distributor will carry a program using it, and no sane user will keep it on his disk—registered or not. In essence, the author threatens to reformat the hard disk or erase users' data if he or she isn't paid on time.

An Unconventional View of Using Shareware

The shareware metaphor has always been educational television. People bemoan the fact that only a small percentage of viewers support the programming financially. I think that children's television may be a more useful metaphor. After three-year-olds spend an hour watching *Sesame Street*, what do they want? A Cookie Monster puppet, of course! Having observed my daughter poring over her Disney Babies books, I suspect that Disney Corporation and others like them could profitably produce and deliver their programming with no "advertising" at all.

Shareware is not necessarily at its most effective as a marketing channel. It can be a very effective advertising medium. A television show's sponsor spends money developing a show that will attract and hold an audience in order to deliver the sponsor's message— sometimes more money than to develop the sponsor's product itself. Shareware can be used in much the same way.

Many, if not most, of the recently successful shareware products have built at least some of their success on a strategy of using shareware as much as an advertising medium as a marketing channel. *The ShareWare Book* was an example of that strategy. I wanted people to buy the book (paper and glue) and author's kit (diskette) that were registration incentives offered by the program. I couldn't afford to print thousands of copies and distribute them so people could visit a bookstore and thumb through one while deciding to buy. I couldn't even afford the advertising necessary to get people to walk into a bookstore and ask them to special-order the book.

With certain unusual exceptions, no single registration encouragement technique will be sufficient. I suggest that you combine as many as you can to encourage your potential customers to register.

In summary, I see successful shareware marketing as having five steps:

1. Get widely *distributed.*
2. Get the program *ordered.*
3. *Hold customers* once you get the program into their hands.
4. Convince customers to *send you money.*
5. Continue to provide services and products desired by customers, resulting in *repeat sales.*

Think of these five steps as an equation:

$$\$ = \text{Distribution} * \text{Orders} * \text{Holding power} * \text{Registration rate} * \text{Repeat sales}$$

Distribution is largely a matter of getting your product to the largest number of effective distributors possible, making it easy for them to carry your product, and convincing them that your product offers more to them than other products competing for the same space. Choosing a market appropriate to shareware distribution is an essential first step. Avoiding challenging entrenched competition is the second. After those two first steps come presentation and the quality of your product.

Orders are primarily a function of the text describing your product. If a potential customer with a problem can perceive your product as a potential solution, you've done your job here. This is a matter of writing effective copy and making it easy for your distributor to use it. As a secondary issue, any pull that you can create through press releases and reviews also will help.

Holding power is directly related to your installation routine, tutorials, and the immediate impression your program makes. It doesn't matter how powerful the program is if people never get there. Your potential customers must be able to visualize in the first couple of minutes how their problem is going to be solved. To avoid distracting customers from seeing your product as an immediate solution, hide configuration options, any complex choices, and registration reminders until potential buyers have gained an overview of the product.

Registration rate is influenced primarily by your target market, the long-term usefulness of your product, the additional value that registration offers, and your price—in that order.

Repeat sales are where the profit occurs. The job of a direct marketing company is to acquire loyal customers; the profit is an outcome of an ongoing relationship, not a single encounter.

"Writing a great program and sending it to a few distributors" does not work. As a matter of fact, the great program part is really a minor part of the entire equation.

OFFERING SUPPORT

Support can be a wonderful market research tool. It also can be a source of revenue. It can be the way you discover for the next four years just where version 1.0's wording on installation was ambiguous.

One of the things I've learned is that people often use different words for the same thing. This results in a fair proportion of support calls where the customer really couldn't use your documentation, even though the information was there. This wastes your time and frustrates potential customers. Try to log customer support calls in the customer's language; that is, write down the questions and problems in the words the customer uses to describe them. When it's time to revise the manual, list those words as synonyms for your own in the index and the glossary.

Software Updates

An upgrade is an update that was released when you really needed the money. You'll have to decide what your policy will be regarding the price of upgrades and updates—and when your customers will be entitled to them for free. Having a well thought out policy is more important than what your policy is.

My impression is that most shareware authors allow registered users to keep the same registration within a major release. This means that the branding key or magic code that works with release 2.0 will also work with release 2.99 if the user cares to download the new version, but it won't work with release 3.0. Unless serious bugs are found, users will not be sent minor releases automatically.

For products sold through other channels, it seems that most publishers will send out a free update within a release if it fixes a bug reported by a customer. Otherwise, the customer is generally not informed of bugs or the availability of fixes.

For higher-priced products or products that offer other benefits (such as an update of the data or a newsletter), a subscription service can be used. All upgrades issued during the life of the subscription are sent automatically.

Diagnostics

Three tools have helped me in providing support:

The first is an undocumented *diagnostic switch* in my programs. Invoked from the command line, the program shows (on the screen or a file) breakpoints and critical values as it executes. Based upon the last known breakpoint and value, I can usually find, duplicate, and correct bugs based upon users' descriptions fairly quickly.

The second tool is *ASQ.EXE* (from Qualitas) that will do a very good job of showing a complete system configuration. It is bannerware, available for free (they do ask that you register). You can prepare a disk with a batch file and have the program write its findings to the disk. Simply send the disk with some instructions to the customer and ask him to run the batch file and return the disk to you. A copy of ASQ is included in the Software Publisher's Kit.

Finally, if your customer has a copy of MSDOS dated 1990 or later, he has a copy of *MSD*. This is a MicroSoft Diagnostic utility that will give you a very good snapshot of the machine's actual configuration. If you run it with the /P switch, it will throw its output to a file of your choosing. You might want to include a call to it in your diagnostic routine.

CHAPTER 5

Classified Ads and Direct Mail

The shareware marketing channel reaches only a very small proportion of your potential customers. This fact was brought home to me dramatically when I spoke at a meeting of the Independent Computer Consultants Association. I was astounded to learn that fully two-thirds of the audience had never heard of shareware. The few who had were enthusiastic about the concept, but many others were suspicious of "something for nothing" and "small software houses." By selling your product in new channels, you will reach the potential new customers who comprise 95 percent of the rest of the PC software market.

At first, you may choose simply to ship your shareware "preregistered" version. You can create these versions of your products by removing files vendor.doc and register.doc discussed in Chapter 4 and by including the registration key file.

Once you begin to get serious about using classified ads, you'll probably want to spin off your second entry-level product. Besides having a different name and price point, it may have a different set of features. Typical shareware buyers are fairly sophisticated; they both demand more features than the typical classified ad buyer and are more able to sort through the complications those features involve. You may wish to strip your product to the bare essentials for this channel so that buyers' frustration level and your support costs will be lower. This does not necessarily mean a lower price; the price may be higher. It's your job to experiment with different prices to see where sales are best. Too low a price can scare classified ad buyers as effectively as too high a price.

CLASSIFIED ADVERTISING

Classified advertising has a number of real benefits:

- *It's cheap.* Besides the fact that the actual cost of the ad is low, you don't need to spend money on layout.

- *It's great for testing your offer.* You can run different versions of your offer at different times in different magazines. As long as you have some way of tracing the source of orders, you can put together a preliminary model of which offers work well with which markets.

- *It identifies your market.* For $200 you can find out if your product might appeal to private eyes or women thinking about getting married.

- *It finds the people who are serious about the subject.* By and large, the people who are really interested in the subject are the ones who scan the classified ads in a magazine. These are your best first prospects.

- *It is oriented toward asking the prospect to take action.* Other advertising may try to project an image or impart information. Classified ads ask the reader to take action—either to request more information or to send money.

Do not expect fast results from any form of advertising. Beyond the sixty days that it takes to get the ad into the magazine in the first place, it seems that ads begin to draw after they have been in three consecutive issues. I've heard a lot of theories about why this is true and don't claim to know why myself—but I've seen it often enough to believe that this is generally true of classified ads. Don't use single classified ads. Commit to a period between three and six months. If the ad isn't paying for itself in six months, it never will. Then either change your offer or drop the magazine.

DIRECT MAIL

Direct mail is an essential marketing channel because it is your only way of keeping in touch with your customers. Used wisely, it is also the first channel that can bring in large numbers of new customers. Direct mail can be very effective with a targeted list, targeted advertising, and the right offer.

If you are going to be successful in software, you will be in the direct mail business. Even if you never rent a list or participate in a card deck, if your business is managed well, eventually you will receive more money from existing customers for upgrades and add-ons than you do from new customers.

Why prospect using direct mail? Simply because shareware typically reaches less than 5 percent of your potential market, and even fewer people read the classified ads in magazines. (Bulletin board software and products for shareware authors are obvious exceptions.) This fact implies that direct marketing might *increase your installed base by a factor of 30 or 40* over other channels.

The emphasis in direct marketing is not on making sales—it is on acquiring customers. Once a customer is acquired, the profits flow from the ongoing relationship. Most large direct mail companies don't make a profit on a customer until the third or fourth purchase. In software, given the low cost of manufacturing your product, you are in a position to make a profit earlier.

The minimum cost of experimenting with direct mail prospecting (looking for new customers) is probably somewhere between $5,000 and $10,000, but a larger budget is advised because of the cost of the artwork and setup, which is constant no matter how large your list.

Unlike shareware and classified advertising, direct marketing is fast. Half of the sales will be made within a month, and over 95 percent of the sales will be made within three months of your mailing.

Products that do well in direct mail:

• *Appeal to a well-defined audience.* A program for keeping track of pedigrees would do well using the membership list of the American Kennel Club. A 1-2-3 template might do well using the subscription list of *CFO* magazine.

• *Don't have serious retail competition.* Generally this is true because the people who form the market for this software are too spread out for retail stores to cater to them. If the product (or a competitor) were available at the store, the customer would already own it. Given the very small number of retail software products, this means that most software fits this channel very well.

• *Have a moderate price.* A "one-step" sale is most effective in direct mail. (More on this on page 138). For this to work, buyers must perceive little risk.

• *Are easily explained.* If potential customers can't see immediately how the product will meet an existing need, they won't spend any time on the ad.

• *Are perceived by customers as having low risk.* An unconditional guarantee helps, but trying to sell a product that would have disastrous consequences to users if it failed is not a good candidate for direct mail.

• *Will result in repeat sales.* While you may not be able to make a profit selling a $20 product through direct mail, if finding a new customer will result in repeat sales over time, the possibility of turning a profit increases greatly. Software is a natural for repeat sales—for upgrades, additional products, or subscription services.

Calculating Direct Mail Costs

Before you start trying to sell through direct mail, work the numbers carefully. For planning purposes, you can figure that the unit cost of direct mail will be in the $.50 range for quantities of 5,000 and that your response rate will be about 2 percent if your materials are professionally done and you have an effective list. Given these numbers, each response will cost you $25. If the price of your product is $20, you're planning to lose money before you begin. If you are offering a $40 product and the response drops to 1 percent (not an unusual number), you will have lost money on the mailing.

For example, one publisher broke down his actual costs as follows:

Postage	.146
Envelopes (2)	.08
Sales letter	.07
Order card	.023
List rental	.065
Total	$0.384

Plan things so that you can break even on a 1 percent response. At first, you won't even achieve this. Direct mail is an iterative process, where testing and modifying the campaign slowly increases the response rate. No one really knows what works best for any one product; that's why testing is so important. Do not, under any circumstances, allow yourself to roll out your campaign too early. The trick is to run lots of tests that cost a little until you find out what works for your product. It's at that point that mailing to thousands begins to make sense. Generally, a good software product using the right list at the right price will typically see a response rate between 5 and 10 percent. Most people familiar with direct mail for other products will tell you that this is impossibly high, but it isn't because of the specificity of software—it can be targeted more precisely than other products.

Working these numbers, if you have a product that sells for $49, achieves a response rate of 12.5 percent, costs you $.45 to send and $5.50 to fulfill, the numbers would work like this for a 10,000-piece mailing:

```
10,000 pieces @ $.45 = $4,500
1250 responses @ $49 = $61,250 (gross income)
1250 responses @ $5.50 = $6,875 (cost of goods)
so. . . 61,250 - 4,500 - 6,875 = $49,875 profit
```

All this sounds great, of course, but first you have to find the key that will result in a 12.5 percent response and find a way to put up a bit more than $11,000.

Using the same example, if you managed to miscalculate or have the bad fortune to mail into a major news event (people don't open their mail when the country is about to go to war) and your response rate dropped to 1 percent, you'd see a loss of about $5,000 (you'd still have to pay for the product, but the other response costs would disappear) and you'd have 1,150 software packages stuck in your garage.

The price point that works for your product in shareware and in classified advertising probably will not be the optimal price point for direct marketing. You may want to launch a second (or third) "product" (it may have only a different name and price) in order to sell your product at a profit. Frequently, the direct mail product will have fewer features (to reduce support problems with new users) and a higher price. A formula for estimating the potential of direct mail and catalog campaigns is given later (see page 161).

Keys to Success

According to Bob Stone (one of the best authorities), there are six keys to success in direct marketing:

1. The right product. It's essential that you be able to demonstrate to customers that this product is a great value for them. It's essential that the product offer features they cannot obtain at their local retailer and that the product have the potential for repeat business.

2. The right list. You'll know only by testing the list, but it's important to know when the list was last cleaned, by whom it was used immediately prior to your use, and whether the people on the list tend to be direct mail buyers.

3. The right offer. There will be lots more on this later (see pages 130 to 131), but the guarantee and deadline are essential, as is testing the price. You also may test the effectiveness of free gifts, time-limited discounts, and special "bonus" coupons.

4. The right format. Postcards, fold-out brochures, self-mailers, traditional direct mail letters, and flyers each have their place. Once you settle on the basic format, you'll also want to experiment with the optional elements—everything from using window or nonwindow envelopes, to glossy or flat paper. I actually had a good response rate mailing shareware copies on disk to the right list.

5. Thorough testing. Test all of the variables, and then establish reliable controls so that you *know,* not guess, what made a difference from one mailing to the next.

6. Analysis. Learn from both successes and failures and refine the way you cultivate repeat business.

Bob Stone's book is the second best single resource I've found in the area of direct marketing:

Successful Direct Marketing Methods
by **Bob Stone**
Crain Books
740 North Rush Street
Chicago, IL 60611
(312) 649-5200

The best resource I've found has been collecting as many direct mail pieces for software products as I could find and studying them very carefully.

If you have already been using shareware and classified advertising, you have a reasonable shot at the first three keys to success:

1. The product (and your understanding of how it appeals to your market) will be refined through the feedback you get through shareware publishing.
2. The magazines producing the best results from your classified ads are the natural source for your first lists.
3. Experimenting with different offers in your classified advertising has resulted in better refinement of your offer. The benefits and price that work well in classified advertising are similar to those that work in direct marketing.

List brokers work similarly to travel agents: The party renting the list pays a 20 percent commission to the broker for generating the rental. Most lists have a "data card" available that quotes a price per thousand, extra selection options (and associated charges), media available (labels or magnetic media), terms (typically thirty days from drop at the post office), and whether subsets of the list are available for testing.

Generally, you'll have to agree to the following terms:

- You must submit a copy of your mailing to the list owner and mail out *exactly* what you presented.
- You must agree to a specific date that the piece will be mailed and keep to it. The list owner needs this so that mailings don't overlap.

- You must agree to use the list just once. If you are ever caught holding on to names after a mailing, your chances of working with any broker in the industry become very slim.
- On the other hand, anyone who does order from you becomes "yours." You may reuse these names for your own purposes and even rent out your own list containing these names once your list is long enough.

In choosing a list for testing, you might keep a couple of things in mind:

- If the list was generated with a sweepstakes offer, you'll almost certainly have to make a sweeps offer yourself in order to get a decent response.
- Try to get a copy of the piece that actually generated the responses. The closer your piece is (the offer, the type of product, the price range, freebies and incentives, and so on), the higher your response is likely to be.

Direct marketing is fundamentally different from advertising. To quote George Duncan, a specialist in software direct marketing: "The dynamics are exactly opposite to one another. Advertisers produce many impressions over time that are designed to bear fruit later in another place—a grocery store, for example. Direct marketing tries to get a response right now, to make you a proposition you can't refuse. Direct mail sells an offer, not a product."

An article by George Duncan on the dynamics of direct response marketing is included in the Software Publisher's Kit.

SOFTWARE DIRECT MARKETING PIECES

As you read the next couple of pages, I suggest that you examine some software direct marketing pieces. I find that real-life examples really help in understanding the way a package is put together. The traditional direct mail piece is made up of these following parts: the envelope, the sales letter, the brochure, the order card, the return envelope, the lift note, and the involvement device. Let's examine each part in detail.

The Envelope

The envelope's job is to get opened—no small task.

• You need an *attention grabber*. Dazzle, impress, or tease. Double entendre works well. Quotes from favorable reviews that don't tell readers just what this product actually does have worked well for me.

• Experiment with the *back of the envelope*. Half the mail comes facedown, doesn't it? One technique that has been used effectively is a "handwritten" note on the back of the envelope that mentions the key benefit and teases at the same time.

• Unless your company name is recognizable to the majority of your target audience, do not include it on the outside of the envelope. I sometimes use a return address of "03802-0117 USA." It is enough for the post office and, again, creates curiosity. I've read reports that putting no return address at all will also increase the response rate. Custom-made rubber stamps can arouse curiosity as well. Using labels, of course, destroys much of the magic.

• Many people automatically throw away "junk mail" without opening it. Using stamps rather than metered mail or bulk mail indicia may raise your response rate—especially if you use discount postage, paste the stamp on slightly crooked, and do whatever else you can to make the piece look interesting. Many businesses instruct their mail rooms to throw out all third-class mail. Most mail clerks simply look for a multicolored stamp and assume, if they see one, that it's first class. Mail with two different stamps almost always gets opened.

• Gimmicks work. Making the package lumpy or noisy does get it opened. I found that mailing a diskette was very effective; while I don't have a control to compare against, I think that envelopes with disks in them got opened more than most others.

• Try experimenting with different sizes of envelopes. It's not uncommon for people to sort their mail by size and give a different amount of attention to different-size pieces. If you use window envelopes you also may want to experiment with the number of windows in the envelope.

The Sales Letter

Of course, as soon as customers look at the postcard or open the envelope, you must hit them between the eyes with the primary benefit (not feature!) of your product. "Get out of debt fast!" is a benefit; "Organizes your finances" is a feature.

The letter is typically between two and six pages long. Its job is to *sell the dream,* not the product. Little mention is made of features; it describes in detail how the buyer's life will be different after the purchase. A good letter follows these guidelines:

• *Don't use your letterhead.* You're not selling your name. If you feel the need for a letterhead, make one up for the product instead.

• *Use a headline* that is aimed directly at the person most likely to take action on your offer right now. Do not try to use one headline for your entire possible market—you risk losing your most probable sale. Think about all of the characteristics of the people most likely to buy from you and write the headline for them alone. Long, bulleted multiline headlines sometimes work well; don't reject them out of hand.

• You may opt to *use a Johnson Box,* which is slightly different from a headline. It is a box at the beginning of the letter that promises the single most powerful benefit and hints at the offer to come. For example, see the Johnson Box for an Ami Pro mailing in Figure 5.1.

THE BEST WORD PROCESSOR
FOR WINDOWS: AMI PRO 3.0

YOUR OPPORTUNITY TO OWN NEW AMI PRO 3.0 FOR JUST $99.90—AND RECEIVE 2 FREE GIFTS!

Figure 5.1   A Johnson box.

• The first line (if readers got that far) is critical. *Speak to their needs, not yours.* For goodness sake, don't "introduce" yourself!

• *Don't discuss the great issues of the day;* you are trying to sell an offer, not change an opinion.

• *Be very careful with humor.* It backfires more often than it sells.

- *Don't pose rhetorical questions.* They transfer control to readers.

- *Use the words now, free, announcing,* and *discover.* They are powerful. Try to use as many of them as you can in your headline and first line.

- *Include a hook*—either a contest give-away or a special gift that tries to get customers to respond quickly. You might want to give a double discount to the first 100 who respond. Sell this premium first. Once you have established an interest level, you can begin discussing the advantages your product offers.

- In addition to a hook, you might want to *use a deadline.* Typically this is done with a limited time offer where there is a temporary price reduction.

- *Use color* in the letter—but use it sparingly and strikingly. Use it only to bring attention to the one or two things you want prospects to notice immediately.

- You also might try to *use the fake highlighter trick.* If you do, be sure to use an appropriate fluorescent yellow.

- *Colored stock works well sometimes.* Yellows and yellow greens seem to work best.

- *Include a photograph or a screen shot* in the body of the letter—sometimes it helps. Illustrations (drawings, etc.) rarely do.

- Your headlines and bold type should *extol the benefits*, not the features of the product. For every "benefit" you list, ask and answer the question "So what?" Eventually, you'll get down to the real reasons (not more than three or four) people might want your product. After all, perfume isn't sold because it makes you smell good.

- If it's a multipage piece, *keep them reading.* One way to do this is to change pages in the middle of a paragraph, in a sentence where they'll really want to see the rest of that paragraph at least. Every time you ask potential customers to turn the page, you risk losing them.

- You know how we all laugh at the *Reader's Digest* personalized letters asking us to subscribe? *Personalized letters work.* Even with sophisticated people. If you are running that side of the piece through your printer anyway, why not put their names in?

• People scan direct mail in a Z pattern: They read the top line, travel down the page from the top right to the bottom left, then read the bottom line. *Try to put your important selling points along the path of the Z.*

• *Try to work things so your benefits list appears in the middle of the page*—right in the middle of the Z. Use no more than five benefits, with no more than six words per benefit.

• That Z also accounts for the reason you'll frequently see a P.S. on the bottom of a direct mail piece. *Put your most important hook in the P.S.*—this is the part of the letter most likely to be actually read.

• For some reason, perfect letters work less well than the ones that are a little rough around the edges. *Don't polish too well;* leave out a period at the end of a sentence occasionally. You may find that a spelling mistake increases response.

• Once you've established the benefits, make them credible. *Use features and testimonials* to show how the benefits are achieved. A feature not linked directly to a key benefit is a waste of space.

• *Get personal* in your copy. Even if your company is a "we," you should write your copy on a person-to-person basis. Refer to yourself as "I" and the customer as "you." This helps customers visualize you as a person and trust you. Emphasize the point that customers get to talk to the author when there's a problem.

• One very effective way to keep them reading is to *include a lot of good information and tips* that are useful to your target readers.

• *Use larger type.* If your dad can't read it without his glasses, neither will many of your potential customers. Typically, you'll want to use 12-point type. It may be necessary to play with the margins, line spacing, and font size in order to get your key points to fall on the page where you want them.

• This is not an English Lit course. You are trying to quickly establish a personal relationship and sell a dream. Excited people use *short, choppy sentences.* You should too.

• *Include a clear offer.* Exactly what does the customer get, and for how much? Write at a sixth-grade level. Repeat the offer a number of times, both to reinforce it and because people who are skimming will be more likely to see it. Try to close the sale once within the first four paragraphs, at the bottom of the first page, once on each subsequent page, and on the order form.

- *Don't stop at twelve reasons to buy;* give them twenty-two if you can. Think of the Ginsu Knife commercials on late-night television and include so much stuff at a bargain price that readers feel compelled to take advantage of your offer.

- *You absolutely, positively must have a money-back, cheerfully refunded guarantee*—the first step toward making the customer comfortable. In addition, you might join (and prominently display the logos of) your local Better Business Bureau, Chamber of Commerce, and Direct Marketing Association. A "real" (street) address, hours of operation, and telephone number help in providing assurance. Customer testimonials also can boost the comfort level.

- You need to *be from where they expect* you to be from. If L.L. Bean had a Brooklyn address, it would lose half its sales. Be from someplace appropriate to your target market and someplace thought of as "trustworthy."

- *Use an incentive to respond now.* Such incentives can boost your response rate by a couple of points. It's estimated that 95 percent of the reply cards that get put on the pile to be mailed later don't. Typically, the problem your product solves goes away on its own, or the user finds another (frequently more expensive, but more convenient) solution to the problem.

- *Respond to the customer's objections.* Doing so also can boost the response rate. Try to anticipate the reasons a person might hesitate to take action, and respond in a positive way without naming the objection directly. For example, computer phobia is widespread. Many people are uncomfortable about trying software without someone around to help. Your response could be to emphasize the ease of installation, and add that personal help is available by phone.

- *Offer overnight delivery* for a reasonable fee.

- Tell them what they will give up if they don't order now. *Contrast "the dream"* with their own sorry current reality.

- *Use lots of clichés.* Write at a sixth-grade level; they won't "obtain" the software, they'll *get* it.

- Expect to *spend at least a month preparing the letter.* This is something that requires many, many drafts. You also need to put it down and get some distance from it as a part of the process.

- *Maximum paragraph length is six lines*; do not justify the right margin.

- Use bullets, <u>underline</u>, **bold**, *italics* to make key points—if you use two colors, use the color for three points maximum.

- *Experiment with fonts*, but a courier typeface usually works best.

- *Be sure to say why it's possible to offer such an incredible deal.* People may think that this is too good to be true.

- *Get personal.* Use a first-person, conversational style.

- *Ask for the order.* Tell them to call your 800 number right now.

- It's important to *provide social support* for the decision to buy. Everybody has somebody ready and willing to say "Isn't that the fourth program you've bought in a month? Do you really need it?" Provide the answer to that question if you can. Say "This product is so complete it will be the last astrology program you'll ever need" or "You won't need to purchase upgrades for a year; they're included if you buy now!"

- *Reduce their sense of risk* by including testimonials. The people quoted do have to be real, but they don't have to be recognizable names.

- Puffery will work against you, *facts will work for you.* Don't say this is "the best" or the "most powerful"; but do search for ways to quantify the good things you want to say. If your product is 30 percent faster or is twice as accurate (and you can prove your claims), use those facts in your pitch.

- *Emote like crazy* (I know it's tough; that's why I hire somebody for this). This is an impulse sale. People are buying on the basis of wants, not because they need the features you're offering. Share some personal information about yourself. Tell them what you have in common with them and why you like the product.

- Keep their imaginations going. *Tell an interesting story* about an unusual use of the product.

- If you're printing in two colors, *use the second color for the signature*. The letter should be signed by either the president or the programmer—never someone with a sales title.

- *Use at least one postscript (P.S.)*, maybe two. This is the second most read part of the sales letter. Reinforce the dream here, and assure buyers that they will have the dream. The risk must be yours, not theirs.

The Brochure

The brochure describes the product in detail. Its job is to explain the features and benefits to people who have already tentatively decided to buy, to make them feel that this product is, in fact, right for them. It should:

- *Use simple and attention-getting artwork.* Look at it under bad light with a scratched-up pair of cheap sunglasses. If it still looks good, you have a good design. Photographs generally do better than illustrations.

- *Include your features list* . Once prospects have decided to buy, they'll turn to the brochure to see if there's a reasonable match between their requirements and your features.

- *Mention the full list price*—if you mention price at all—so that your irresistible offer in the letter and order card is that much better.

- You may choose to have the brochure *show the entire product family.* This assures buyers that they have a growth path and that you are a "real" company with a family of products.

- Make sure it has full contact information; *include your toll-free phone number.* Brochures have a way of getting separated from the rest of the package and found later.

- Don't let your graphics person run away with this. While you do want to use glossy paper and color, be sure to *use high-contrast* colors and avoid any kind of pattern behind the text that could make it hard to read. Make sure that the screen shots you use are easy to see and have high contrast as well.

• *Avoid bleeds.* A bleed is a place where you want the color to go right to the edge of the page. This is accomplished by using larger paper, printing beyond the "edge" of the page, and then cutting the paper to put the edge where it should be. It both uses more paper and creates extra steps. A bleed is almost never necessary to increase sales.

Usually, only the brochure needs to be in full color. One source for full-color printing (and a free Color Printing Handbook) is:

Rapidcolor
705 East Union Street
West Chester, PA 19382-4937
(800) 872-7436

The Order Card

While it certainly has to be designed to take the order, the order card's real job is to describe the offer clearly and exactly, and let the buyer know the terms of the sale. Be sure to include:

• An 800 number for placing orders with a credit card. Print it on both side of the card in large type. State your policy of shipping the product the same day it's ordered—and stick to your policy. Include a toll number for foreign orders and a fax number.

• An order form (self-mailer) for people who don't like placing phone credit card orders. The customer information should be preprinted on the form so the customer doesn't have to do this and so you can correct your mailing list. Always restate the offer including benefits and savings on the order form. If someone starts to be interested in your offer, they typically turn there to find out "how much." Be sure to turn them on with the benefits at the same time.

• This is where you use check boxes to gather marketing information. As long as you're not too outrageous, most people will give you half a dozen pieces of information about themselves.

• Another technique is to print your offer—and then cross out the price by hand, using a pen to write in something like "$20 until October 3rd." Be sure to use a colored pen that can't be mistaken for printing. An alternative is to print stickers and attach them next to the price.

• *Repeat your guarantee* here. A phrase like "If you're not absolutely delighted with this ..." or "You'll have your data converted the same morning or your money will be cheerfully refunded" goes a long way toward reducing your buyers' perception of risk.

• You also may want to *offer a 60-day free trial*, where you bill at the end of 60 days. This reduces the customers' sense of risk greatly. By the time the 60 days are up, you have inertia working for you; they are very unlikely to deinstall the product.

• *Use an involvement device*—it may raise your response rates (see pages 137 to 138). An involvement device is anything that gets prospects involved. It might be solving a riddle to get the "bonus" gift or putting yes/no stickers on the order form.

• Try to *offer* as many *different payment terms* as possible; do take personal checks. If this is a business application, consider taking purchase orders. (Most people who can write a purchase order have to go through hell to prepay for an order.) If you have an international market, you might even say that you take cash.

• Always *code your response form* so you know where the sale came from. If you are using telephone credit card sales, use a slightly unique product number or "operator." Then use this information to refine your approach. Avoid using the letters B, D, and E in your order code, since they are hard to tell apart when taking a telephone order.

• If you are testing the price or the terms of the offer, do use different order codes, but, more important, *use different telephone numbers* and different colored response cards and envelopes. If the order comes in garbled, you'll know which offer to fill.

• *Allow customers to keep the free stuff* even if they decide to return the product.

• *Test your response mechanism!* Have at least six people try each (mail, phone, fax, credit card, check, and so on) method. Have them actually mail or phone. You'll discover typos and omissions only in this way. One publisher forgot to say to whom to make out the check. I managed to reverse two digits in my ZIP code. These are expensive mistakes.

- *Don't get fancy with shipping and handling fees.* If people get confused, they won't order. Make it a single round number if possible.

- *Consider adding a tear-off stub* to your order form that restates the guarantee and the offer. Maybe include a spot to write down the order confirmation number when customers call to order. This gives people the assurance that they still have a copy of the terms after they send in the reply form and reduces their sense of risk.

- *Fill in as much of the order form as you can* for them while leaving it easy for them to correct the information.

- It helps if your "special offer" is at least a 65 percent discount from the price listed in the brochure.

- *Throw in as much "free" stuff as you can.* You may be able to swap with another publisher for this free offer.

- If you're going to attempt an *"upsell,"* this is a good place to put a special offer.

The Return Envelope

The return envelope may or may not be postage paid. (You'll have to test this for yourself.) It seems that the act of addressing an envelope is a major barrier to consummating the sale.

- Consider using a *postage-paid reply.* Experiment if you can; sometimes this boosts response, and sometimes it has no effect.

- Include a box on the outside to check for "priority handling" and/or *express delivery.*

- You can usually get a *unique color* (or at least a unique bold graphic design) for the same cost. This doesn't do a thing for the buyer, but does help the dyslexic postal workers get the envelope into your box on their first try.

- Include the postal service's *bar code* for your address. This will add to the accuracy and speed of the response.

The Lift Note

The lift note is that small, folded piece of paper with *Open this only if you've decided not to order* "handwritten" on the outside.

The purpose of the lift note is to reinforce the benefits outlined in the sales letter. Typically, it is your last chance with a potential buyer who has decided not to buy.

- This may (word for word) be the most important words you write. You need to *establish trust and restate your offer* and benefits in the shortest possible note.
- Ask them to *call you collect at your personal direct line* if they aren't going to order. Besides lifting response (few actually will call), the marketing information you get from the few calls actually made will be well worth it.
- *Offer another freebie.* In fact, you're going to send this last freebie to everyone, but it feels to the customer like you're making your last best offer to them. You might want to try the "secret box" technique where you tell them to put a check mark in the box in the upper left-hand corner of the reply card to get this extra premium.

The Involvement Device

This is some kind of gizmo (like "yes" or "no" stickers, or a riddle to solve) that holds the prospect long enough to get your message through.

Collect and examine as much direct mail as you can, and you're likely to find an involvement device that will work well with your product.

Do not attempt to sell more than one product in this type of piece; that's the job of a catalog. You should be stressing the sale of a single product, with a single vision. At most, you may wish to attempt an "upsell" to a more expensive version of the same dream on a separate piece of paper.

It ought to be obvious, but the order form has to fit easily within the return envelope, and all the pieces have to fit easily within the envelope.

The rate for bulk mail in the U.S. is the same for up to 3 ounces. You'll find that your response rate climbs as you approach this limit.

One- and Two-Step Sales

It is important to decide on an objective before designing your direct mail material and selecting your list. Are you trying to generate leads for later follow-up, or are you trying to close the sale? A *one-step* inquiry/response model sets things up so the majority of sales are made directly from the materials sent out. Usually this is an impulse purchase and must be presented and priced as one.

Closing a sale using the one-step method requires that you give complete information and make buyers feel assured they will get what they expect.

A *two-step* process assumes that you are testing for interest and will follow up with more material and a telephone solicitation. As you might imagine, a higher price is necessary to turn a profit in a two-step sale.

If lead generation is your goal, the ad should arouse curiosity rather than try to close the sale. Do not give potential customers the entire story, but leave enough questions open that they are motivated to ask for more information. Time is of the essence in following up leads—research shows a dramatic drop-off in interest just days after potential customers give a positive response. For this reason the best two-step campaigns try to get the customer to call an 800 number immediately.

The nature of direct mail is such that even a professional rarely hits upon the right combination the first time for a new product. Budget for and plan to do many mailings, refining your choice of lists, materials, and techniques as you go.

Hints for Effective Direct Mail

My miscellaneous list of direct mail hints:

• *Get your customers to join or lead the group.* If you have a state-of-the-art product that attracts people who like to be on the leading edge, let them know this is their chance to be the first on the block with this exciting new software. On the other hand, if you sell a product that appeals to more conservative types, imply that almost everybody will be upgrading to this new release—certainly they will not want to be left out.

- If you've followed my advice and have a family of products, *try for an upsell* to the next product level in a separate lift note.

- *Allow for as many response options as possible.* Let the customer select "Yes," "No," and some form of "Maybe" at the least. I don't know why it lifts the response rate, but it does.

- *Keep the offer simple.* Complexity breeds suspicion and depresses response.

- *Experiment with a separate gift slip.* Make it look like only the special prospects get this special extra incentive.

- *Use many different sizes, shapes, and colors in your direct mail piece.* It works. I don't know why it works, but it does.

- When you really get going big, you'll be able to use a number of lists simultaneously. Negotiate to *use* these *lists on a net-name basis* and use mailing house software to eliminate the duplicate names. The best software will allow you to use the cheapest name.

- Always *use the best lists you can get.* Even if a list is outrageously expensive, test it. It may in fact be a bargain if the response is high enough.

- Do *save as much money as you can on printing.* Quality stock, accuracy, and bleeds almost never add to the response rate. Don't let your graphics person drive up your costs unnecessarily.

- If you use a mailing house, *get a copy of the Postal Services mailing verification form for the mailing.* Insist on it. Not everyone is honest; this form will tell you when the mail was really dropped and how many pieces there were.

- *Stress the availability of upgrades and new versions.* People want "live" software.

- *Don't* do anything that might *distract readers' attention.* For instance, don't ask them to refer to an illustration on another page. Don't use a word that has a potentially negative meaning in another context—for instance, don't sell fully "integrated" software.

- *Don't simply drop previous customers* from the list after an arbitrary number of mailings with no response. Instead, schedule them for every other mailing, then every fourth mailing, before dropping them. This will keep you in contact with them if they have a temporary reason for not buying right away.

- *Hold on to your old names.* If and when you make a platform change, you may get a good response. It is also common for people to skip major releases if a single release doesn't offer enough new features to warrant a response. I personally tend to do this with DOS and Quicken.

- *The best time to mail is early January.* You'd think that everybody would be tapped out from the holidays, but in fact many people will buy themselves something they really want this time of year. Try to avoid mailing into the television sweeps periods, when audience-grabbing miniseries are being presented.

- It may not be possible to control when your mail is delivered but, if you can, try for the end rather than the beginning of the week. Try to *avoid Monday delivery*.

- On the other hand, be sure to *get more offers out to buyers* shortly after you ship the product. People are most likely to buy again while they still have that good feeling from acquiring a new tool or toy.

- *Use a positive or a negative approach.* Notwithstanding the Anacin ads that gave you a headache, positive ads are generally more effective. Trying to mix positive and negative approaches in a single mailing is a recipe for disaster.

For products under $150, you can reasonably use a one-step process. Over $800, a two-step process with personal follow-up makes sense. Between those two prices, it's very difficult to use direct marketing.

You can convert a high-end item to a low-end sale by selling an inexpensive product to the same market. The easiest way to do this is to offer a subset of the full product. Alternatively, you might offer a book, a seminar, or a useful tool at a low price. Once you have acquired the customer (and established some credibility), you can then begin the process of selling them the more expensive product.

In putting together your second-step materials, design them to respond to specific questions, rather than try to create a one-size-fits-all "book." Mail or fax only the chapters that customers require to get the information they need. They're much more likely to read something targeted to their concerns than they are to try to find it in an inch of literature.

Don't send demos. Or at least don't send demos the way they're usually sent. Make an appointment for a "phone demo," then send a complete product that includes a demo data set. Walk customers through the demo, setting the product up for their organization. Get them fully up and running, then tell them that they can continue to use the full product if they'll just give you a purchase order number. If they don't buy, don't ask them to ship the product back—instead, call in a month to see if you can get them to use the product again. If you can get a corporation to use your product, eventually you'll be paid for it.

For a really high-end product, schedule "hotel demos." Plan a week to be in selected cities. Have the entire product set up in a hotel suite and have support staff in attendance. Invite individual prospects in by appointment to spend half a day exploring whether your product meets their needs.

I think that full-color postcards are a great way to sell *upgrades and new releases* by direct mail. The advantages of postcards include:

- Lower cost of printing (compared to sheets of paper and envelopes).
- Much lower labor (compared to folding and stuffing).
- The sales message is guaranteed to be seen for at least a split second.

About half of the people who will upgrade at all will respond to a postcard with a list of key new features, an 800 number, and a deadline. Wait about 60 days from the postcard mailing and follow up with a more traditional piece to those who didn't respond to the card.

There's an interesting (apocryphal) story about a software house that got its lists mixed up and mistakenly mailed an upgrade notice to a general list. According to the story, the response rate was better than any other mailing the company had ever done. You might want to give this a try if you develop an upgrade piece that works well for you.

For those who still don't respond, you might want to try the "fake carbon" approach. This is a second copy of the direct mail piece with a yellow sticky back attached that reminds your customers that they may miss this opportunity to keep current with the product unless they respond now.

The cost of a full-color postcard campaign can drop as low as $.30 per piece. Using a one-step response with a 2 percent return, you'll need a margin of $15 to break even. For a software product that people are actually using, you can expect about a third of your users to upgrade to a major new release that offers needed features.

Full-color (meaning you can use photographs) postcards go for about:

Quantity	Price	Size
6,500	$450	3.5" x 5.5"
12,500	$700	4" x 5⅞"
25,000	$1,500	5⅜" x 7"
50,000	$2,800	6" x 9"

Two sources for full-color postcards are:

American Color Printing
1731 NW 97th Avenue
Plantation, FL 33322
(305) 473-4392

US Press
PO Box 640
Valdosta, GA 31603
(800) 227-7377

For doing your own two-step direct mail, I really favor the *double postcard* technique. In essence, you print a single large postcard expressing your message in a colorful way. A portion of this postcard is designed to be returned to you with the mailing label on it (leave room for corrections). Even people who throw "junk mail" away without opening it will notice the main message on a postcard if it's a bright color and printed on both sides. If you don't have a bulk mail permit, this technique can still be used, but you will have stricter postal regulations (size, shape, and a required fold) to deal with.

For a two-step response, a good postcard campaign can yield about 150 good inquiries per thousand dollars, or about $7 per inquiry.

TESTING YOUR MAILING LIST

When you do decide to use direct mail, test your list before sending out thousands of pieces. One thousand pieces should give you a reasonable estimate of the return you can expect from a list. If the yield isn't acceptable, buy another list. The cost of materials and postage is high enough that it makes sense to abandon a list rather than invest more in it.

There are a lot of rules-of-thumb in direct mail, but no magic answers. Every list and every product is different. It will be necessary to test different approaches to see what works for your market and your product line in order to refine your approach. When you find a list that produces good yields, continue to reuse it periodically. This forms a baseline against which you can measure the effects of new approaches. Use old lists with new materials and new lists with old materials. In this way, you have a standard from which to decide if the list or the collateral is making a difference in yields.

In testing, it is essential that you *change only a single variable* at a time. For instance, if you are trying to see if a four-color postcard will outperform a two-color postcard, perform a mailing where you:

- Randomly use half of the list for two color and the other half for four; do not use different lists.
- Use the exact same copy and (to the extent possible) art.
- Mail all of the cards on the same day from the same post office.

Make the test big enough that you can reasonably expect to receive at least 100 responses for each variable. In a two-variable test with an expected 2 percent response, this implies a minimum mailing of 10,000. Any test smaller than this is not necessarily statistically significant. Since you can run an experiment in about a month, you should have a good feel for what works and be approaching your optimal response rate in about six months.

Why test only one variable at a time? If you test two variables and you do see a difference, there's no way to know which variable actually made the difference. At times, you may suspect that two variables work together. To test this, you need a four-part test. The first part is no change (to act as a control); the second and third tests work the variables independently; and the last test works them together. As you can see, testing more than three variables requires enormous mailings.

On the other hand, there will be times when you will need to try out entire new concepts. Treat the new concept as a single variable, and compare it with your "control" in testing. You may find that you will end up with different "best" mailings to different audiences. I found that private eyes, lawyers, and corporate staff functions had totally different "hot" buttons when it came to time tracking, for instance.

The primary variables with which you will be experimenting are:

- The *medium* (postcard, letter, etc.).
- The *copy* (the text of the message). Some of the major things you might experiment with include the length of the letter, the font, and which benefit you select to promote as the key benefit. I fool with the Johnson box and the P.S. last, and find that subtle changes in these two elements really can make a difference.
- The *art* (layout, photos, typefaces, color, and so on). Experiment with the change in yields as you use one, two, four, or full color. The higher response rate may or may not pay for itself.
- The *price* of the product—including two-for-one deals or time-limited offers. The most responsive prices seem to be $19.95, $39.95, $69.95, $97.50, $134.50, and $195. Again, I don't know why; they just are.
- The *delivery* (type of mail, stamps vs. meter, and so on).

• The *seasonality*—day of the week, period within the month, relationship to major holidays, season of the year. You may never know why, but some periods will be more effective than others. My offers do best if they arrive on Wednesday or Thursday near the end of the month—but never during tax season. According to *World Book*, the best months for direct selling are January and February, followed by October and August. You might choose to schedule major new releases for early in the year for that reason.

• The *method of payment*. In general, the easier it is and the more options available, the better. Consider experimenting with a "soft offer"—the "send no money, we'll bill you later" offer. For inexpensive products, the response rate often rises high enough to overcome the deadbeats. This is, of course, especially effective where you deliver the product over time, as with a subscription product.

• The *offer*—the actual details, the wording, and the positioning of the offer.

Since testing is essentially "free," it makes sense to devote a fair percentage of your mail volume to testing. In the early stages when I didn't know what was going to work, as much as 50 percent of my outgoing mail was marked for testing. Once you think you know what works, it makes sense to devote about 10 percent of each mailing to testing one new variable.

Lists generally rent (single-use only) for about $40 to $60 per thousand. There are *two kinds of lists*—compiled and mail order. A mail order list is a list of people who have actually purchased something through the mail in the recent past. A compiled list is a list of people that was constructed from the rolls of associations, licenses, the telephone book, voter registrations, or other public records. In general, a mail order list will be much more effective than a compiled list because these people have demonstrated that they can read, they open their mail, and they are inclined to purchase products through the mail. Obviously, you may not have a choice. If your package is written for astronomers, the only list available may be a compiled list—but if given a choice, obtain a mail order list.

Copywriting and designing direct mail is something that few people can do well. It may be well worth your time to work with a professional. Some people who have reputations for understanding the software industry and getting results include:

George Duncan
16 Elm Street
Peterborough, NH 03458
(603) 924-3121

Bill Mirbach
301 Riverside Avenue
Westport, CT 06880
(203) 454-2594

Ivan Levison
14 Los Cerros Drive
Greenbrae, CA 94904
(415) 461-0672

You can get lists from brokers, magazines, and associations. Some of the larger list brokers include:

Hugo Dunhill Mailing Lists, Inc.
630 Third Avenue
New York, NY 10017
(212) 682-8030
general list broker; free marketing guide

SpeciaLists
120 East 16th Street
New York, NY 10003
(800) 888-3462
general list broker

Dun's Marketing Services
3 Sylvan Way
Parsippany, NJ 07054
(800) 624-5669
broker; lists of businesses

Ed Burnett Consultants
99 West Sheffield Avenue
Englewood, NJ 07631
(800) 223-7777
list broker and direct mail services

American List Counsel
88 Orchard Road
Princeton, NJ 08543
(800) 252-5478
general list brokers

Research Projects Corp
Pomeraug Avenue
Woodbury, CT 06798
(203) 263-0100
(800) 243-4360
general list broker

Dinner+Klein
600 South Spokane Street
Seattle, WA 98134
(800) 234-6637
complete direct mail service; U.S. and Canada

Best Mailing Lists
38 West 32nd Street
New York, NY 10001
(212) 868-1080
(800) 692-2378
general list broker

Card decks are another form of direct marketing. These are the often cellophane-wrapped stacks of cards you get in the mail; each card advertises a different product. Their effectiveness is limited by the surrounding cards and by the size of the card itself, so yields are significantly lower. A typical price is about $.02 per card for a fairly targeted list of over 100,000. The normal rules for direct mail, such as quality of the list and effectiveness of the message, apply. If you use a card deck, have it designed as a horizontal because that's the way most people hold the deck as they go through it.

Position is also critical; you may be asked to pay more for a spot in the first dozen cards.

If you do decide to investigate card decks, obtain back copies of the deck from the publisher. Take a look at the cards and try to figure out how you can both fit in and stand out. If the majority of advertisers are using two colors, consider using four. If the majority of the cards are printed vertically, print yours that way too. Pick out the cards for the products most like yours in market, price, response type, and card type. Call these advertisers and ask about their experience. If you can get multiple back decks, note which advertisers repeat and which ones don't. This can help you figure out which types of products do well in this deck.

In a card deck, you can use a one-step sale only for products that are easily explained and present minimal risk to the buyer. Most card deck sales for software are two-steps, for this reason: Getting a person who has never heard of you to send you money based on the information you can fit on a card is asking an awful lot. The upper limit for a single-step card deck sale seems to be about $25.

To start educating yourself about direct marketing, start collecting your junk mail instead of tossing it. A collection of pieces that you find interesting will be valuable later on. Also, request controlled circulation subscriptions from:

Target Marketing Magazine
401 North Broad Street
P.O. Box 12827
Philadelphia, PA 19108

DM News
Mill Hollow Corporation
19 W. 21st Street
New York, NY 10010

Direct Marketing Magazine isn't free, but it is worthwhile for someone serious about direct marketing:

Direct Marketing Magazine
224 Seventh Street
Garden City, NY 11530
(800) 229-6700 $56 year

It may make sense to have a professional be responsible for the entire campaign the first time. You can find people who specialize in direct mail by looking in your yellow pages under "Advertising Agencies" or by using:

The Direct Marketing Marketplace
Hilary House Publishers
980 North Federal Highway, Suite 206
Boca Raton, FL 33432
(407) 393-5656

This directory seems to list everybody in direct marketing, including catalogs that might carry your product, printers, list brokers, creative services (art and copy), events and seminars about direct marketing, and separate sections for Canadian and foreign organizations. Using this directory, I was able to find three agencies within twenty miles of me in New Hampshire. When you do contact agencies, try to find one with recent successful experience selling software—ask for and check references.

There are a number of local direct marketing clubs across North America. Joining one is an excellent way to both learn a lot and meet people who either are or can lead you to local resources. The following list is sorted by state (or Canadian Province), then phone number. It was checked just before publication, but these contacts do tend to change annually; updates can be found in the Software Publisher's Kit.

Phone	State	Ask For
(602) 990-8868	AZ	Murray Hill
(604) 736-3024	BC	Cathi Flanigan
(310) 374-7499	CA	Jan Edwards-Pullin
(415) 434-1696	CA	Walt D. Abraham
(619) 270-6230	CA	Gil Mombach
(714) 939-1785	CA	Al Ingallinera
(818) 567-2885	CA	Glen Giles
(818) 995-7338	CA	Joan Mullen
(303) 534-2508	CO	Sabrina Luce
(203) 691-1260	CT	Ned Haley
(202) 347-0055	DC	Gene A. Del Polito
(202) 962-8342	DC	National Infomercial Marketing Association
(703) 821-3629	DC	Sherryl Marshall

Phone	State	Ask for
(305) 472-6374	FL	Betty Kaufman
(407) 347-0200	FL	Robert Dunhill
(407) 352-3207	FL	Debi Bushnell
(813) 278-5778	FL	Anthony Correnti
(813) 447-8406	FL	Danene Martinez
(312) 642-1377	IL	Pat Wheelless
(312) 761-1232	IL	Rob Jackson
(317) 471-8246	IN	Scott Macy
(502) 585-3403	KY	Larry Kass
(508) 473-8643	MA	Gregory Sullivan
(301) 249-7800	MD	Eva Watson
(301) 490-9143	MD	Camille Chioini
(301) 559-5715	MD	Terri LaGoe
(800) 441-1850	MD	Maryland Direct Marketing Association
(313) 292-3200	MI	Duane E. Dub
(612) 339-8141	MN	Mark Lamberty
(314) 291-3144	MO	Margaret Forster
(913) 236-6699	MO	John Goodman
(919) 990-1441	NC	George A. Wehmann
(402) 333-4777	NE	Tom Dudycha
(201) 222-0404	NY	Pat Giassa
(203) 637-4777	NY	Hunter M. Marvel
(212) 536-5185	NY	Susan Sherwood
(212) 645-0344	NY	Stan Winston
(212) 661-1410	NY	Ken Ketzler
(212) 689-8920	NY	Nicholas Veliotes
(212) 768-7277	NY	Jonah Gitlitz
(516) 746-6700	NY	Direct Marketing Club of New York
(516) 868-1732	NY	Susan Johnson-Soules
(513) 294-4000	OH	Marilyn Smith
(513) 397-7227	OH	David Rose
(614) 846-1800	OH	Don Nichols
(416) 391-2362	ON	J. Gustavson
(416) 502-0433	ON	Luci Furtado
(503) 228-4000	OR	Richard Rosen
(215) 540-2257	PA	Arlene Claffee
(514) 281-5725	QU	Paul Poulin
(713) 869-8551	TX	David E. Mackey
(817) 640-7018	TX	Blair Y. Stephenson
(703) 519-8160	VA	Norman Scharpl

Phone	State	Ask for
(703) 836-9200	VA	David Weaver
(802) 655-4442	VT	Sam Cutting IV
(703) 821- DMAW	WA	Jeanne Davis
(414) 873-9362	WI	Grant A. Johnson

Jim Johnson is one person who claims to be a guru of direct marketing for software. Each year he offers a one-day seminar on software direct marketing in a wide range of cities for $99. While the day was one-third sales pitch, I felt that it was worth my time and my money. He also offers a newsletter; eight issues for $101.50. For more information (ask to be put on his mailing list, if nothing else), contact:

Jim Johnson
400 Seaport Court #100
Redwood City, CA 94063
voice: (415) 306-1555
fax: (415) 306-1556

CHAPTER 6

Working with Software Publishers

 If you're getting the impression that running a software business is more about marketing than it is about programming, you're right. If you feel that you'd be happier writing code than writing press releases, you might be well served by working with a publisher.

LOW-COST RETAIL (LCR)

If you wander through the computer sections of the major discount stores (Wal-Mart, Kmart, and so on) or through the gift shops in airports, you'll notice that there are now racks of low-priced consumer-oriented software. Much of this software was written specifically for this market, and much is shareware that has had a facelift and been retitled. The name of the "publisher" is almost never the same as that of the (usually anonymous) developer. Publishers who specialize in bringing this kind of software to market typically go trolling in the major information services, looking for shareware that might have mass appeal. Then they make an offer to the developer, retitle it, and include it in their line.

In order to maximize "turns" on this impulse item, rotating the titles is important to the distributor; the rack must look fresh to potential customers every time they browse through it. A typical rack might hold twenty-four to forty-eight titles. Each month the publisher will kill the slowest-selling 10 percent to 20 percent of the titles to make room for fresh products.

A single product generally stays in a line for about six months before it is burned out. Given the right clauses in the contract and an engine that allows you to change the "look and feel" of the product, it's possible to have a number of publishers publish the same base product for a number of years.

Since the product must be priced as an impulse purchase, the retail price ranges for LCR software are usually between $6 and $30.

Games make up the biggest part of this marketing channel (especially arcade games). Right behind the games come educational products purchased for kids. How-to and information-based products take up a big segment ("Wedding Planner" and "Train Your Dog" type products). Finally, a couple of staples (a spreadsheet, a form generator, etc.) take up a few slots.

Like other "shelfware," this channel presents a problem in acquiring customers (as opposed to simply making the sale), first, because many publishers want the developer to remain anonymous and, second, because of the difficulty in offering purchasers an opportunity to identify themselves.

You can expect a typical product to sell one copy per month per rack. While this doesn't sound like very much (especially when you consider the low royalty), remember that both Wal-Mart and Kmart each have over 2,000 stores in their chains. A large publisher will move about 1,000 copies per month of a moderately successful product. Typically, sales will fade after about six months, since all the rack browsers who are likely to buy your product will have done so by then.

As a developer, your costs basically are limited to development costs. Once your product is accepted for publication, the publisher assumes all responsibility for manufacturing and distributing it. In most cases, advances are not paid unless you are in an extremely strong negotiating position. Royalties are usually based on net receipts. This means you will be paid a percentage of what the publisher actually receives minus any returns. Usually, some royalties are held back to provide for the time when the product is pulled from the racks.

The royalty rate varies tremendously, depending on the nature of the product, how exclusive the contract is, your track record, your rights to sell other products to the buyers of the product, and your negotiating skills. In general, the low end seems to be about 7 percent and the high end seems to be about 15 percent. Alternatively, you might be offered a fixed amount per unit sold.

At the very low end, it hovers around a dime, and at the high end, it may reach a dollar.

Given the typical numbers in this type of distribution, you should insist on a minimum royalty of $.25 per unit and a minimum royalty of $200 per month starting three months from the date the contract is signed. If the publisher fails to make the minimum, he or she loses the right to publish the product.

The most common bad experience with this type of publishing is to have the publisher sit on a product for an indeterminate amount of time and finally do nothing with it. This happens either during negotiations where you fail to negotiate simultaneously with a few publishers or, worse, after the contract is signed.

The second most common bad experience is to have the product published but never have it reach full distribution. In this case, a publisher will make up a few thousand copies and then test the product. If the tests don't turn out well, the remaining copies will be shipped to some locations where sales are slow anyway and the supply will be allowed to run out over time. This makes sense for the publisher, since it limits losses. It can be devastating to you, since it can be a very long time before you regain the right to sell the product through someone else.

Some of the larger publishers with decent reputations include the following:

GoodTimes Software can be found in Wal-Mart and other very large discount retailers. The company is reported to be looking primarily for children's educational software, and it seems to have the clout to insist upon an exclusive contract. It will republish a shareware product if the new product has a new interface and exclusive features. Dave Snyder, a software publisher himself, is the acquisitions representative for this company:

GoodTimes Software
c/o **Dave Snyder, MVP Software**
1035 Dallas SE
Grand Rapids, MI 49507-1407
voice: (616) 245-8376
fax: (616) 245-3204

Sofsource has three product lines (Who, Personal Companion, and Pro One) and massive distribution. It will insist on an exclusive contract and will resist including anything that encourages the buyer to contact you directly.

Rick Trask
Sofsource
3186 Pine Tree Road
Lansing, MI 48911-4205
(517) 393-8197

Expert Software works mostly with DOS games and Windows special-interest products. It will rename the product using its name and ask you to rework the interface and add some exclusive features. You'll find Expert Software mostly in Radio Shack and department stores. Its target price range seems to be from $15 to $20.

Khan Lowe
Director of Product Development
Expert Software
800 Douglas Road
North Tower, Suite 355
Coral Gables, FL 33134-3128
voice: (305) 567-9990 ext. 234
fax: (305) 443-0786

UAV Corporation is a big and established videotape publisher, just starting to publish computer software. It seems to be working to increase its distribution and find its niche. Based on its success in video, I'd guess that it has the talent to figure out the retail software distribution business. For right now, it seems to favor inexpensive games. It probably will ask for an exclusive relationship but has been known to settle for a unique name and interface:

Jeff Taylor
UAV Corporation
P.O. Box 7647
Charlotte, NC 28241
voice: (803) 548-7300
fax: (803) 548-3335

Villa Crespo Software is primarily an under-$10 games publisher; its "Coffee Break" label may be familiar to you:

Donna L. Corson
National Sales Director
Villa Crespo Software
501 South First Ave., Suite L
Arcadia, CA 91006
(708) 433-0500

National Systems Technology may be familiar to you as Software Concepts. It publishes mostly games and seems to have wide distribution:

John Mayo or Jim Crabtree
National Systems Technology
1990 N. Alma School Road #348
Chandler, AZ 85224
(800) 489-8355

Do:

• Concentrate on easily explained products. These are impulse purchases.

• Be sure to have screens that are designed with selling the product in mind. These will prove important when the product packaging—including screen shots—is developed.

• Keep it simple. If it's a productivity product, accomplish your task with the simplest solution possible. Support calls to the publisher will get you booted off a rack faster than anything else.

• Make sure that you and the publisher agree on whether and how you may solicit your customers. If you can sell the hint books for an adventure game, you can afford to give away the royalties. If you won't get the names of your buyers and can't sell them more products, you'll have to make the royalties support the entire deal.

• Be absolutely honest with your publishers. Tell them how the product they'll be publishing is similar to and different from products you developed for other publishers.

• "Exclusive" is a critical word. Make absolutely certain that you and the publisher agree on just what this means. Most publishers will insist only on a unique name, visual interface, and some exclusive features. They also may insist that you not compete in the same market.

• Try to structure the product and the deal so that you can republish your product with successive publishers as it gets stale and so that you are building a mailing list of customers interested in your type of product.

• Submit the product with packaging and an interface that is similar to the publishers'. This will help them to visualize your product in their product line. Tell them exactly who will be buying the product, and why.

• Check out a publisher very carefully. Check references, then get all the information you can through other software developers that have dealt with this publisher—both the company and the people involved.

• Insist upon a Dun & Bradstreet report and an audited financial statement from your prospective publisher. You need to be sure that he can pay you.

• Tour the stores. New publishers spring up all the time, and they are more likely to need new developers. You are most likely to find these new publishers by tripping over their products in the stores you'd like to be in.

Don't:

• Even think of taking on product support in this environment. There is no way you can answer the phone and teach beginners how to insert a diskette into the drive with the royalties available here.

• Do business on a handshake, or without the advice of a lawyer familiar with this type of publishing.

• Sign a contract that allows a publisher to sit on a product without paying you or releasing the product back to you. Insist on a minimum royalty once some reasonable period has passed.

• Believe any promises that are made to you unless they are in the contract with a performance guarantee.

• Expect an advance unless the contract is exclusive and you have a track record.

• Sign a right-of-first-refusal clause. If you must sign a clause of this type, define the conditions very carefully.

• Agree not to develop competing products. Do agree on how you're going to limit the competition.

• Allow the license to be transferred or assigned to another company. If the publisher won't move on this issue, insist on a minimum cash royalty and certification by a national accounting firm (at the publisher's expense) as to how many units were shipped. Transfer of a license with a royalty based on net receipts is an invitation to have the publisher sell the product to his wife's company for a dollar a copy, and then have the wife's company distribute it for a much higher price.

• If you are on a royalty as a basis of net contract, be sure that the costs that can be assigned are very clearly defined. By charging the company limosine to your product, a publisher can cut your royalties substantially.

PUBLISHING UNDER A PRIVATE LABEL

There's no reason you can't provide product to other publishers as well, either a complete product that will be renamed and sold as part of that publisher's product line or one that will be integrated into another much larger product.

For instance, most generalized manufacturing packages don't have their own, written-from-scratch accounting software—reinventing that wheel would simply be wasteful.

Elfring Softfonts probably makes most of its money through this type of deal. I worked with a software firm that found some of these fonts on a bulletin board and incorporated them into their product as it was developed. When the time came to release the product, licensing the fonts being used already made much more sense than either developing their own or finding another font supplier. While Elfring Softfonts doesn't make most of its money from shareware, it does seem to do most of its marketing through shareware.

Most private-label deals do not provide for adding customers who buy your products to your base, so the deal has to stand on its own.

BUNDLING

Simply put, bundling is when you make a single large sale to a company that will in turn offer your product as a premium or incentive to buy its product. You are probably aware of the systems sold with preinstalled copies of DOS, Windows and half a dozen applications programs. That's bundling.

Depending on what you are supplying, a bundling deal may bring anywhere from a couple of cents to a couple of dollars per unit. Typically a bundling deal will bring you half a percent to 2 percent of the list price of your product if you are supplying only a license (a master copy of the disk and manual, with no support).

It is very easy to lose money on a bundling deal and very hard to make much. The least risky way to bundle is one in which you license the product to the bundler to be sold under a different name, with the bundler responsible for production of the disks and manuals as well as support.

On the other hand, the way to (potentially) make money on bundling is by having your product distributed under your name and providing support to users who have returned their registration cards. You won't make much at first, but, with the list of registered users, you have a potential upgrade base that can be converted into an annuity using direct mail for upgrades and add-ons.

Don't restrict your thinking to computer manufacturers. If you produce a program that helps bicyclists keep track of their runs, call a distributor of bicycle accessories to suggest that your product be a premium for customers who order during the snowy months.

REFERRALS

We all hope that software will be sold on the recommendation of one friend to another, but referral selling raises this to a fine art. The basic idea is to find a company that needs to exchange information with many independent agents. Insurance companies, franchise operations, and multilevel marketing operations come to mind immediately. By having the parent company endorse your software product as the preferred way to keep and transmit business records, you can offer it a way to standardize and computerize its relationship with its agents at no cost to the parent company.

For example, all of the larger real estate brokerage franchises offer relocation services. You might design a software product whose format standardizes the relocation service information across the entire organization. Usually your product will be distributed by the parent company to the franchises as a part of the start-up kit and will be promoted in the parent company's newsletter—you might even want to write a column.

Another reason that this method of distribution is attractive to your customers is because independent agents generally prefer to use generic or industry-standard software rather than be locked into the product of a specific supplier. By obtaining the recommendation of two or more suppliers in the industry, you can become the standard.

CATALOGS

Catalogs offer a way to sell to a "legitimate" market without the cash commitment that wholesale distribution/retail involves. Catalogs generally work in one of two ways: either they take the risk, or you do. As you might imagine, it's much easier to get into a catalog where you assume the financial risk.

A quick formula for estimating the net yield of participating in a catalog or card deck is:

$$\text{Net Yield} = ((G - U) * T * Y * O * (A / S) * F) - C$$

Where:

Y is your estimate of the catalog yield. Unless you have experience that leads you to believe differently, 2 percent (.02) is about the best you can hope for.

O is the average number of items ordered in each order. A lot depends on the catalog, the market, and the relationship between the ordering costs (shipping, handling, and whatever else is charged) and the product costs. If nothing else, the maximum number of items that fit on the order form will give you an idea of what the highest number is. For most catalogs, something between one and three is about right.

T is the total number of catalogs that will be mailed.

S is a measure of size for the entire catalog or deck. Use product pages, square inches, or cards. Be consistent in using the same unit of measurement as in A. You are figuring out what proportion of the entire publication your ad accounts for.

A is the size of your ad; use the same unit of measurement as in S. I haven't included placement (cover, first twelve pages, and so on). You may want to adjust the formula for this as well.

G is the gross price (price + s&h) you will receive for each product.

U is the unit cost of producing and shipping an item. This includes your materials and shipping fees, the cost (value) of direct labor in assembling them, and some prorated part of your up-front costs.

F is the fudge factor. Almost certainly, your information is going to be too optimistic. Use this factor to cut it back to size. A value of 1 assumes there is no optimism inflation. A value of .5 is reasonably conservative.

C is the actual cash cost of participating in the catalog.

For example, say you were offered the opportunity to place a quarter-page ad in a sixteen-page catalog to be sent to 100,000 potential customers for $1,200. Also assume that your gross price is $34 and your unit cost is $5.50. Is this a good deal?

If you assume a yield of 2 percent and that the average order will be for 2.5 products, then use a fudge factor of .5, the formula predicts that you will lose $86.72 on the deal.

This formula assumes that you will make only a single sale to each customer. If you are selling a family of products or a product that can be renewed, you will need to project those later campaigns as well (they may be done through direct mail if you obtained the customers' names and addresses), and sum the results. For instance, in the preceding example, if you were to add a follow-on mailing to the thirty-nine customers you did attract and had a 20 percent yield (not unusual for an existing customer) on a second (net yield) $25 product, you will predict an additional $195 in revenue, resulting in a profit for the campaign.

As a rule of thumb, you can figure that previous buyers are ten times more likely to buy than people named in an untested list. Two-time buyers have a rate half again higher than one-time buyers. Three-time buyers are three times more likely than one-time buyers to buy more.

You are most likely to be successful in catalogs that are tailored to your target market. These are probably not "computer" catalogs but "toy" catalogs for adults. Use the *Direct Marketing Marketplace* (cited on page 149) to find these catalogs. Companies that publish catalogs of low-priced software include:

Parsons Technology
One Parsons Drive
P.O. Box 100
Hiawatha, IA 52233-9904
(319) 395-9626

Tiger Software
800 Douglas Entrance
Coral Gables, FL 33134
(800) 888-4437

Power Up Software Corporation
2929 Camput Drive
P.O. Box 7600
San Mateo, CA 94403-7600
(415) 345-5575

DAK Industries
8200 Remmet Avenue
Canoga Park, CA 91304
(800) 888-7808

If you do participate in a catalog where the company does the fulfillment, be sure to include a postage-paid registration card in the package. If you can, *add an incentive to registration* to make the percentage of people who register as high as possible. Immediately add these people to your direct mail list, even if you're just "keeping in touch."

One way to get discovered by a catalog is to exhibit at or attend the Consumer Electronics Show, the National Mail Order Merchandise Show, and/or the Premium Incentive Show.

The Consumer Electronics Show is an enormous show held in Las Vegas in January and in Chicago in June. If you have a product that belongs in an electronics catalog, it might make sense to attend or exhibit:

Consumer Electronics Show
2001 Eye Street NW
Washington, DC 20006
(202) 457-8700

The National Mail Order Merchandise Show in New York is fairly small, but it is a heck of a lot cheaper than Consumer Electronics. This is a good bet if you have a product that belongs in a non-electronics catalog:

Division Expo Accessories, Inc.
300 Allwood Road
Clifton, NJ 07012
(201) 777-5802

The Premium Incentive Show is all about cheap stuff that can be sent through the mail as a reward. Held each spring in New York, it is a natural for many kinds of software (especially the entry-level version). The people at the show are generally very interested in entry-level products; if you can be paid for something that you'd normally give away, that's a pretty good deal. The trick, of course, is to be sure that the product has a registration incentive so that you can later identify and upsell your users. You can get information on this show through:

Thalheim Expositions, Inc.
P.O. Box 707
Great Neck, NY 11021
(516) 466-2038

RETAIL

As soon as you saw the word "retail," you started thinking "Egghead," right? If you are selling a niche application you'll sell the least number of copies in a traditional retail computer or software store—if you can get on the shelves at all. Instead, *get on the shelf where your customer shops*. If you sell a dog breeding program, get on the shelves of the grooming and pet supply stores. If you have a design-a-sundeck program, find out who wholesales do-it-yourself books to lumber yards.

Computer retail begins to make sense when you have an extremely broad market and enough "pull" to interest the large wholesale houses and local retailers. Jim Button of Buttonware is said to have made the jump from shareware to retail by changing his registration reminder to read "If you find this product of value, please purchase a copy at your local Egghead store." The interesting point about the story is that at the time he changed it, Egghead did not stock his product. Enough people walked in looking for the product so that Egghead wound up putting him on its shelves.

The retail channel is terrible at accomplishing your primary goal, acquiring customers. Why? Because users register generally less than one-third of the packages sold through retail channels. If you don't know who bought the package, it's hard to sell them more!

Some ways to encourage people to register the retail package they purchased include:

- Use some of the shareware registration encouragement techniques listed earlier. (See pages 95 through 114.) Many of them are equally effective in the retail channel.
- Offer some kind of bonus for registering. This could be more fonts, or a newsletter with tips for using the software more effectively.
- Refuse to supply tech support to unregistered users.
- Use the sledgehammer approach and refuse to run (or nag them to death like Dell does) until they call an 800 number to get the registration key.

The first (and hardest) step in getting into the retail market is getting into the wholesale market. There are a very small number of wholesalers in the retail software industry. These wholesalers are very demanding about having assurances of minimum volumes before committing to carry a product.

Ingram Micro, one of the largest distributors, carries 13,000 different products from just under 700 publishers. As a practical reality, in order to be carried by Ingram, you must first displace one of its current 700 publishers. Ingram receives serious pitches for over 100 new products each month, of which it accepts about a dozen. By and large, it is getting pitches from companies already well established in other marketing channels that are trying to make the jump to retail shelves.

Your chance of making it with a nonestablished product and without a marketing staff is close to zero.

Major distributors will not carry a product until they are convinced that they will move at least $25,000 worth (wholesale) of that product per month.

They do not pretend to "sell" or create demand for the product; that's your job. Their job is to service their customers by always having what they want in stock at a low price. Prior to approaching major distributors you'd be well advised to:

- Have enough of a market presence that you can demonstrate demand.
- Penetrate at least two other reseller channels.
- Demonstrate that you have a national presence and can service accounts nationally.
- Have a support function that has shown it is capable of adequately handling end-user problems. Neither the distributor nor the retailers want to deal with your problems.

Pricing is critical here, and the optimal retail price will probably be different from the optimal price for shareware or direct mail. A shareware price must be low enough that buyers feel good after writing the check—or they won't mail it. A retail price must be high enough to keep the sales clerk (who is probably paid on commission) interested in it. If you publish a $30 product and sell it to a distributor for $15, who resells it to a retailer for $20, who has to discount it down to $25 (so customers feel they're getting a "break"), the salesperson's 10 percent of that $5 margin isn't too exciting, especially if he or she has to put any time or effort into learning what your product does and who it is designed for.

The discount rates you offer to distributors are negotiable. In general, the rate will approach 55 percent in quantities greater than 100 and be close to or at zero for quantity one.

Do:

- Offer a "clean channel." If retailers can obtain the product in any way other than from this distributor, the distributor is less likely to carry the product. If your product is sold through catalogs, it may be necessary to offer the product at retail under a different name.

- If you have established your own dealers, do expect to have to deliver them to the distributor.

- Expect to take back all copies of earlier versions on the shelf when you announce a new release.

- Try to have a strategic alliance with larger software companies that your product works with. This way your product can be sold as an add-on when the primary product is sold.

- Be prepared to show a strategic plan that shows how you are going to continue to be the market leader as your market matures.

- Present a comprehensive marketing and advertising plan that will show how you are going to generate "pull" for your product.

Don't:

- Even think of presenting a "brown bag" product. All of the retail packaging, store display material, and promotional stuff must be complete and in production.

- Propose a product that will have to take market share away from an established competitor before it can become successful.

- Ever demonstrate a beta version. The very first minor problem will set off so many warning bells that the rest of your message will be totally lost. The one exception to this is a product that is leapfrogging on a technology that is itself in beta.

According to *Computer Reseller News*, the advertising budgets for companies such as Computer Associates, Borland, Microsoft, Corel, Lotus, and Oracle range between $250,000 and $750,000 *per month*. Participating in the retail channel normally takes this kind of money.

If you would like to pursue getting shelf space with individual computer dealers, whether through direct mail or telemarketing, Chromatic Communications sells a database of 6,000 computer retailers (U.S. and Canada; minimum of $500,000 in sales, a storefront, and factory authorization for at least three major brands) with the names of the key contacts, phone and address, and major lines they carry. For $595, you get the database and a search engine that will export. You may use the list multiple times; the only restriction is that you may not resell it. You can order or get more information about the *MicroLeads Dealer Directory* from:

Chromatic Communications
P.O. Box 30127
Walnut Creek, CA 94598
(510) 945-1602
(800) 782-DISK

CHAPTER 7

Organizing Publicity for Your Product

❖❖
❖❖   Planning for publicity (what you're going to say about your product) comes before product development. If your ideas about the product and its market are not defined enough for you to write clear, concise, and exciting prose about the product and why people should pay attention to it, you need to go back and spend more time on concept development. In other words, if you haven't figured out how you're going to sell a product, don't start designing it.

It is during this early conceptual phase that the real systems specifications get hammered out. When you have a good idea of how you're going to sell the product and what you're going to say about it, you have the first phase of a working specification.

There's an apocryphal story about a producer for a major motion picture studio. He insisted that new story ideas be written on the back of the proposer's business card. If you can't summarize your idea in an exciting way on the back of a business card, you are unlikely to be successful in marketing.

The difference between marketing and sales is that marketing is the process of listening to potential customers and designing the product and delivery systems to match their real needs. Sales is the process of taking an existing product and convincing people they need it. In my opinion, marketing is a much more satisfying process, makes sales much easier, and is the first step in systems specifications for a commercial product.

Try to think in terms of *push* and *pull*. When potential customers browsing through a catalog encounter your program description, you have to "push" them to be interested and order it. When people are trying to solve a problem, are led to believe that your product might help, and go looking for it in a catalog, you have "pulled" them. Up until now, this book has discussed only "push." To use marketing channels effectively, you will need a combination of both push and pull. This chapter is oriented primarily to helping you create pull for your product.

A good primer on public relations for software companies is:

> **How to Publicize High Tech Products and Services**
> by **Dan Janal**
> Janal Communications
> Suite 7-301, 1063 Morse Avenue
> Sunnyvale, CA 94089
> (408) 734-2092

WORKING WITH THE PRESS

You and the press can have a mutually beneficial relationship. Unfortunately, the burden is on you to maintain this relationship. What do members of the press want? What we all want. They want their job to be easier, and they don't want their time wasted. Most people who write for a living are very pressed for time and have rapidly shifting priorities. They don't have the time or the inclination to look for deeper meaning in 99 percent of the material presented to them. Additionally, you will probably be telling them about things outside of their areas of expertise (if they know computers, they don't know your vertical market, and vice versa), and they are likely to find what you are saying both difficult and boring.

What do you want? You want two things. First, you want an occasional mention of your product in their publications. More important, you want them to think of you and your product when some outside force (probably an editor or breaking news) makes your area of expertise or product interesting.

A press release is the orthodox way of accomplishing the first objective. In a moment we'll dive into the mechanics of writing and distributing press releases.

The second, more important objective should be your long-term goal. The way to get the press to associate you with an area of expertise and/or product is by maintaining a low-key, cordial relationship and by keeping it simple. Really simple. One word. The word may be different from one writer/editor to another, but for the two of you, that word is your mantra. Use it consistently and frequently. Gary Elfring is probably one of the best at this. When I hear "font," I think "Elfring"; it's automatic. Every time the press does a story on viruses, McAfee is quoted. That's no accident.

A press release is the normal way of communicating with most of your press contacts. The advantage of a press release is that it can be sorted, filed, retrieved, and used directly by a publication. On its own, however, a press release won't build the relationship you want. You want writers to think of you and pick up the phone when they need information. A regular series of press releases will help.

Build a List of Publications

The first step is to *build a list of publications that correspond to your product's market*. While you certainly want to include the computer press, unless you are marketing a horizontal application or a product appealing only to sophisticated users, you want to concentrate on the trade magazines covering your vertical market. For this reason, "computer editor" mailing lists are limited in their usefulness. Unless you develop compilers, most people who can use your product don't read *PC Magazine*. The publications you want are oriented toward your customer base, whether they are butchers, bakers, or racing car makers. See pages 3 and 4 for a short list of directories that will help you find these publications.

Using this list, subscribe to the publications for which you qualify or can afford. If you can convince the marketing department that you are a potential advertiser, you may get a free subscription. Also obtain a copy of the editorial calendar from the ad department; usually the focus of each issue is planned as much as a year in advance. If you fit into a particular issue, get on the phone and find out which editorial staff person will be responsible for coordinating it. The lead time for many of these articles is at least three months. Contacting someone nine months before the scheduled publication is not unreasonable.

There is an additional way of finding magazines that may be interested in news of your product. The *Reader's Guide* lists every article published in almost every major magazine, arranged by subject. If you publish a program that helps people plan for their retirement, you might look up this subject in the *Reader's Guide* and discover which magazines have printed articles recently on this subject. Almost every library has a copy of:

> **Reader's Guide to Periodical Literature**
> **H.W. Wilson Co.**
> 950 University Avenue
> Bronx, NY 10452

Build a List of People

The second step is to *build a list of people*. Many people who write for magazines are freelancers. They generally have an area of expertise and have to sell their story ideas to editors before getting a commitment. You can cultivate these people and obtain an occasional mention by keeping them informed of what is going on in the industry and alerting them to new trends and ideas useful to them in earning their living. Most magazines will supply direct addresses for their freelance contributors if you ask for them. Usually, you can tell who the freelance people are because they will not be on the masthead at all or they will have a "contributing" title.

When *The ShareWare Book* was published, there were three magazines devoted to shareware. As this volume is going through final revision, there are none. The people who wrote for those publications are still around and are still writing about their specialty; they're just not doing it in a "shareware" magazine. Some who were full-time employees are now freelancers. Some of the freelancers have found permanent positions. My point here is simply to note that publications change, the holders of positions change, but the people in the community pretty much stay the same. Concentrate on and follow the people. If you remember them when they're "out," the good ones will remember you when they're "in."

It might be useful to mention a fact of life here. Many, if not most, writers have a hidden agenda related to other work he or she does. Unless a writer is very prolific, writing for small magazines doesn't pay very well. One very effective way to gain recognition for a company and product is to write articles. Consultants do it all the time; employees of equipment companies are encouraged to do it. I was surprised to discover that a writer I was trying to cultivate wrote a shareware program that competes directly with mine. (He writes under his own name; the software is published under his company's name.) This hidden agenda seldom is divulged to the public. The chances of your getting a favorable mention from a competitor or someone closely allied with a competitor are low. Try to find out as much as you can about the writers you want to cultivate; they will have innocent and not-so-innocent biases.

You also might want to consider becoming a columnist yourself, of course. I helped support my consulting practice by writing articles on computers in manufacturing. Writing these articles required little additional research since it was an outgrowth of my ongoing work. The extra dollars came in handy, and I found that having a publications list gave me a great deal of credibility with prospective new clients. It is not uncommon for readers to call to discuss issues I deal with in my articles. Some of these people become clients as well. What better way to give your product a (discreet) occasional plug than to write a column showing your target market how your product solves their problems?

One way to stay in contact with writers is to attend trade shows. Before you leave home, call the writers you want to cultivate. If they'll be attending, arrange to meet them for a drink. If they're not attending, you may be in a position to do them a favor by picking up literature or passing on your impressions of the show.

Any time you're taking a business trip, do a quick search: If writers are near your destination (usually a similar ZIP code), invite them to lunch. It'll make your trips more interesting and may encourage them to call you the next time "your" subject area comes up.

Plan Your Campaign

The third step is to *plan your campaign*. Try to manage things so you have something newsworthy for your press contacts to tell their readers every two months or so. At first glance, this might seem like a lot, but it's only four to six releases a year. When you consider the possibilities, it isn't hard to come up with that number of bits of news. For example, some of the things you might choose to announce include:

- A major new release. You'll probably want to do this slightly more often than once a year anyway.

- A new distributor. If Budgetware in Australia has agreed to act as your agent, announce it to the world. A small software company selling a breeding program halfway across the globe is interesting news to *Pet Grooming Monthly*.

- Your offer of a free, fully functional evaluation copy to anyone who writes on a business letterhead by a certain date. We know you do this all the time with shareware, but to the trade press in your niche market, this is a revolutionary idea. The time limit and letterhead requirement make the offer seem more exclusive and prod potential customers to take action right away.

- Your offer of a free pamphlet as a public service. Don't make it a blatant ad—it isn't necessary. Just provide good, solid information relevant to your potential customers. Of course, it makes sense that people who requested the pamphlet are potential customers for your product, so you'll also want to add them to your in-house list.

- The signing of a site license. This will, of course, be of no interest to *Byte Magazine*, but the people in your target industry are interested in what each other is doing. This is newsworthy for their trade press.

- The annual meeting of your user group.

- A synopsis of a talk you gave at an industry trade show or computer user group.

- A contest you're running that involves your product. If you publish a design program, the best product wins. Even if it's a bookkeeping package, the most original chart of accounts could be worth a prize.

Jim Samuel, a professional publicist, wrote:

For example, I may send out a release announcing a client's new software. Two months later, I may send out a release about the same product, this time featuring one of the things that can be done with the product. Something like "Managers can now track their employees' sick days with Sick Days from Catchfraud Software." The release would then go on to explain how the product works for that application, as well as list other features. This type of release can also be sent to vertical publications as well as the computer books.

Next, start clipping. Go through a couple of issues of every magazine you will be mailing to, and clip the short articles releasing product information—stories like those you envision for your own product line. Try to determine why these releases got printed, what reading and technical level they were written at, and how long they are.

Finally, develop a press release, planning it as part of an ongoing series. Figure 7.1 shows an example of a press release.

As a writer/reviewer I get many "professional" press releases from large organizations. There are very few hard and fast rules about format, so don't feel that you have to copy any format exactly; do what works.

Ordinarily, release date and contact information will appear first, typically left-justified.

Dates are an ongoing item for discussion. Some people advocate not dating the release at all, on the theory that late publicity is better than no publicity at all. The flip side of that policy is the risk of embarrassing the publication because it publishes a "release 3" announcement when release 5 is actually shipping. Rather than making your release "immediate," you might want to consider using a date about a month in advance. This allows time for the distribution process and makes the news "fresher" for the monthly periodicals. I prefer putting the date in the body of the text for newspaper press releases and in the release date only for magazine press releases. Remember that you are trying to make the writer/ editors' job as easy as possible. If your target publications don't normally include a dateline, don't make them cross it out.

Just under release date and contact information, center your headline. The headline is about the only thing guaranteed to be read, so make it a good one. "DataMumble announces better User-Friendly TechnoNoise Groupware" is not a good headline.

FOR RELEASE 1 FEBRUARY 1992

CONTACT:
Tim Campbell
(514) 345-9578

ZERO-MAINTENANCE BULLETIN BOARD SOFTWARE UPGRADED
TO VERSION 4.00

Sapphire emphasizes ease of installation and operation

MONTREAL, QUEBEC–PINNACLE SOFTWARE has announced the release of Version 4.00 of their Sapphire builetin board system software. The new version enhances the system operator's customization capabilities while continuing to concentrate on Sapphire's main strengths, which are ease of installation and operation.

Particular attention has been paid to ensuring that the installation can be performed very quickly. A new demonstrator mode enables the sysop to try out the Sapphire system literally within seconds of copying the program files to the hard disk. This is in sharp contrast to many other BBS packages which require extensive configuration before the software can be used.

Sapphire's zero-maintenance design is aimed chiefly at small business users who need to transfer files but feel they do not have time to set up and run a BBS. Because of this orientation, Sapphire is well received by people who are setting up a personal BBS for the first time. Sapphire is popular with typesetting and translation companies.

"Over the years, Sapphire sysops have identified EASE OF INSTALLATION as the most common reason for choosing Sapphire over other BBS software," said Tim Campbell, a spokesman for PINNACLE SOFTWARE. "Small companies usually can't spare a person for a few days while he or she configures a BBS, so they tend to see Sapphire as their only real choice."

Sapphire can run on any IBM-PC compatible computer equipped with a smart modem. A hard disk is recommended but not required.

PINNACLE SOFTWARE is a computer consulting company with offices in Swanton, Vermont and Montreal, Quebec. PINNACLE SOFTWARE, Box 714 Airport Road, Swanton, Vermont 05488. (514) 345-9578.

A fully functional evaluation copy of the program may be obtained from PINNACLE SOFTWARE for $3, or may be downloaded from PINNACLE SOFTWARE's support BBS at 514-345-8654 (9600 bps v42). The license fee is $51 and includes a printed manual, plus voice support and privileged access to PINNACLE SOFTWARE's BBS. Source code is available.

###

Figure 7.1   A sample press release.

"New Products Editor Regains Sex Drive" is. Lead with the problem you solve in simple yet attention-getting words. If you have a secondary headline, center that next. I use a laser printer with soft fonts, so I differentiate my major and minor headlines with font-size changes. This writer chose to do it with all caps/mixed case.

The body of your press release should be in a comfortably large type size (I usually use CG Times 12 point). Leave enough space in the margins and between the lines for handwritten changes. Beg, borrow, or steal a laser printer for press releases; they won't be taken seriously otherwise. While doing all this, of course, you want to limit yourself to a single page.

The headline and first paragraph are your only opportunities to convince the reader to continue. If you don't pass the "So what?" test here, your press release will never appear in the magazine.

Who, what, when, where, why, and how are the "five w's" (and one h) taught to freshman journalism students. Make sure that you cover the necessary bases.

The key to a good press release is to write it so it can be inserted into the publication without any changes other than deletions. Like a newspaper article, press releases are written to be cut. The most important information is placed first, and the article can stand on its own as one, two, three, or many paragraphs. You also may choose (especially with magazines) to structure your press release so that everything but the first and last paragraph can be cut. The sample release used this strategy.

Publications are very uncomfortable with calling a product "wonderful," "advanced," "easy," or even "good" outside of a formal review. You, of course, want the reader to be left with exactly that impression. The way to accomplish this is with a quotation, preferably of a very happy customer who reads the publication to which you are sending the release. If you can't find a happy customer, use yourself, as was done in the example.

Finally, at the end of the release, you'll note that "###" was centered. Sometimes you'll see "-30-" instead. Both of these are journalist codes for EOT (end of transmission), to ensure that readers have the entire story. If it is necessary to go to a second page, the bottom of the first page should have either "(more)" or "(page 1 of 3)." If your release is more than one page, reprint the headline and "continued" at the top of all subsequent pages.

Your release will, of course, be too long when first written. One of the first steps in paring it down is to edit phrase by phrase, asking the "So what?" question. If you can't justify the phrase in terms of both reader interest and sales, leave it out. Using the previous example release, I would question the last sentence in the third paragraph. Unless the release was sent to typesetting or translation magazines, I don't see how it adds to the punch of the release.

Having a consistent "look" can be valuable. I use my business stationery for press releases. The letterhead is in a left-hand margin and doesn't interfere with the release, while making it a little different and thus creating an impression as it is used from one time to the next. When a writer needs a quote from "that guy with the time and expense program," it's easy to pick out my release from the pile without reading any words at all—that left-hand letterhead and logo jump out.

Writers/reviewers are very concerned about writing articles on products that disappear before the article is in readers' hands. This only has to happen once, and the writer will never work for that magazine again. By becoming familiar to your press contacts, you reassure them you're likely to be around the month after they mention your product.

I almost never mention the channels my software is sold through (especially including shareware) in press releases, for two reasons. The first is that I want readers concentrating on my product, not the marketing channels I use. The second is that some magazines won't mention nonretail software, since it is unlikely to ever pay for advertising. Some corporations have policies against using shareware. I offer large corporations "full-featured evaluation copies" instead, when they call.

The other reason is that I want readers concentrating on the product, not the marketing channel. In order to mention the word "shareware" in something other than a sophisticated PC-oriented magazine, you have to describe it. Like a good preacher, I try to limit myself to one topic per sermon.

If you can afford it, send both black-and-white and color prints of your product (the box, manual, disks, and so on) or, better yet, a shot of your program in action (people and screen together), plus one of the main screens illustrating how the program is used (data, not menus).

If you wish to communicate information to the editor that should not be included in the release (for instance, to offer a review copy), do it on a separate sheet of paper with an inside address. Be sure it looks like a letter, not a press release. Otherwise, you may find it printed with the release, to your (and the editor's) embarrassment.

Keep sight of the reason you are putting out a press release. If you want people to pick up the phone, you will write a press release very different from one aimed at having them recognize your product name while looking through a catalog.

Mail your press releases via first-class mail, addressed to the correct person's name. Bulk mail generally doesn't get opened. I suggest you avoid using a postage meter because some people assume that metered mail is bulk mail. Don't use address labels. Envelopes addressed to "New Products Editor" will get opened by a secretary some time after all mail addressed to that person has been delivered.

One additional way to save money and get noticed is to use discount postage. Reviewers sometimes notice the strange stamps and tend to remember you. (Details on discount postage can be found in Chapter 14.)

PR Newswire is a service that will take your press release, do some minor editing, and send it by wire to any of its prepackaged lists of magazine, newspaper, and radio/television journalists, including the Associated Press, Dow Jones, and trade publications. For more information:

PR Newswire
150 East 58th Street
New York, NY 10155-0097
(212) 832-9400
(800) 334-6692

If you don't want to promote your own software products, these people have experience in the field:

David L. Shank
Shank Public Relations Counselors
2611 Waterfront Parkway
East Drive, Suite 310
Indianapolis, IN 46214
(317) 293-5590

Richard Sater
1704 Spear Street Suite #2
Logansport, IN 46947

REVIEWERS

Sure, you want reviews, but don't expect just a review to bring in a lot of requests for copies of your software. Reviews are used most effectively after the fact. Sending a diskette wrapped in a copy of a glowing review is an effective way of getting a distributor to consider carrying your product in its catalog or rack. Short quotes from reviews also can be effective in your direct mail pieces and other advertising. Unless you are getting a full column in a major magazine, a review actually is unlikely to do much for you initially. It's what you can do with a review that makes it valuable. Remember also that copyright laws restrict your right to use reviews. Most publishers will give permission to copy their reviews for specific purposes, but be sure to ask.

Many reviewers are freelance writers specializing in specific types of software. As with press releases, call the magazines to identify those who specialize in similar products, and find out the names of the people who are likely to do the reviews. Address all mail to these people by name and begin cultivating them. Call occasionally to confirm that this information is still correct.

Don't send a review copy until you've already sent a number of press releases to the same person. If your name doesn't sound somehow familiar, the package is not likely to be opened. Your goal is to get people to request a review copy from you, so that you can write "Per your request Tuesday at 10" on the envelope. Don't get your hopes up, however. One particular reviewer has requested three copies of one of my products. To the best of my knowledge, he has never written a word about it.

When you do send review copies:

- *Get your main message on the outside of the envelope*—something like "Consumer Debt Reduction review package inside." The envelope is likely to be thrown on a pile unopened; but when the writer is covering the topic of consumer debt, he or she may fish it out and look at it. I use my laser printer to make up large stickers and paste them to both sides of the envelope.

- *Be as professional as you can be,* but don't try to look like something you're not. If you manage to look like a big, established company, reviewers will send their readers to Egghead to purchase the product.

- *Give the readers an easy way to get the package.* "Call 800 BUY-DISK and, using your Visa card, you can have this package for $29.95."

- *Don't overlook radio.* This may be one of your best ways to stimulate the curiosity of your target audience.

- *Don't forget the lead time.* Remember that it will take at least five months from the time you mail out the review copies until the first review is in the reader's hands.

- *Use stickers to highlight important facts.* Put together a sticker and label it "Reviewer's Information" that contains all the information that you'd like a review to include: product price, how to order, and so on. Put the sticker on the back cover, the diskettes, and anywhere else that seems appropriate. Until I did this, many reviewers got essential facts wrong; since I've used the stickers, they usually get things right.

GETTING A LISTING IN PRODUCT DIRECTORIES

Eighty-five percent of the calls I get from computer consultants or corporate MIS departments come through *Data Sources* or its companion CD. On the other hand, you never know where buyers or reviewers will look to get a snapshot of the market. Since getting a listing in these publications is free, it makes sense to contact all of them and fill out their forms:

Data Sources
Ziff-Davis Publishing Company
20 Brace Road
Cherry Hill, NJ 08034
(609) 354-5000

Business Software Directory
Information Sources, Inc.
Box 7848
Berkeley, CA 94707
(415) 525-6220

Buyer's Guide to Microcomputer Software
Online, Inc.
11 Tannery Lane
Weston, CT 06883
(203) 227-8486

DataPro Directory of Microcomputer Software
DataPro Research
600 Delran Parkway
Delran, NJ 08075
(609) 764-0100

ICP Software Directory
International Computer Programs, Inc.
9100 Keystone Crossing
Indianapolis, IN 46240
(317) 844-7461

Micro/Personal/Small Business/Home Computing
Directory Resources
P.O. Box 1067
Cambridge, MA 02238
(617) 825-8895

Microsearch
Information, Inc.
7700 Old Georgetown Road
Bethesda, MD 20814
(301) 215-4688

Software Encyclopedia
R.R. Bowker
Dept. D-62, 121 Chanlon Road
New Providence, NJ 07974
(908) 665-2849

Business Software Database & Directory
Information Sources, Inc.
1173 Colusa Avenue, Box 7848
Berkeley, CA 94707
(415) 525-6220

Microleads
Chromatic Communications Enterprises
P.O. Box 30127
Walnut Creek, CA 94598
(415) 945-1602

TSP Software Directory
Technical Processing Services, Montague Publishing
P.O. Box 3159
Gardena, CA 90247-1359
(213) 770-6929

Office Automation Buyer's Guide
Thomas Publishing
One Penn Plaza
New York, NY 10019
(212) 695-0500

For getting calls from potential buyers, however, this next directory may be the most important for you. Very few end users know about computer directories. Lawyers look in law directories; architects look in architectural directories. This directory will help you find the directories you really need to be in:

Directories in Print
Gale Research
835 Penobscot Building
Detroit, MI 48226

In my experience, directories where you pay to be listed result only in calls from advertising salespeople. The American Bar Association's software directory comes to mind immediately in this context.

TRADE SHOWS

Trade shows are:

- A great way to meet people in the industry, including writers, potential customers, and people with whom you might start cooperative ventures.
- Sometimes a great way to begin opening up a second marketing channel.
- A good way to gather a lot of information about your market quickly.
- Expensive, tiring, and frustrating if you don't prepare for them.

As with other communications vehicles, differentiate between trade shows that reach your target market and trade shows that reach you. While it might be fun to spend a week in Las Vegas at COMDEX, the chances that a lot of soon-to-be brides (if your product is a wedding planner) are touring the show are low.

After deciding to attend, *decide whether to exhibit*. Examine your reasons for going to the show—it's entirely possible that you can achieve all or most of them without exhibiting at all. If your product is in the catalog of a company that will be exhibiting, it may make more sense to share its booth. As long as you work with them, most companies will be glad to have an extra hand and will be pleased to have one of "their authors" on board.

Many trade shows also have concurrent educational seminars occurring on a regular schedule. For many software products, a seminar is a much better way to sell than a booth exhibit. You have a chance to deliver a planned presentation that explores the user's problem and how your product contributes to the solution. Usually it is not necessary to be an exhibitor in order to *deliver a seminar.* In those cases where you must pay for a booth in order to deliver a seminar, it is possible that a wholesaler or catalog house that carries your product will be exhibiting anyway and will not want the seminar slot.

If your goal is to give away shareware copies of your work, almost any exhibitor will be glad to give away free disks— especially if your product complements theirs. You even may be able to talk a computer hardware dealer into splitting the cost of duplicating the disks if the dealer's name and address appear on the label. Shareware vendors generally are happy to give disks away for you or sell them for $.25—it brings people into the booth who will then become prospects for their other offerings. This is also a good way to build the mailing list; presumably, the dealers will be building their own lists and may be willing to share it with you. They may even be willing to include your flyer in the follow-up materials they send out to their booth visitors.

The only reason I can think of for actually paying for your own booth at a trade show is if you are going to try to sell your product at the show itself and can't find someone else to do it for you.

One way to *exhibit without exhibiting* is to have a banner or table cover made up for your product. If you can get one of your distributors to display it as a part of their booth, you'll have presence without the expense. You also can split the cost of printing bags with distributors—one side for your product, the other for them. Both of these ideas can give you visibility at trade shows you don't even attend.

Banners and table covers are available from:

Britten Banners
22510 Sterling Boulevard
Sterling, VA 22170
(703) 471-8009
(800) 426-9496

Carrot-Top Industries
437 Dimmocks Mill Road
P.O. Box 820
Hillsborough, NC 27278
(800) 628-3524

You can get custom-printed tote bags to hand out at shows for as little as $120 for 500 (plus setup charges) from:

Art Poly Bag Co.
140 Metropolitan Avenue
Brooklyn, NY 11211
(718) 388-0866

If you've never worked a show before, or if your goal in attending a show is to learn about the computer industry, you might consider joining the Association of Shareware Professionals (ASP) (a membership application is included in the Software Publisher's Kit) and attending COMDEX, PC-EXPO New York, or PC-EXPO Chicago as a booth volunteer. The ASP has booths at these shows every year and hosts parties for the working computer press. It's a great way to learn how to use trade shows effectively.

Some key points to making the most of trade shows:

- *Have a single specific goal in mind.* Are you there to sell your product for its retail price? Hand out freebies? Get name recognition for your product? Gather information? Your goal will dramatically affect how you prepare and what you do there.

- *Be sure the show audience corresponds to your goal.* If your goal is name recognition, a small local show that doesn't attract press won't help you. Trying to retail a product at COMDEX is a waste of time and money.

- *Dress comfortably,* especially your shoes—you will be on your feet almost the whole time. Plan for lots of rest. If you need to shmooze, bring a person who will work the booth while you rest and visit.

- Keep it simple. *Carry everything you need.* The power you expected will be at the other end of the hall. The chair will arrive on the last afternoon of the show.

- *Create a flyer* specifically for the show, headlining a single reason why reporters should stop by and see a demonstration. Tape the flyer up in the press room.

- Most shows have a paper handed out to all attendees. *Call the editor* months before the show and explain personally why your product is interesting to those attending. The chances are very good that your product will end up with a couple more column inches than the others.

- *Have duplicates* in the hotel. Anything you carry onto the floor will get stolen eventually.

- *Make appointments* with writers before the show. Get their hotel phone numbers and confirm the appointments.

- If you are selling a product, arrange to *take credit cards.* If your aim is to get names for a mailing list, *have two imprinters* and ask for business cards besides.

- *Have a large, simple sign.* Use your product name and your one-sentence slogan.

- *Bring lots of press kits.* Leave a few at a time in the press room.

- *Be aggressive in meeting people's eyes.* Have a standard question that brings them in. If you're an introvert like me, bring an extrovert along to do this. Your job, then, will be to hang around in the background to field the technical questions.

- Go to every party you can get into. *Wear a button* with your product name and slogan on it. Meet as many people as you can.

- *Keep your goal in mind.* Don't spend time doing anything that does not contribute to the goal.

- *Follow up all leads,* by mail and telephone, *immediately* upon your return.

Complete portable display systems are available from:

Professional Displays, Inc.
746 Arrowgrand Circle
Covina, CA 91722
(416) 291-2932
(800) 222-6838

Skyline Displays
1301 Cliff Road East
Burnsvilie, MN 55337
(800) 328-2725

ShowTopper Exhibits
P.O. Box 10247
Raleigh, NC 27605
(919) 544-6504

TOURING

If you have the time and money, it is possible to speak to two or three user groups a week, at an average attendance of about 100 people. If you have stage presence and your product appeals to a large proportion of the kind of people who attend the meetings and demos well, this may be an effective way to get the word out.

ADVERTISING

Advertising is used primarily to heighten the awareness of people who will be in contact with the product in the near future. It is most effective in influencing consumers to choose between products rather than in getting consumers to buy in the first place. Generally advertising is ineffective in getting consumers to go into a store they wouldn't have been going into anyway or even in getting them to pick up the telephone.

The classic advertising model is a situation where a mother sees an ad for baby food in a magazine she respects, hears the name of the product again as she watches television, and then, when shopping for baby food, chooses that brand as opposed to the other brands on the shelf.

Advertising works for software sold through retail outlets by inducing customers to choose or consider one product as opposed to others also on the shelf. Because consumers have "heard" about the product, they are more comfortable choosing it.

Unless you are selling to a truly horizontal market and have your product sitting on retailers' shelves, advertising in general computer magazines will waste much of your money. Advertise instead in magazines targeted to your application's market, especially in those magazines that also carry articles about using computers.

The second way in which advertising can work is by announcing the only source of a solution to a particular problem. People buy those figurines from the Franklin Mint through advertising because they really want them and can't get them easily anywhere else. If that kind of item were available in local stores, the advertising strategy would have to be completely different.

The next time you're looking at a magazine that carries ads for mail order products, notice some of the characteristics of the ads and the products. Usually the products claim to be higher quality than generally available in stores and have a price to match. Consumers are likely to buy from the same source repeatedly—either the same consumable item or similar items. The premium price is largely a function of the high costs and low yield of magazine advertising. Most companies plan on losing money on the first sale, hoping to make up the loss with future direct mail sales. Advertising can be used in this way to feed direct mail sales. However, for the small operator, renting a list is usually cheaper. Unless you have potential for repeat sales, magazine advertising is probably not for you.

Before you commit to advertising, do some arithmetic. The numbers just don't work for most software products.

If you still think that advertising makes sense for your product, there are two keys to using advertising successfully: your purpose and repetition.

Your purpose is what you are trying to accomplish with the ad. Do you want people to mail in money? Pick up the phone? Recognize your name in the future? Ask for more information? Your purpose will directly affect the layout, copy, and placement of the ad. If you want people to take action, you must give them a reason to do it now, and you must make it easy for them. Almost no one will put a magazine aside, find it later, then write a letter, address an envelope, and write a check. If you do want people to take action, have a "special offer" that expires on a specific date (about a month after the magazine is expected to be in people's hands) with a toll-free number for ordering via credit card.

Repetition is the second key in advertising. Orders don't start to come in (if they ever do) until after the third or fourth ad in a magazine. If you can't commit to at least four ads in a publication, don't start. Tombstone ads (small ads in the body of the magazine) don't get noticed. Ads in classified sections at the back of a magazine can be productive if they are coupled with an 800 telephone number or a "bingo card" where the prospect circles a number.

For some vertical market applications, advertising in specialty magazines using tear-out business reply postcards has produced significant leads, especially if the cards are coupled with an ad that has run for a number of months and the ad with the reply card is run at the time of year buyers are most likely to need the product.

One money-saving way to reach your potential customers is to form a cooperative with other publishers who wish to advertise to the same target market: Sell or give away a "sampler" featuring a number of programs, thus cutting the per-package and per-ad cost. A real estate broker's software sampler, for instance, might result in enough interest to justify itself.

While many salespeople will deny that their magazine will do it, most magazines occasionally will accept "PI" (per inquiry) advertising. Much as cruise ships often sell cruises at deep discounts at the last minute if they can't get full-fare passengers, PI advertising allows a magazine to get some revenue from space that would otherwise have to be donated to public interest advertising.

In essence, PI advertising works this way: You have to supply camera-ready ads in a number of sizes and shapes to the magazine since no one knows in advance what space will be left unsold. The ad must sell a product at a specific price and be keyed so you will know that the sale came by way of that particular magazine's PI ad. Whichever party processes the order remits 50 percent of the revenue to the other, together with a list of the buyers (to keep the deal honest). Assuming that you're willing to sell your product at a 50 percent discount for some free publicity, PI ads can be a good deal for you and the magazine.

The main disadvantages to you are not knowing when and if your ad will run and the necessity for having extra camera-ready mechanicals for the ad made up.

PI deals are made by the advertising manager or magazine publisher, not by a space salesperson. The best way to get a PI deal is by writing a letter to the advertising manager of the periodicals you think are likely prospects, including a copy of your proposed ad. Any success you have had with a PI deal with any other periodical will make the magazine staff much more likely to take you seriously. Your letter might read like the one on pages 191 and 192.

<<date>>

<<inside address>>

Software Entrepreneur advertised our book on a P.I. basis and pulled in over 300 orders for a gross of $7,185.00, netting the newsletter $3,592.50. This is more money than if they had sold the ad space at one-time full rate!

This success occurred with "A Software Entrepreneur's Cookbook"; a copy of the ad is enclosed. The book outlines all of the steps necessary for a software entrepreneur to take an idea from the initial concept through to marketing through multiple channels. As you can see, a significant portion of your readers share that dream. At $24.95, it is priced to have a very attractive cost/benefit ratio to your readers, while at the same time having a high enough price that retaining 50 percent of the gross proceeds will be very attractive to you.

I'd like to offer you a camera-ready ad for P.I. insertion in *<<pub name>>*. Please choose any one of these three alternatives:

- We can place your name (or the name of a fulfillment house of your choosing) on the ad. You take the orders and remit 50% of the gross proceeds with a list of the buyers. We will ship to that list.
- Run the ad with our name; we will add a key to the address so that we know that your publication was the source. We will remit 50% of the gross proceeds with a list of the buyers, so you can test and be assured that we are keeping our end of the bargain.
- Run your own ad (or editorial piece) and choose from one of the two fulfillment methods described above.

No matter which alternative you choose, we will pay you $12.50 for each order—and handle the entire fulfillment operation (packing, shipping, postage, returns, and refunds).

As each issue approaches the publication date, seldom do editorial and advertising space happen to exactly fill your magazine. This is an opportunity for you to take space that you would otherwise fill with material not directly associated with your editorial mission and turn it into revenue—without any risk or additional expenses.

Please call if you have any questions. I hope that we'll be working together in the near future.

Sincerely,

Robert Schenot

P.S. I'd also be happy to send a review copy of "A Software Entrepreneur's Cookbook."

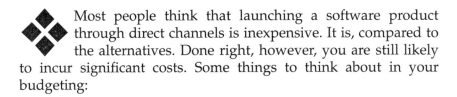

CHAPTER 8

Making Money

COST

Most people think that launching a software product through direct channels is inexpensive. It is, compared to the alternatives. Done right, however, you are still likely to incur significant costs. Some things to think about in your budgeting:

- *Beta testing* can be expensive. On top of telephone costs, there will be times you'll have to go to the customer site and watch what is actually happening.
- *Shareware distribution* will probably run about $1 per distributor. While I advocate a reasonably slow rollout, you will probably need a minimum of $500 for distribution the first year.
- *Online services*—I spend over $100 per month on CompuServe, and I dial up during the least expensive hours of the day. When you add in telephone costs and BBS long-distance charges, it's easy to spend $200 to $400 per month on digital communication.
- *Publicity* is very expensive. This can include renting lists, printing and postage, and long-distance charges. In-person visits are very effective but, again, expensive.
- *Art and documentation* are mostly up-front costs. A letterhead and a manual that are professionally done go a very long way in making the right impression.
- *Material costs* are primarily diskettes and envelopes.
- *Travel and trade shows* are indispensable for gathering information and contacts. Just attending one runs about $300.

- *Equipment*—there's always something you don't own that you'll need.
- *Lawyers, accountants,* licenses, trademarks, copyrights all cost money.

THE CUSTOMER AS AN ANNUITY

Your real profits come from an ongoing relationship with your customers. In this section, I hope to give you some ideas of how to accomplish this. There are three major ways to turn new releases for your customers into a reasonably steady cash flow:

Low-priced products lend themselves either to sequels or to outright purchase of new versions. Quicken generally doesn't try to sell "upgrades" to its users; it makes sure users know about major new features and generally encourages them to go to their retailer and purchase the new version.

Mid-priced products lend themselves to new version announcements. You probably get these announcements now for your compilers and major applications. Customers are notified of major releases and will be offered an opportunity to purchase them at a significant discount, usually somewhere between 20 percent and 40 percent of the initial purchase price.

High-priced products lend themselves to a software maintenance agreement. Typically set at 1.5 percent of the retail cost of the software per month, this type of agreement offers both all major new versions and pretty much unlimited support. An alternative to this is simply to lease the software with no up-front payment. A joint venture I was involved in was pretty successful doing this with a not-for-profit application where a high up-front price would have killed the sale, but an ongoing monthly cost could find its way into the budget.

Additional sources of revenue include:

- Renting out your list of customers once you have at least 5,000. Depending on the nature of your users, you may be able to rent out the list as frequently as every three weeks for between $40 and $80 per thousand. Using optimistic numbers, that could be as much as $7,000 per year for a fairly small product.

- Including complementary products in your mailings and obtaining a commission on each sale made.
- Selling support separately from the price of the product.
- Selling add-on products. A hint book for an adventure game is an obvious add-on. Less obvious is how Intuit made much of its early money by selling checks to Quicken users.
- Selling a subscription to a newsletter that specializes in your product. Microsoft does this with most of its major products.
- The ever-present upsell.
- Hook-in products. If you sell a financial package, work with a mutual fund.

Software publishers often keep in touch with their customers using a *newsletter*. By releasing a single newsletter for your entire product family, you save on printing and postage costs while also encouraging your customers to upgrade. As they see announcements of new releases of the standard product, features now available in the professional-level product, and/or interfaces to other modules, you may generate sales. Newsletters are often also passed on to friends and associates, resulting in subsequent sales.

If you want your newsletter to be read, be sure to include short humorous pieces and clip art. You may choose to write most of the text yourself and farm out the actual desktop publishing task. Besides the fact that desktop publishing requires a substantial investment in software, if not hardware, you'd be an unusual software entrepreneur if you also had the skills necessary to turn out a good-looking newsletter.

If you supply the edited text on a disk and want copy ready for the printer, it will probably cost you about $100 per issue to have desktop publishing done. This assumes that you commit to multiple issues with the same layout and don't try to change things after the job is done. Pick a format and keep it—your readers will recognize it and read it. Every time you change your format, you run the risk of being mistaken for junk mail.

Software Support

Strange as it may sound, some companies will pay you to do your support. They do this by charging the user, either by way of a 900 number or by charging the support time to a credit card. The idea is controversial, but most publishers who have used the system are reporting both good results and few complaints from users. In order to comply with the ASP's requirement for free support for ninety days and to deal with those people who object to paying for support, many publishers continue to offer free support by mail and Email. Others offer free telephone support only during specific early-morning or evening hours.

These companies will pay you about 20 percent of the gross revenues collected in supporting your product. They charge the customer about $2 per minute.

One problem with these support methods is that corporate switchboards frequently block 900 numbers, and few people at the operational level have access to the corporate credit card. While support agreements are available, that doesn't help the person who needs assistance right away.

My major concern with this type of support is that I get most of my market information from support calls. This service may be best suited to widely used, mature products.

One company that offers this kind of deal is:

Advanced Support Group
11900 Grant Place
Des Peres, MO 63131
(314) 256-3130

Forms

If your software prints its output to standard forms, many forms suppliers will pay you for recommending their forms. You simply put a notice in your documentation that a certain supplier will provide a discount if customers call to order forms and mentions a certain order code unique to you. Besides customers getting a break on orders, the forms company also pays you a commission based on the value of the orders you send its way. Major forms suppliers that may work with you in the United States include:

Moore Business Forms
P.O. Box 5000
Vernon Hills, IL 60061
(800) 323-6230

NEBS Computer Forms Division
500 Main Street
Groton, MA 01471
(800) 225-9550

GETTING PAID

This section is devoted to the surprisingly difficult mechanics of getting paid and to some techniques that can add to your revenues in other ways. The easier you make it for customers to pay you, the more customers you will have.

Pricing

If anything is black magic, pricing a software product is. Some basic rules for pricing include the following:

- Your price must be the price the customer expects to pay. Too low is just as deadly as too high. If you are selling to two different audiences, it may even make sense to sell the product under different names and prices for each of those audiences.
- In shareware, your price should be lower than the value of your registration incentives.
- The price must be a reasonably small fraction of the cost of continuing on without the use of the product.
- The price must be the same or lower than other reasonable alternatives. This includes the use of manual methods or simply not solving the problem at all.
- If the program is not valuable to the person considering it, it doesn't matter how low the price is.
- Price competition may play a part—but it is usually a small part. Usually you either don't have competition (that is, the customer doesn't know about it) or your competition isn't convenient enough. Since most people have a very limited

number of software sources, very few people know that they
have a choice.

- The size of your target market will probably affect your price.
  With a smaller target market, you will need a higher price to
  justify the front-end work of developing and marketing the
  product.

- A minimum for personal programs is probably $20, because of
  your cost of doing business. Under $40, businesses won't take
  you seriously; it costs them more than that to cut the check. On
  the other hand, there are very few successful shareware programs selling for much more than $50. Interestingly enough,
  according to *PC Data*, 77 percent of all PC products sold in 1993
  had a price of under $50, 25 percent sold for under $20, and just
  over 7 percent sold for more than $100. The magazine also
  reported that half of all business products sold for between $50
  and $100. Clearly, this is the general area in which to begin your
  price testing.

Some things that absolutely don't have to do with setting the
price (because they don't add value to customers) include:

- How much effort you put into the product. Whether it took you
  a day or a year to develop it, the program is the program. Its
  utility doesn't change.
- How badly you need the money.
- How technically sophisticated the program is.

Invoices

If your product will be sold to businesses, accepting purchase
orders and presenting invoices are very important. Accounting
departments demand invoices before they will pay a bill because
it's a part of the financial control system. By providing an invoice
to customers that they can then present to the accounting department, you are much more likely to be paid.

For business shareware products, you can have the software
itself print out the invoice.

I find it very useful to print a *questionnaire* as a second page.
About 80 percent of the people registering my products answer at
least one of the questions. I have found this to be one of the best

ways to obtain information from customers. Some of the questions that you might ask include:

- *Where* they actually obtained their copy. While your vendor identification in the sales code identifies to whom you sent the distribution package, this will tell you who is actually distributing it for you.
- If they felt that anything was *missing* (installation, features, or documentation), inaccurate, or misleading.
- If they have any *additional suggestions.* I always try to ask a very open-ended question so they can put in whatever they think might be helpful. You might even ask them what question you should have asked.

Payment Methods

Cash

For shareware and direct marketing, I really like paper money. It doesn't bounce, and it can't be canceled. I have much more faith in my local post office's honesty than I do in its competence. In general, I encourage my customers simply to mail cash or to obtain a "Certificate of Mailing" (USPS form 3817), which costs only $.50 and provides evidence that something was mailed to a specific address. Figuring that sending the money by certified mail costs about $2 and that the post office loses one first-class letter in 500, even on a $50 order the insurance of certification isn't worth it ($50/500 = $.10 average loss). Of course, I leave that decision up to my customers. For international payments, sending currency is second in convenience only to credit cards. Please see the international section (Chapter 12) for more discussion of these issues.

If your customer decides to send cash, there is always a possibility that the Postal Service will fail. I use the following method to deal with the problem; you may choose to use a similar policy.

- First, I ask the customer to write or call me to determine the direction of the failure. (And to please give the system a couple of weeks to work.) If my package failed to reach the customer, I will tell him or her when it was mailed.

- I ask the customer to obtain a USPS form 4314-C (U.S. Postal Service Consumer Service Card) from the local (U.S.) post office, or I will send one upon request.
- Depending on the circumstances, I will send another copy of the product at a nominal charge or no charge at all. To obtain a replacement registration package, the customer can fill out the USPS form and send it to me. I will make a copy of it and then mail it to the postmaster.
- If I received a registration payment and my package failed to reach the customer, I will send another package at no charge.
- If a customer sends a registration by return receipt or recorded delivery mail and includes a copy of the document with the Postal Service complaint form, I will send another package at no charge.
- If the customer obtained a "Certificate of Mailing" when mailing payment and included a copy of that document with the Postal Service complaint form and $5, I will send another package to the customer.
- If the customer simply mailed payment and has no documentation, I ask that he or she send the Postal Service complaint form and $10—I will send another package to the customer.

While there is always some possibility that someone would lie about sending money, by insisting on the USPS form you are accomplishing two things. First, you make it more likely that your local post office will put some emphasis on proper delivery of first-class mail. Second, anyone filling out a complaint form and stating the facts falsely is committing mail fraud, a federal felony. The Postal Investigative Service is very aggressive about investigating and prosecuting these cases.

Checks

For domestic customers, checks are easy. Very few people pay for software with rubber checks. Checks are a near impossibility for international customers, though. Unless a check is drawn on a member bank of the United States Federal Reserve and has the MICR encoding across the bottom, it will cost you anywhere from $20 to $35 to process the check. Clearly, except for site licenses, this is unacceptable.

Credit Cards

Depending on the situation, credit cards can be very convenient or totally unworkable. Given that the typical software purchase is an "impulse" purchase by an individual—at the moment, perhaps, when your humorous Times Square registration reminder travels across the display showing the 800 number to call ("I'm not Jerry Brown, but . . .")—being able to accept a credit card order by phone will help avoid many lost sales.

In order for you to accept a credit card for payment, you must have a "merchant" account, usually issued through a commercial bank. Bankers are not known for their imagination and flexibility. Most banks will not authorize merchant status to mail order businesses, businesses without a storefront, or any business processing less than $2,000 in charges per month. You probably lose on all three counts.

A couple of companies can help you serve your customers who wish to pay with plastic. The easiest and cheapest (for a new author) in the United States is probably *Public (software) Library*. PsL offers an order-taking service through both toll-free numbers and fax. It will accept many different types of payment. In order to be effective, you must have a CompuServe account, since that is how PsL transmits the information to you. It remits monthly. I use this service and have found it to be absolutely reliable and helpful. For more information, contact:

Nelson Ford
Public (software) Library
P.O. Box 35705
Houston, TX 77235-5705
(713) 524-6394
(800) 242-4775

Especially if you market to a professional or international market, you should participate in *CompuServe's SWREG*. This service allows CompuServe members to register shareware products and have the amount added to their CompuServe bill. This plan is especially convenient for corporate employees who don't have access to a company credit card and to international customers who would otherwise have trouble making the currency conversion. To sign up, simply GO SWREG. A coupon for a very large discount on a new CompuServe membership is included in the Software Publisher's Kit.

Teleflora CreditLine is a third-party credit card processor that offers merchant card accounts to software publishers. The fact that your business is run from your home and that many of your orders come over the phone is not a problem for them. It will process Visa and MC for a fee of about 3 percent. There is no minimum transaction requirement, but it does require a $100 application fee and that you purchase a $475 credit card terminal. (Why can't this be done with software?) In general, you must be at least eighteen years old, be based in the United States (you will be able to accept foreign cards), have a software product out on the market for at least six months, and have a clean personal credit record. It will want to review your product as a part of the application process.

For more information and an application:

Teleflora CreditLine
12233 West Olympic Boulevard
Los Angeles, CA 90064
(800) 325-4849

If you are an ASP author member, *Indiana National Bank* offers what is probably the lowest-cost merchant card processing. The sign-up fee is $35, the rate is generally under 4 percent, and there is a $10 monthly minimum fee (which means you need $200 a month in charges to rise above the minimum). You use your computer and modem with the bank's specialized communications software to call in your charge sales through its 800 number:

Marla Cole, Merchant Representative
INB National Bank
1 Indiana Square, Suite 1370
Indianapolis, IN 46266
(317) 266-6999

Money Orders

A great idea—money orders don't bounce and you process them like checks.

Purchase Orders

Corporations use purchase orders, bills of lading, invoices, and checks to protect and control their financial systems. For any application that is subject to site licenses and purchase orders, I highly recommend a branding technique. When I receive a purchase order, I charge a premium for the extra service and exposure, ship up to 100 manuals, and withhold the license file (the brand) until I receive the company check and it clears.

Accepting a verbal purchase order is sort of like accepting a verbal check, only worse. Why? First, you need the physical document with signature in order to submit an invoice. Additionally, the purchase order contains shipping and billing instructions as well as other contractual language—which you may or may not choose to accept. Finally, purchase orders are controlled in much the way checks are. If you have a purchase order from a company, you have the right to assume that the person signing it had the authority to issue it. Someone simply using the telephone does not imply authority.

CHAPTER 9

Legal Issues

This chapter is an overview of some of the issues involved in starting any new bootstrap business, with special emphasis on the issues that specifically affect software companies selling through the mail. It is not a substitute for buying a couple of starting-a-new-business books and getting competent legal and accounting help.

I run my business as a cash-basis fictitious-name sole proprietorship, with a business telephone listing and a post office box as my address. The next few sections go into the implications of these decisions. Having had a couple of experiences, I am convinced that you can buy any justice you want in the United States if you're willing to pay the price. The reality is that if a large corporation decides to hijack your code, use your product name, or use your product without a license, you cannot begin to afford to stop it, should it be willing to outspend you.

The main purpose of this section is to give you a head start on understanding the issues you'll need to discuss with your lawyer and to help you control the costs of obtaining that help. You'll go broke if you try to "do it right" right away. Try to find a lawyer who is willing to "do it okay for now" and then make it better as you can afford it.

When you meet with a lawyer, he or she will want to:

- Incorporate your business for $500.
- Do a trade name search and register your corporate trade name and logo, both federally and in surrounding states, for $1,500.

- Do a trademark search and register your product trademark and logo federally for $1,000.
- Write a distribution license for $1,000.
- Write a user license for $1,000.
- Do a review of your general legal situation for $1,500.

If you can find a lawyer willing to work with you, it is possible to get by with some basic advice until you can afford to do everything. The problems you are most concerned about in starting your business include:

- *Liability* for doing some damage to someone else.
- *Defense* against attack. This means both being well protected and being an uninviting target, so opposing lawyers working for contingency fees will be unwilling to take the case.
- *Protecting yourself from liability losses* by having someone else take the hit, whether it is a corporation you own or an insurance company to which you paid premiums.
- If you get tagged anyway, *making sure you have very little* that can be taken away from you.
- *Other people ripping you off.*

As I see it, there are two possible sources of trouble—something you (or your product) does and something that someone else does to you. Your software may do damage. If you publish software that could hurt a person or a business, spend the money early on competent legal help specializing in software issues. If doing damage with your product is not an issue, your main exposure will be if you trample on someone else's intellectual property—you use a name that is too close to theirs (trademark), develop a product using a protected technology (patent), or put your name on their work (copyright). The following sections give you some basics about the issues and how to research existing claims.

A free booklet ("A Legal Guide for the Software Developer") covering many of the topics of concern to you is available from:

Merchant and Gould
Wells Fargo Center, Suite 1650
333 South Grand Avenue
Los Angeles, CA 90071
(213) 485-0100

When you reach the point where your local counsel needs specialized help, you may choose to call Merchant and Gould or the lawyer who handles much of the work of the ASP and many of the larger shareware companies:

Lance Rose, Esq.
236 West 26th Street, Suite 7NW
New York, NY 10001
(212) 691-4560

WHAT TYPE OF BUSINESS ARE YOU STARTING?

What are you (legally)? Generally speaking, a business may be a sole proprietorship, a partnership, or a corporation.

Sole Proprietorship

A sole proprietorship is what you are if you are in business alone and have taken *no legal steps* to be anything else. The advantage of a sole proprietorship is that it is easy to form (it's the default setting) and is very simple to run. For federal tax purposes, you simply attach a schedule C to your federal tax return. (Local taxes are a separate issue.) The main disadvantage is that all of your personal assets are exposed if you are sued in your capacity as a business.

I do business as a sole proprietorship. I deal with the problem of asset exposure largely by not having any personal assets (everything is in my wife's name and has been for years) and by carefully selecting the problems I deal with. The chances of my doing major damage with this book or my time and expense system are pretty low. Of course, if you choose to put everything in your spouse's name, do keep him or her very happy.

Partnership

A partnership is the *worst thing* you can do from a liability standpoint. If you and someone else are running the business together and have done nothing legally, you are a partnership. In a partnership, all of your personal assets are exposed for your own as well as each and every one of your partner's mistakes. If your partner, en route to a business meeting, were to crash into a school bus—once her assets were exhausted, all of your business and personal assets would be fair game for the lawyers representing the aggrieved parents.

Do not enter into a partnership without legal advice and a formal partnership agreement.

Corporation

A corporation is a separate and distinct "person" in the eyes of the law. The main advantage of incorporating is that, done right, the corporate form will *protect your personal assets,* should your business be sued. Depending on your situation, incorporation may offer some tax advantages as well.

A corporation is major lawyer magic. The very first thing lawyers who want to sue you will do is to thoroughly check everything from the moment of incorporation. If there's a single mistake anywhere, they will try to "pierce the corporate veil" (sort of like annulling a marriage) by finding just one place where the lawyer magic wasn't perfect. If they succeed, your personal assets are totally exposed once again. Do not even think of do-it-yourself incorporation. If you choose to incorporate, have a good lawyer look for cracks every year and every time someone makes lawyer noises at you.

You may have heard of a "sub S" corporation. It is not a different kind of corporation; it is an option you pick at tax time with a normal corporation. It has tax implications only and carries some restrictions having to do mostly with size and ownership. You might want to get a copy of Publication 589, "Tax Information on S Corporations," from your local Internal Revenue Service office. In practical terms, this option is useful either if you are making big bucks personally and your company is losing money, or if your company is earning over $500,000 a year. If you are in either situation, you need professional accounting help anyway.

Usually, incorporation represents higher legal and accounting fees and may present you with a problem of double taxation. Depending on your situation, the limits to financial exposure and some tax breaks may make incorporation a good choice for you. Almost certainly, your accountant will advise against it and your lawyer will be for it. It's up to you to decide. If you do incorporate, be sure to observe all of the formalities and pay your lawyer to double-check your work.

If you start out as a sole proprietorship or partnership and then incorporate, you will still be exposed in your original form for all business you did prior to incorporation. To some extent, an "assignment" clause that assigns all rights and liabilities to a "successor" corporation will shield you from suits brought against you after you incorporate on licenses sold before you incorporated. This is more lawyer magic—it is not a do-it-yourself project.

NAMING YOUR BUSINESS

Who are you? As a sole proprietorship or partnership, you may do business under your own name or a "fictitious" name, sometimes called a d/b/a, or "doing business as." A corporation needs its own name.

Names are legal property, governed for the most part by trademark law. In some situations you can't use your own name in business because someone else owns it. That's why there is a no-name winery in New York State: The person who owns it is related to a family that started a major corporation with the family name.

It is generally easier to start business as a sole proprietorship under your own name. If you choose to incorporate or rename your company later, there is no reason you can't. If you choose to use a fictitious name, you will have to fill out some kind of form locally. In New Hampshire, it was with the secretary of state; in other locations, it may be in your city or town. You may have to publish a notice in a newspaper. If you choose to use a name other than your own, you are well advised to read the section on trademark and check with your lawyer.

I find it advantageous to use a somewhat ambiguous company name (Compass/New England) because I can be whatever I need to be in acquiring resources.

Another part of your identity is your *Dun's number:* Dun & Bradstreet Corporation provides credit reporting on businesses. As a part of this process, it assigns a unique number to each business. Many large corporations and government agencies use this number as their primary identifier for suppliers. A Dun's number does not cost money and may add to your credibility if you can supply it when asked. Look up your local Dun & Bradstreet office and ask for the appropriate forms (it's best to work through the local office) or call (800) 227-3830.

LOCATION

Where are you? You have to have an address to get paid. Your choice of address has legal, marketing, and efficiency considerations.

Zoning is your first concern if you are doing business out of your home. It is usually possible to drop by your local planning board to find out which "home occupations" are allowed. Very frequently, freelance writer and author are allowed. I suggest you call yourself that, rather than "shareware author" (what's that? when in doubt, don't allow it) or "software publisher" (probably going to bring in printing presses).

If you don't care to visit in person, a phone call is sometimes sufficient. Call yourself a self-employed writer, make it clear that you have and will have no employees, will not have any kind of sign out on the road, will not have people come to your house for business purposes, and that all transactions occur through the mail or the telephone—delivery vehicles and inventory will not be involved. If you can demonstrate that it is necessary to go through your living quarters to get to your work area, this will generally work for you.

Alternatively, you can do what I do. I maintain a post office box and keep a very low profile as a business. My street address is never published, so I get no business mail at home, and I rarely have a delivery truck stop at the house. Technically, I'm not in compliance with my local zoning laws (which require a hearing for anything) but none of my neighbors cares, since I don't create the traffic problems a business normally does. And we're still hoping to build that house on the lake. By using a post office box, I can continue picking up registrations until some time after the stale messages in my software kick in.

Learn from my mistake. If you open a post office box, use a small post office and don't rent a box with the numbers 1 or 7 in it. At the large post offices, P.O. Box mail is sorted by the people who got last choice of job assignment. These people tend to have difficulty telling a seven from a one, so I'm constantly swapping mail with boxes 111, 171, 711, 777 . . .

If you need the fiction of a street address and the benefits of a post office box, certain services will accept your mail and packages at their address using a "suite number." UHaul operates quite a few of them in my area. The main concern with this type of arrangement is that they won't guarantee you five years' notice before discontinuing the service or moving.

If you need the appearance of a street address, but will never, ever, ever actually need a real street address (as for UPS or Federal Express), use the street address of the post office itself (let's say the post office is located at 100 Main Street) in this form:

Your Company Name
100 Main Street
P.O. Box 6789
Anytown, U.S. 12345-6789

The post office rules require that mail be delivered to the address nearest the town/state/ZIP code line, so mail will always go to your box anyway. If somebody messes up, it's hoped that the postal carrier will figure it out when the mail gets delivered to him or her. The post office will not accept packages from "competitors," so don't use this technique if you'll ever need deliveries from other sources using your "published" address.

An alternative form that does work with UPS and FedEx is to list your street name but not the number. These services will refuse to accept a package without a street address on it, but once it gets to your town and it's lacking a house number, they will call you to find out where to deliver the package. Using this method, your address would look like this:

Your Company Name
Oak Street
P.O. Box 6789
Anytown, U.S. 12345-6789

If your state charges a sales tax on prepackaged software and you live near a state that does not, it may be to your advantage to "locate" your business in that neighboring state. Check with your lawyer for a conclusive local definition of "business presence." Collecting sales taxes is a major hassle.

You are probably going to move while your business is operating, so do plan a way to gain access to your mail or have it forwarded for a couple of years if you use an address other than a P.O. Box.

COPYRIGHT LAWS

You establish (claim) intellectual property rights (the right to have, sell, modify, and so on) through notice given by copyright, patent, trade secrets, and trademarks. You transfer limited privileges to those rights to your customers by way of a license. Never, ever refer to a customer as "owning" or "buying" the program. We'll go into more detail later (and you will really need to have an attorney review your materials), but every copy of your product should have a ™ or ® next to the product name to show that you claim rights to the product name.

Copyright

If it was possible to copyright an idea, I'd be in trouble. Most of what I've learned, I've learned from others. A copyright protects the *expression of an idea, not the idea itself.* The actual copyright law is 17 United States Code, sections 101 through 810. Most libraries have a copy.

You do not need to do anything in the United States (since 1989) to have a copyright—it is automatic. On the other hand, it is definitely to your advantage to include a "notice" in your work, since that will head off a defense of innocent infringement. It is also useful from the standpoint of deterrence.

If an individual claims a copyright, that claim is good for his or her lifetime plus fifty years (certainly long enough for most

software). A copyright claimed by an unnatural person (corporation or partnership) is good for seventy-five years from the date of
publication. This is why you will see a spread of dates on works
published by corporations.

A complete "notice" is composed of the letter c inside a circle
or the word "copyright," the year of first publication, and the name
of the owner of the copyright.

Some people use a "(c)," since a PC in text mode does not have
the copyright symbol. This method of showing a copyright is not
explicitly recognized in the law and has never been conclusively
tested in court. The conservative advice is just always to spell the
word out in full. On the other hand, the Universal Copyright
(Berne) Convention, by which your copyright is recognized by
other countries, requires the © and doesn't recognize the word
"copyright."

In order to have a "year of first publication," your work must
be published. In this case, the word "published" does not necessarily mean what you might expect. To quote the copyright act:
" 'Publication' is the distribution of copies or phonorecords of a
work to the public by sale or other transfer of ownership, or by
rental, lease or lending. The offering to distribute copies or
phonorecords to a group of persons for purposes of further
distribution, public performance, or public display, constitutes
publication. A public performance or display of a work does not of
itself constitute publication."

Additionally, our lawmakers were very concerned with the
physical distribution of "published" materials. To quote Circular 1:
"The reports also state that it is clear that any form of dissemina-
tion in which the *material object does not change hands . . . is not a
publication* no matter how many people are exposed to the work."
To be on the conservative side, I'd make sure I sent a diskette and
a manual to somebody out of state (and could prove it) if my
primary mode of distribution was by uploading to bulletin boards.

If you are claiming a copyright on an unpublished work and
wish to place a copyright notice on it, the correct form is to print
"Unpublished work" ahead of the rest of the copyright notice.

Copyright registration is easy, cheap, and offers a number of
advantages:

- You can take legal action for infringement only after the copyright has been registered.
- If the infringement occurred before copyright registration, infringers can attempt to use an *innocent infringement* defense.
- If the infringement occurred before copyright registration, you may not be able to sue violators for *your costs* in pursuing them or for the economic damage they may have done.

Registration seems to take about four months. You can obtain the appropriate forms and get information from:

Register of Copyrights
Library of Congress
Washington, DC 20559
Public Information: (202) 707-3000
Forms Hotline: (202) 707-9100

The copyright office publishes free circulars that will be useful to you—Circular 1, "Copyright Basics"; Circular 2, "Publications on Copyright"; and Circular 61, "Copyright Registration for Computer Programs." As always, if in doubt, pay a specialist. There doesn't seem to be an all-purpose software copyright form. You'll have to decide which of the following forms is the most appropriate:

TX: for registering "literary works." This is the normal form used for computer software and documentation.

PA: for "performing arts." Some arcade-type computer games have filed under this form.

VA: for works of visual art. If you're worried about "look and feel," this is probably the one.

SE: for serial publications, such as magazines. If you market your product in this way, you may need this form.

SR: for sound recordings. Multimedia seems to belong on form PA, not SR.

CA: for supplemental filings.

RE: for renewal filings.

I question whether it makes sense to register (as opposed to claim) a copyright for software. My reasoning is that, because you cannot copyright an idea, having protection for the source code is not very useful.

Registering a copyright requires you to submit the source code to the copyright office, where it is available to anyone. While the copyright office instructs you to submit the first and last twenty-five pages of your source code and blank out all the trade secrets (up to 50 percent of the code), the legal community has questioned whether this would be sufficient, or if only that which is deposited would be protected.

In any case, there is general agreement that copyright is not a defense against reverse engineering. Instead, I never let my source out to anyone (only my wife has a copy), but since my documentation contains all the "public" information about the program, such as descriptions of key combinations and screen layouts, I register a copyright on the documentation and help files and claim (but not register) a copyright on the program. Since my documentation is embedded in the .exe, and the .exe won't run without it, I can't imagine how someone could violate my copyright on the program without simultaneously violating the registered copyright of the documentation.

If you do register a copyright on the program itself, be sure to read Circular 61 very carefully.

If your product contains any work you did as an employee or a contractor, see a lawyer. You may fall under the work-for-hire section. If so, you will need a release from the company for which you did the work.

If you choose not to register, the law requires that you deposit two copies with the Library of Congress if the work is "published." There are fines and other penalties for failure to comply. One additional thing you may wish to consider: A very unusual key combination in all of my programs (it differs from one program to another) blanks out the screen, then prints "This is the original executable code from program x, copyrighted by x in 19xx." As you might imagine, I took some pains to hide this particular routine. You won't find the literal "copyr" using a hex editor. If someone were simply to hack my code, this module would probably survive. Imagine the look on the opposing lawyer's face as that message appeared on the screen!

Trademark

A trademark or trade name is an *exclusive right to use a particular name* or mark (logo) in connection with a specific kind of trade. It is rooted in English common law and is thus largely free of both the bureaucracy and certainty that a more modern method might bring. Essentially, you establish a mark in the United States by claiming it, using it, and defending it. Unlike a copyright, it does not have a fixed expiration date; it expires when "abandoned." The exact mark and any other mark that could reasonably be confused with it is then protected as long as you continue to claim, use, and defend it. In case of similar marks, the first user retains the right to use the mark. The subsequent user loses the right to the mark. There is no obligation to register a mark in order to retain your rights, but doing so does have some advantages.

The idea behind giving protection to a mark is that this protects the public from thinking they were buying one thing when in fact they are buying another. For this reason, the test for similarity has more to do with people's impressions or recollections than an exact match between words or designs. If you've ever seen a Russian can of Pepsi, you'll know it immediately, even if you can't read the label. Some years ago, Coke had, in effect, established through widespread usage a trademark on the shape of a bottle. (Remember them?) Anyone trying to bottle a soft drink in a similarly shaped bottle would have been taken to court. For this reason there is a Cadillac dog food not associated with General Motors—the courts felt the public was intelligent and discriminating enough to tell the difference. If you ever note a somewhat out-of-place item in a name-brand catalog, what the company may in fact be doing is establishing its mark in another area of trade for future protection.

If you fail to defend the mark vigorously, you may lose it. Aspirin and escalator once were trademarks. The companies that owned them lost them as they became so successful that the words passed into general usage. This is why Xerox is so careful to be sure its name is never used as a verb, and Burger King has to explain that they don't sell "Coke" if you ask for that instead of a cola or a Pepsi.

The problem of losing rights to a trademark or trade name arises when two companies or products unknowingly use similar names or logos. Years of marketing and thousands of dollars' worth of advertising might be spent on fostering name recognition before they became aware of each other, resulting in company number 2 losing all that momentum. You can display the fact that you are claiming a mark by putting ™ next to the mark the first time it appears in anything you distribute. It really won't buy you much, but it doesn't cost you much either. If you fail to put those magic letters there, an opposing lawyer can assert that you didn't really claim the mark and thus can't defend it.

Having said all this, it is possible to register a mark. It just doesn't do exactly what you might expect. Even with a registered mark, if someone has been claiming and using a similar mark prior to your first use, theoretically you will lose the right to that mark.

Federal registration of a trademark offers some significant advantages:

- Once the mark has been registered for five years, the grounds under which a mark can be challenged are very limited, even by someone who can prove first use, the logic being that the person had five years to defend the mark and didn't.
- You can sue in federal court for infringement only after your mark is registered.
- Registration allows you to sue for recovery of damages and costs.
- Registration should eliminate the good-faith defense against an infringement suit.
- The U.S. Customs Service will block imports infringing upon U.S. trademarks that have been registered. To those without registration, it will offer only sympathy.
- All things being equal, if one person has registered a mark and the other hasn't, the registered mark will be viewed as having established the stronger claim and defense.

The registration period is ten years, with each renewal also ten years. Between the fifth and sixth year after registration, you must file an affidavit certifying that the mark is in active use in commerce. Lack of this affidavit will result in automatic cancellation of registration.

Trademarks come in four flavors: generic, descriptive, suggestive, and coined.

Generic marks are words that would ordinarily be used to describe the product and cannot be protected at all. You cannot prevent someone else from using the phrase "computer program" or "spreadsheet," for instance.

Descriptive marks are words that modify the product name in a way that would ordinarily not be exclusive. The mark "Joe's Pizza" could be protected only if it had been in use and aggressively protected for a period of years, since it implies that no other Joe could make pizza.

Suggestive marks are slightly stronger. They do not directly describe the product, but use the language to suggest what the product is about. VisiCalc is a good example of this type of mark. Certainly, the word was not in general use prior to its being used as a mark, even though it is made up of English syllables.

Coined marks are the strongest of all. Xerox is a good example of this type of mark. Without the efforts of the company that coined it, it would mean nothing.

Unless you have a great deal of money for promotion, you will probably want to select a suggestive mark. The time and money to make a truly coined mark recognizable to the public is formidable.

It costs $200 to apply for a federal trademark. (The address for the forms is given on page xiii). If the Patent and Trademark Office finds that a similar mark is already registered, you will lose the application fee. The process takes about eight months. Given the high cost (money and time) of applying for a mark that could be turned down, I suggest you use the following strategy:

First, come up with a list of names (both for your company if you are not using your own name and for your product), then whittle it down to the top half dozen or so.

Next, go to the computer directories listed on pages 3 and 4 and look in the product and company name lists for anything similar. Changing a letter or two won't be enough of a difference. You probably won't be able to register "MikroSoff" or even "SoftMicro."

If you have a CompuServe account, you can use the IQuest (go IQuest) service to check what's left of your list to see if your preferred names are registered at a state or federal level. It costs about $15 to check each name. This is a quick and easy way to get negative information (that the mark is already registered and in use). It isn't safe for "clearing" a name, however, since it doesn't search for unregistered names. You have to be skilled in using the service to find similar names, and you really need to know trademark law to interpret the results.

If you live near Washington, D.C., you can do your own search for free from 8:00 A.M. to 5:30 P.M. at the:

Patent and Trademark Office Search Library
Crystal Plaza 2, 2nd floor
2011 Jefferson Davis Highway
Arlington, VA 22022

Otherwise, use one of the services your lawyer would use and then mark up 500 percent. A search costs about $300. Feed the service one name at a time unless you're in a big hurry with lots of money to spend. To find these services, look in your phone directory under trademarks or call one of the big names in the industry. (Yes, Thompson & Thompson owns Compu-Mark, but their price lists are different.)

Thompson & Thompson
500 Victory Road
North Quincy, MA 02171-1545
(617) 479-1600
(800) 692-8833

Compu-Mark
500 Victory Road
North Quincy, MA 02171-1545
(617) 479-1600
(800) 421-7881

Another (slightly cheaper) source for trademark searches is the

Trademark Research Center
300 Park Avenue South
New York, NY 10010
(212) 228-4084
(800) 872-6275

Its searches run from $120; Thompson & Thompson starts at just over $200.

Assuming you get a clean report on one of your names, if you're a gambler, submit your application form. If you don't want to gamble, see a lawyer who deals with federal trademark issues and give him or her a copy of the search you've already paid for. This type of lawyer will be cheaper than a local lawyer who will charge you for the learning curve. Merchant and Gould provides this service, as does Lance Rose. (See p. 207.) Lots of others do also.

Once you have gotten confirmation from the Trademark Office that your mark is registered, you can put ® instead of ™ next to your product name.

It is also possible to register trademarks with the individual states. The benefit to be gained by this is debatable at best.

Patent

You probably don't have the money or the time for a patent. If you did get one, you'd could quite possibly go broke trying to defend it.

If you're still interested, a patent does actually protect an idea, but that idea must be "novel" and "nonobvious." It can't be an algorithm (the traditional reason that software is generally not given a patent) or a law of nature. The process of getting a patent takes years and costs many thousands of dollars. Once you have a patent, it can be challenged by anyone at anytime—and if you don't have the money to defend it, you'll lose it. Simply writing and publishing an article describing a process similar to yours prior to your patent application may be enough to invalidate the patent years after it was granted.

On the other hand, if you really do discover a "novel" and "nonobvious" idea with broad application that could be reverse-engineered, a patent is the way to protect it. For seventeen years, you will have the exclusive right to use the process you patented, whether someone uses reverse engineering to duplicate the process or not.

In general, you must apply for a patent within a year of when your new invention is first offered for sale or disclosed to the public. Your best advice is to disclose your new invention to your patent attorney first.

Licensing Your Software

Most software requires a single (end-user) license from you to your end user.

Shareware uses three distinct licenses. The first is a distribution license, which allows distributors to copy and ship your product. The second is the trial use license, which allows a prospective customer to use the program for a limited trial. Finally, the customer license (in common with software distributed through other channels) is granted to those people who register your program. There are lots of lawyer magic words involved in licensing. Even upper and lower case have their own magic in certain situations. Your best bet is to cut and paste from existing licenses that you like, then take it to a lawyer who specializes in the field to have him or her properly chant over it.

Distribution

Distribution allows vendors to copy and ship your product, and charge for the service. I have my distribution license embedded in "vendor.doc." I suggest that you keep your distribution terms simple. Many good vendors will just discard programs where they feel they don't have a clear right to distribute the program or have to comply with onerous provisions.

Trial Use

Trial use is the right to use the product for a trial period. Most authors limit by time, but other limits may be used. Again, keep it simple, but protect yourself from liability claims.

Customer

The customer license is the license you've seen shrink-wrapped on all the compilers you buy. Personally, I really like Borland's license—short and to the point.

You may choose not to use a formal license at all. First, there is some doubt about whether most licenses are enforceable when customers do not have the opportunity to examine them prior to purchase (typical of direct mail, catalogs, and retail), and there's a question of how much licenses add beyond what you already have with your copyright.

If you do choose to use a customer license, you need to decide whether you are licensing a single person to use as many copies of your product as he or she wants. (If a person has laptop and desktop machines, is a single license enough?) Are you licensing a single machine? Or are you licensing a single copy of the program, as Borland does? Be explicit.

One thing I do recommend is having a clause that makes a disgruntled customer sue you in your own neighborhood. If you ever have to go to court, this will save you a lot of money and will let you carry on some semblance of a life while the whole thing is going on. I also can tell you that a jury made up of New Hampshire Yankees is unlikely to give a big award to a bunch of Noo Yawk lawyers. If you have a home court advantage, use it.

Site

A site license is a customer license that allows more than a single person/machine/copy to be used.

Be explicit in your documentation about how you are going to handle disks, manuals, and support. Since my site license fee is considerably lower than a number of licenses purchased individually, I send a single master disk and as many manuals as the customer's license calls for. Additionally, I require that all support calls be made through the same person—this generally avoids answering the same question multiple times for the same license.

THE FEDERAL TRADE COMMISSION (FTC)

If you use the U.S. mail in your selling cycle (either soliciting the order through the mail or accepting the order or payment through the mail), you are subject to the Federal Trade Commission's "Mail Order Rule." While the requirements of this rule are good business and should be done anyway, deviations from the rule are not something you want to fool around with. The FTC is very serious and will follow up aggressively if someone makes a complaint. Your best bet in making sure you are in compliance with the rule, and in demonstrating to the authorities that you are in compliance (at least as important as the first), is to have formal procedures for dealing with orders and complaints and contemporaneous records that can show exactly what was done and when. The rule requires:

- That you not advertise something that you probably won't be able to ship within thirty days of the order.
- That you either clearly and conspicuously show your order processing time or process orders within thirty days.
- The clock on order processing starts when you have a "properly completed" order. Basically, this means you know what customers are ordering and have their address and their money. If you have a check or money order, you have their money. If you have their credit card number, you have their money as soon as you submit the charge.
- The clock on order processing stops when you deliver a properly addressed package to the shipper.
- If you cannot process the order within the prescribed time, you must provide an "option notice." This is a postage-paid notice that asks customers to indicate whether they wish to cancel the order or to agree to a delay in shipping. You must provide a specific date for shipping in order for this option notice to be in compliance.
- If you cannot reasonably give a specific shipping date on the option notice, you may provide a detailed explanation for the delay so that consumers can make an informed judgment. The option notice must be sent before the order processing clock runs out.
- The notice also must state what action you will take if they don't respond. Basically, if the delay is over thirty days, you must take a nonresponse as a cancellation of the order; if it is under thirty days, it must be treated as a consent to a delay in shipping. The rules get complicated here, so if you are in this position (unlikely in software), you'll need to check the rules yourself.
- If things are really screwed up and you're going to blow the option notice date, you must then send a "renewed option" notice. With a renewed option notice, a nonresponse from customers is an automatic cancellation of the order.
- If you cancel an order, you must provide a prompt refund. Effectively, your best method is simply to not deposit a check until the package is in the mail. Incidentally, this is a good practice anyway, since sometimes the only address that is legible is on the check itself. For international sales, the

returned money order presents a real problem to customers. In that case, I cash the money order and send currency as a refund by registered mail.

- Credit vouchers are not a refund under this rule.
- Refunds must be sent by U.S. first-class mail within a week of the cancellation.
- You must ship exactly what customers ordered or provide an option notice. You may not substitute something "better." What this means is that you must ship the version a customer ordered, or not state a version number in the solicitation, or state in the solicitation that the "current" version will be shipped.
- If you use the word "free" (as in "try this free for thirty days"), you may not require that payment accompany the order. If you include a bill-me-later option as well as a way to send money, you meet the requirement. A no-risk trial may require payment as long as there's provision for a refund.

The state out of which you operate your business may have additional rules that go beyond the federal rules.

After you read the preceding rules, I hope it is obvious that it's a really dumb idea for a software company to accept orders for (or advertise) a product before it is fully tested and ready to ship. Besides the ill will it can generate, it is both costly and likely to get you in a lot of trouble with the federal government. While the feds' rarely pull out the big guns, they can levy civil penalties of up to $10,000 per violation (customer).

As a practical matter, I've found that people get angry if you don't ship within two days of getting the order. I make a point of catching the last mail out with all orders received that day.

It's a really good idea to put a "Return Postage Guaranteed" sticker on all outgoing merchandise—not because you really want it back, but because you need to know about undeliverable packages in order to head off complaints.

Shareware represents a particular problem, since you can't turn off the solicitation for the order. A stale message helps in this regard, setting a time limit beyond which the software won't solicit the order (if the customer's clock is working). You might want to have a separate post office box for each product and close the box when you discontinue the product. When I get orders for discontinued products, I send out a preprinted postcard explaining that the product is no longer available and that the order has been canceled. I cut out half of the customer's signature and MICR check number from their checks and glue it to the post card so that they know that the check has been destroyed.

CHAPTER 10

Accounting and Taxes

 There is one simple rule from which all my advice springs: You don't want to fool around with the tax collector.

LOCAL TAX

See your accountant. You may have to pay a gross receipts tax, a business profits tax, an inventory tax, sales taxes, and/or other taxes.

SALES TAX

Interstate collection of sales taxes is in a state of flux in the United States as this is being written. In the Quill case, the Supreme Court decided that firms cannot be compelled to collect and remit sales taxes across state lines. Under current laws, you are subject only to your own state's regulations and the regulations where you have a "business presence." As I understand it, the Quill case refined the definition of "business presence."

Many of the news reports analyzing the effects of Quill were misleading. The Court decided that states emphatically do not have the right to compel businesses to collect sales taxes if they do not have a business presence (nexus) in that state. While it is true that the Court stated that the Congress could pass a law making such a requirement, most legal scholars have always assumed that this was the case.

The Court explicitly stated that the Congress could pass a law requiring interstate collection of sales taxes if it chose to do so without a constitutional amendment. Given the feeling on the part of local governments that they are underfunded, pressure is building on Congress to pass such a law.

If your state taxes sales of computer software, you may have to collect sales taxes from your customers in your state and remit them to your state tax department. Under current law, you usually are required to collect and remit taxes only in your own state. Some states, such as New York and New Jersey, have set up reciprocal agreements, so you may be required under your state law to collect for another state.

If you are near a state that does not tax software, it may be to your advantage to locate your business in that state.

It is a very good idea to have a stale message in your products, just in case some form of national taxation (sales or value added tax, or reciprocal agreements between your state and others) becomes enacted—or you need to move to a different state. You also might want to consider adding some words to your license agreement that allow for invoicing for taxes that are enacted after your release.

LICENSES

You're probably supposed to get a local business license. If you use a fictitious name, have a "real" address or business telephone number, or incorporate, there's probably no escaping it.

FEDERAL TAX

Check with your tax advisor about making *quarterly estimated tax payments*. The penalties for underpaying your taxes are high enough that you don't want to expose yourself. Until you have a better feel for your own personal tax situation, remitting 20 percent of each quarter's software gross income will be about right.

Before you release your product, take a trip to your local Internal Revenue Service office, or call (800) 829-3676, and get copies of these books, pamphlets, and forms:

Publication 910   Guide to Free Tax Services
  This booklet lists all the other booklets.
Publication 17   Your Federal Income Tax
  This is an excellent all-around introduction to personal taxation.
Publication 334   Tax Guide for Small Business
  This is the book I find myself reaching for most. It answers such questions as how to deduct business mileage and what records the IRS can demand if it audits you.
Publication 533   Self-Employment Tax
  You'll have to pay FICA on your profits.
Publication 560   Self-Employed Retirement Plans
  The rules are complex, but there are a few good tax breaks left here.
Publication 587   Business Use of Your Home
  If you are going to take this deduction, think twice and read this book carefully.
Schedule C   Profit or Loss From Business
  This is the form used for reporting on the financial activity of your company.
Schedule SE   Self-Employment Tax
  Used for paying more FICA.
Form SS-4   Application for an Employer Identification Number
  Really a Social Security Administration form.
Form 8829   Expenses for Business Use of Your Home.
  Get out the tape measure, and be prepared to swear that you never pay a personal bill from your office.
Form 1040-ES   Payment Voucher
  Pay your quarterly estimated tax using this form. The penalties and interest are high if you don't or you are late.

Here are some general comments on filling out Schedule C, but check with your tax professional before you sign anything:

You may need to get an *Employer Identification Number* (really a company identifier) from the Social Security Administration. It's a short form that assigns a pseudo-social security number to your business. You'll need this number when corporations want to write large checks to you. Without it, they are legally obligated to withhold a portion of the money in case you don't report it. If you are a sole proprietorship and have only a single business, you can simply use your social security number.

In Box B, you'll need to supply an SIC (Standard Industrial Classification) code. You choice of *SIC code* is important because the IRS uses a statistical program called a "DIF" score to determine whether an audit is likely to result in increased revenue for them; the SIC code is used to compare your business to other businesses. You do, of course, want to be honest and accurate, but it is to your advantage to select a code that is not prone to use by people who play games with their taxes and most closely matches your income and expense patterns so that you won't seem unusual. Common choices are:

Code	General Category
7372	Services: Computer software; prepackaged
5961	Trade: Computer software; mail order and retail
2741	Publishing: Miscellaneous, including multimedia
2731	Publishing: books; no printing press
7371	Services: Computer software; custom design

The IRS looks very carefully at codes 7371, 7872, and 7286; these codes are used by job shoppers, who recently lost the ability to use Schedule C as a part of section 1706 of the tax reform act. I am oversimplifying things, but you may want to avoid those codes if you legally can.

Talk to your tax professional and read the rules, but, if you can, you want to use the cash (line F) accounting method. To do otherwise means that you have to pay taxes on your "earnings" rather than on your "receipts." To an accountant, you "earn" money by writing code. You know, of course, that you "receive" nothing until you get paid.

For line G, it is best that you arrange your business affairs so you have no inventory. This keeps things simple and avoids the asking of all kinds of other questions.

ACCOUNTING

I use my personal checking account for everything. The experts will probably warn you against this, primarily because they have seen too many people mess up both sides of their lives with sloppy bookkeeping. How you handle it depends on your self-discipline and willingness to document things. The advantage to using a single account, with a single checkbook, is that you can write one check for many things and then just split it out in the accounting system. Many of my checks are split out this way. Both Compu-Serve and GEnie insist on billing a Visa account, which means that when I pay my Visa bill, I am paying both business and personal bills.

If you are incorporated, a single account is not an option. You must keep the money separate, in separate accounts, preferably in separate banks. This means that you never, ever pay a personal bill with a company check and never give or loan money to the corporation without a formal loan agreement. To act otherwise undoes all the legal magic that created the corporation.

If you are at the point that you are incorporated and are looking for venture capital, you should know that the 1993 Omnibus Budget Reconciliation Act has a provision that may make investing in your company much more attractive to individual investors in the higher tax brackets. Under this law, nonincorporated taxpayers who invest in "qualified small business stock" and hold it for five years or longer get a 50 percent discount on any taxes owed on the gain when they sell or exchange the stock. For people in the 28 percent bracket, this means that the gain will be taxed at only 14 percent. There are limits, of course:

- Only the first $10 million (or an increase of one order of magnitude) is eligible.
- The stock must be newly issued.
- The stock must not be issued in exchange for other stock.
- The stock must be issued by a "C" corporation with under $50 million in assets.

Cash or Accrual

There are two ways of keeping score in the accounting business. Cash accounting simply keeps track of real money as it moves around. The accrual method recognizes the value of effort and records this in the books. For instance, manufacturing companies recognize the value of their inventories as they make and ship the product, rather than as they are actually paid. Accrual accounting is considered to give the most accurate picture of a company's current operations, which is true. What is also true is that accrual accounting is much more work, much more complex, and results in paying cash taxes on money you haven't received yet.

Under certain circumstances, you may not have a choice of accounting methods. Once you have managers and supervisors and workers, the accrual method may very well offer valuable management information. In the meantime, the cash method is much easier and cheaper.

Inventory

This is another check-with-your-accountant issue. Your state may tax all business inventories held on a certain date. Inventories also complicate your tax returns. If possible, have no inventories as the tax man defines them. Your tax advisor will tell you if this is possible in your situation, and how to set up your business so that you won't have to pay taxes because of inventories.

CHAPTER 11

Running a Business

◆◆◆ Learning how to run a business is a full-time job in itself. Local colleges probably offer courses in the subject through their extension schools. There are some excellent books on the subject. Browse your bookstore and pick the book that matches your personal style of learning.

You must learn enough about everything to know if the outside services (legal, accounting, banking, advertising, graphics, documentation, support, and so on) you are using are doing an adequate and cost-effective job. On the other hand, you can't possibly know enough about everything to do a good job of it yourself. Your job, then, is to do what you can yourself, to hire others when the job is beyond your expertise, and to know the difference.

Most programmers make terrible business managers (and vice versa). The personality traits that make a person good at one job generally work against him or her in the other. Seriously consider making your first or second hire your new boss. Quite a few successful software companies are run like this. Then the technical/creative person can continue to do what he or she does best—what makes the company and product different.

Don't borrow. Your accountant will want to talk about accrual concepts, which are legitimate—but bills can be paid only with cash. If you do hit a point where you are having a hard time paying your suppliers, call them early and be totally up front with them. The good ones will work with you. In no case should you ever "borrow" from the government's taxes you are obliged to collect. About the only way a software author can go to jail for business actions is by failing to remit tax monies held in trust (sales taxes, FICA, and income tax withholding) in full when they are due. It's a classic mistake. Don't make it yourself.

TRADE ASSOCIATIONS

Several trade associations for software businesses can give you advice and information. For shareware, the best association is the ASP.

The Association of Software Professionals (ASP)

The Association of Shareware Professionals (ASP) is a trade association that tries to further the interests of the industry (vendors, authors, and consumers). The vast majority of successful authors and vendors are members; a Bulletin Board membership is also available. An author membership application is included in the Software Publisher's Kit.

I should mention that I am an active and happy ASP member. People occasionally criticize the ASP for a number of reasons, typically for being cliquey, for "forcing authors not to cripple," and for "being too consumer oriented." I personally found that I was warmly welcomed into the association, and some members who had been in for some time made an effort to extend their hands to me. I certainly agree that the ASP does not allow its members to "cripple" their programs—but, as I stated earlier, I think crippling doesn't work anyway, so I don't consider it a hindrance. Finally, if part of the purpose of the ASP is to help the shareware market grow, I can't imagine any other way than by being "consumer oriented." Some of the services and advantages offered to author members include:

- ASPects, an excellent newsletter discussing issues of interest to authors, vendors, and bulletin board sysops.
- The ASP distribution CD and the ASP quarterly CD. The ASP used to offer a monthly mailing service that allowed publisher members to pool their disks in order to save shipping costs in getting product to distribution members. This service (which cost upward of $700 at the end for full participation in a single mailing) has been replaced by a CD that is distributed monthly to all distribution members. Being on the CD and receiving the

CD if you are a distribution member is included in the dues. From a practical standpoint, publisher members can be assured that they are on approximately 1,000 bulletin boards that simply "play" the CD and are available to the 600 disk distributors within 60 days of the first release of the product. For $100 a year, there is no comparable distribution service.

- Closed sections on a CompuServe forum for member use only. Many hints, tips, and strategies are discussed there.
- The right to put "<ASP>" next to your product name when you distribute it. To many consumers, this is becoming a significant factor in determining which products they will consider.

Author membership in the ASP also brings some constraints. These constraints exist primarily to better serve the public and thus strengthen the value of the <ASP> notation next to a product's name. Some of the more significant ones include the following:

- *Support* must be provided to registered users for at least three months; the support policy must be stated explicitly.
- If, during the minimum three-month period, registered users discover a bug specific to their computing environment, the author must either fix the bug or offer a refund.
- If you receive money for a *discontinued* (unsupported) product, you must return the money.
- If you are aware of *incompatibilities* between your product and other products, you must include that information in your documentation.
- You have to tell customers *how to register* and what they will receive for registering.
- The registration fee must be a fixed monetary amount. "Begware" isn't allowed.
- You can't *short sheet* the documentation.
- In general, the shareware and the registered versions should be the same, with the following exceptions:
  1. In order to save disk space, you *may condense* some tutorial and documentation files.
  2. You may allow registered users a way to *disable the registration encouragement* techniques.
  3. If you offer *source code* to your registered users, you don't have to provide it in the shareware distribution version.

4. If you produce a large and small version of your product (typically used to keep the distribution package small), the *large product must be available* for evaluation for a small fee.
5. You can't *bait and switch* using a shelfware version of your product.
6. You may provide convenience utilities to registered users, as long as they are *not essential* to the operation of your product.
7. Registration reminder screens may appear up to *two times* each time the program is run.
8. Registration reminder screens may not require more than *two keystrokes* to bypass.
9. If you choose to use a forced minimum display time on any screen, it may not be longer than *three seconds*.
10. Undocumented *hidden files* are not allowed.
11. *Printing* a registration form *without asking permission* first is not allowed.
12. Your registration encouragement techniques can't be obnoxious (just in case you invent a new one that hasn't already been prohibited).
13. Your shareware package must contain the *ASP Ombudsman statement* on a file in the distribution package. (*The Share-Ware Book* distribution package is in file Register.doc.)
14. You must *cooperate* with the ASP ombudsman if someone lodges a complaint against you.

Quite honestly, I'm amazed that anyone would do half of the things not allowed. They simply are not good business. For more information, contact:

Association of Shareware Professionals
45 Grover Road
Muskegon, MI 49442

The Shareware Trade Association & Resources (STAR)

The Shareware Trade Association & Resources (STAR) is a much more informal group. Organized primarily as a reaction to the

ASP's rules regarding members' business practices, it takes pride in its disorganization. The group has a very active forum within UKSHARE on CompuServe, which is well worth monitoring. (Membership in STAR is not required for participation in this forum.) It also has an occasional electronic newsletter, which is also posted in UKSHARE.

For more information, contact:

Shareware Trade Association & Resources
P.O. Box 13408
Las Vegas, NV 89112
(702) 735-1980

The Association of Shareware Authors and Distributors (ASAD)

The Association of Shareware Authors and Distributors (ASAD) has been in the formative stages since 1992; it's unclear if it will ever get off the ground. Based on its literature, it seems to be fairly similar to the ASP, with a couple of interesting differences:

- Dues are much less; membership types can be combined and author dues are $35; distributor dues are $65.
- All members will have an equal vote.
- It plans to offer a registration service for authors.
- It will maintain its own bulletin board for membership use.
- It has a crippling disclosure policy rather than a blanket no-crippling policy.
- It will be similar to the ASP in that it will offer a mailing service, an ombudsman, and require shareware "disclosure" and update of programs on the part of vendors.

For more information, contact:

B. Lee Williams
Association of Shareware Authors and Distributors
2425 North Limestone Street
Springfield, OH 45503-1109
(513) 390-1099

INSURANCE

I found out the hard way just what wasn't covered under insurance when I had a fire in my home office. Your household insurance probably does not cover anything connected with your software business. Even if you bought things for your personal use and are using them for business, they may no longer be covered. Check with your insurance agent to be sure that your software business is not somehow "tainting" your household coverage. If you feel that you do need additional coverage, your agent will be glad to give you a quotation for a rider that includes the additional use and property.

EMPLOYEES

This is serious stuff. Your lawyer and accountant must be consulted. Your exposure and the likelihood that you will unknowingly violate a rule are very high.

CHAPTER **12**

Selling Internationally from the United States

◆◆◆ The software world is pretty much an English-reading world. Many authors report as much as a quarter of their income comes from outside the United States. Unless you've written a program specific to the United States (income taxes or ZIP code lookup, perhaps), you'll be missing out on income and a great deal of satisfaction if you don't include international distribution in your plans. Just wait till you get a registration from a country you've never heard of!

Before you begin distributing your software abroad, add the words "All Rights Reserved" to your copyright notice on all your materials. This notice is necessary to fully protect your rights in some foreign countries. It doesn't cost much to include it, even if it's unlikely that you'll ever have to defend your rights abroad.

EXPORT LICENSES

Export of software is controlled by both the Department of State and the Department of Commerce. The rules and regulations regarding exporting are very confusing. Most publishers simply take the money, slap on a green customs sticker, and mail the package. Since I was writing about international sales of shareware, I attempted to find out what the rules actually are. The results are mixed at best.

I am not a lawyer or any kind of export authority, so before I started investigating the rules, I asked a number of shareware authors how they handled foreign sales. Every single one of them simply used the post office's little green customs sticker and

239

figured that they were doing what was necessary. To the best of my knowledge, nobody has ever had a hand slapped for not following the rules. However, the rules do have provisions for civil and criminal penalties if you don't follow them exactly. So, here are the rules, as best I can figure them out.

U.S. Department of State

The first half in the process of exporting legitimately is to disengage yourself from the Department of State. The Department of State is interested in your shareware only if it can be considered a "munition" found on the United States Munitions List (Part 121 of the International Traffic in Arms Regulations [ITAR]). In general terms, software falls on the munitions list either because it was designed for military use (things like ballistics modeling or design of silent propellers for submarines) or because it falls under the general category of "cryptography"—which is where the trouble lies.

The Department of State says that any software using encryption may not be exported at all (even if you imported the toolkit that may be doing encryption). The department also refuses to define "encryption." According to my computer dictionary, encryption is: "the process of encoding data so that the data cannot be read by users who do not possess the necessary key or algorithm."

Of course, under that definition, a word processing document is encrypted. When I called the Department of State at (703) 875-7041, I spoke to a career diplomat who obviously had never written a line of code. When I asked him what the government definition of encryption was, he responded, in effect, "We know it when we see it," and told me that the definition I had was as good as any. Under this definition, if you:

- distribute your program in an archive (the Department of State considers PKzip to be "static encryption"!)
- do not publish your file formats in your documentation
- do not publish how you store your configuration options
- use any way of storing data on disk other than straight ASCII

you must request a "Letter of Determination of Commodity Jurisdiction" from the Department of State. Your commodity jurisdiction request letter must have the following format:

Subject line: It must read "Commodity Jurisdiction Request for" and then name the items. Name shareware and registered versions separately. Identify the release. If you ship different versions to bulletin boards and vendors (.zip and self-extractors), name them separately. Be sure to keep a copy in your word processor; you will have to send this letter for each release.

Description: State the description of your product and how it works. In all probability, you can use the words from your description or vendor.doc files for this.

Origin of commodity: State why the product was designed in the first place, whether the design took into consideration any military uses, and give examples of both military and nonmilitary use. If the product was designed for (as opposed to sold to) any government agency, state the agency and contract history. Include a product history (your .rev file) as well.

Current use: Describe all known current uses and whether the type of use has changed over time. The Department of State is interested only in what the product is actually used for—it is emphatically not interested in what it *could be* used for. Include an estimate of the percentage breakdown of military vs. civilian sales.

Special characteristics: If your product meets any military standards or specifications or has any special military characteristics, describe them in this section. Also state here what archiving methods you use, in which products.

Other information: Request that jurisdiction be given to the Department of Commerce and state with which Export Control Classification Number (ECCN) the product should be classified (see page 245).

Attachments: If you have any marketing literature or reviews, copy them and attach them. You should also print out your .doc files and attach them.

As of this writing, Major Gary Oncale is the person who decides whether your archived program is a threat to the security of the free world. You must submit nine copies of your commodity jurisdiction request package to:

Major Gary Oncale
PM/DTC SA-6 Room 228
Office of Defense Trade Control
Department of State
Washington, DC 20522-0602

Bureau of Export Administration (BXA), U.S. Department of Commerce

Once you are clear of the Department of State, your next step is to determine the type of license you will need from the Bureau of Export Administration, U.S. Department of Commerce. All exports must be done under license—but an export license is not necessarily a piece of paper with your name on it. As a matter of fact, an export license turns out to be very different from what I (and most people) expected it to be.

First off, an export license licenses a specific transaction, the transfer of something from "domestic" to "foreign" between two specific parties at a specific place and time. There is no such thing as a general license authorizing you to export whatever and wherever.

Next, "domestic" and "foreign" are not necessarily what you might expect. Under the law, allowing a foreign student here on a visa access to your computer via modem is an "export." Uploading a program to a bulletin board that might be called from a foreign country is also an "export."

All exports from the United States must be "licensed" by the BXA. This does not mean what you might expect, however. The BXA issues two types of license; a "general" license and a "validated" license.

A BXA *validated license* is pretty much what you would expect—a lot of paperwork, followed by an official document that allows you to perform a specific export to a specific customer.

A BXA *general license* is sort of like a freeware license for software. The BXA simply publishes permission for you (or anyone) to export your software. You don't fill out any forms or even notify BXA that you are exporting. Nothing is required of you beyond *knowing which* "general license" you are exporting under and *knowing why* you qualify for that license.

Your goal is to legitimately claim a general license that is available to anyone who has not been barred from exporting and thus you won't even need to notify the Department of Commerce that you are doing it (sort of like a shareware evaluation license). If, however, the enforcement division of the Bureau of Export Administration decides to audit you later, you must be able to prove that each export transaction was done under a valid license.

The BXA (and customs) spot-checks exports to determine whether you are in compliance. The chances of your being checked are approximately equal to your chances of being hit by lightning. On the other hand, the discomfort level of getting tagged is similar as well, so you are well advised to do a little research.

Export license availability is determined by when the transaction takes place, to whom the item is exported, what is being exported, where the item is going, the value of the transaction, and how it is to be used. Think of these tests as a series of "if" statements where a negative result means that you cannot export under a general license.

We'll deal with the easy tests first.

You may not export to *certain people* or businesses at all. These people are excommunicated under a BXA "denial order" for past transgressions. The identity of these people and businesses and the beginning date and the ending date of the period during which you may not do business with them (generally a period of greater than ten years; the list is not very volatile) is published as the "Table of Denial Orders" by the:

Office of Technology and Policy Analysis
P.O. Box 273
Washington, DC 20044

You may not export to *certain countries* at all. These countries are either under "embargo" or have managed to get themselves onto lists Q, S, W, Y, or Z. This is a very volatile list, and the potential penalties for shipping to these countries can be severe. If you hear the executive branch saying unkind things about a country and you have an order from that country, you should check before shipping. The current list of countries includes: Afghanistan, Albania, Bulgaria, Cambodia, China, Cuba, Estonia, Haiti, Iran, Iraq, Laos, Latvia, Libya, Lithuania, Mongolia, Montenegro, North Korea, Romania, Serbia, Syria, Vietnam, and (still sometimes) South Africa.

If in doubt, call the regional office of the BXA:

Eastern Region: (603) 598-4300
Western Region: (714) 660-0144

In a conversation with a BXA representative, I tried to explain the concept of shareware, and asked how I could know if someone was calling my computer from one of those countries. I was told that BXA didn't care how I did it—making sure it didn't happen was my responsibility. If nothing else, I suggest that if you ever get a registration check from one of those countries, burn it.

You might consider writing to your senators or congressman to ask if they would consider passing laws that can be complied with.

If a transaction *exceeds* $2,500, you must fill out a form 7525-V. You can get this form and the instruction manual (which you have to certify you read and understood) by writing for:

"Correct Way to Fill Out the Shipper's Export Declaration"
& Shipper's Export Declaration Form 7525-V
from:
Bureau of the Census
Washington, DC 20233

The BXA considers all software to be "data." If you qualify for a general export license, it will be a data (as opposed to commodity) license.

The government document that describes the process and eligibility for export licenses is the Export Administrative Regulations (EAR). You can buy a copy of EAR (stock number 903-017-00000-1) for $87 (check, Visa/MC) from:

Superintendent of Documents
United States Government Printing Office
Washington, DC 20402
(202) 783-3238

Or you should be able to find a copy in a university library or by contacting state or federal agencies that try to encourage exports.

The least restrictive data license is the GTDA (General Technical Data; All Destinations). Technical data that is freely available to the general public can be exported under GTDA. This includes information and technical data that has been released to the public at cost. See part 779.3 of the EAR for the exact wording. Most freeware and bannerware will probably qualify for a GTDA license (since payment is not required). It is unclear whether shareware authors are on firm legal ground when using this license to export evaluation copies of their products, since a "transformation" to a product that does require payment occurs later. If you charge for continued use of your product, you should instead qualify for the GTDU license.

Most software will be exported under a GTDU (General Technical Data, Unrestricted) license. The details are covered in part 779.4 of the EAR.

The first step in qualifying for a GTDU license is to determine that your product's Export Control Classification Number (ECCN) is 4D96G. If your software fits anywhere on the following list, you probably do *not* qualify:

- Is an operating system for a supercomputer, hardened or fault-tolerant computer, weapons control computer, high-speed communications, or any fancy new technology the government hasn't gotten around to yet.
- Has nuclear, military, or security (police) applications.
- Is over 500,000 instructions long.
- Performs "multidata stream processing."
- Does real-time control of equipment with a global interrupt latency time of less than thirty microseconds.
- Is an expert system that supports time-dependent rules.

Next, your software must be sold by at least one of these three methods: over the counter, by mail order, or by telephone, and must be designed for installation by the customer without substantial support by you.

At this point, you can cover your bets by having the BXA confirm that you qualify for an ECCN of 4D96G. You can do this by sending a "Request for Commodity Classification" to:

Technical Support Staff
Bureau of Export Administration
Room 4069A
Department of Commerce
14th Street and Constitution Avenue, NW
Washington, DC 20230
ATTENTION: Commodity Classification

This request must:

- Include a recommended classification for the "commodity" (your product) and explain the reasons for the classification in terms of the technical control parameters specified in the ECCN.
- Include descriptive literature or specifications descriptive enough to enable the commodity classifications specialists to determine if your suggested ECCN is the correct one. In most cases, a copy of your product and its manual will accomplish this.
- Be marked "Commodity Classification Request" at the top of the first page.
- Be marked "Commodity Classification Request" at the lower left-hand corner of the envelope.

This process does not cost money and takes less than a month. Up to five products can be classified in a single request. If you do not qualify for an ECCN of 4D96G, plan on spending a lot of money on lawyers. Be especially sure that you never inadvertently "export" your product. Certainly release through shareware marketing would not be advisable under these circumstances; you will either have to export under a GTDR (General Technical Data, Restricted) or a validated license. This is major lawyer territory and is beyond the scope of this book.

Never put the letters "GTDR" on your product if you can qualify for GTDU status. The GTDR designation means that you must have signed written assurance from each and every customer that they will apply for an IVL (Individual Validated License) from the U.S. Department of Commerce before reexporting the product. If someone in authority happens to stumble on your product marked "GTDR" in a country where it shouldn't be, you will find yourself part of a big investigation. Saying that you didn't really mean it probably won't help you much.

In the process of trying to make some sense of this, I did find a lawyer who specializes in these issues and who seems to be both knowledgeable and effective:

Judd Kessler
Porter, Wright, Morris & Arthur
1233 20th Street N.W.
Washington, DC 20036
(202) 778-3080

Other sources of information that may be moderately helpful are:

Trade Information Center
Department of Commerce
Washington, DC 20230
(800) 872-8723

Small Business Foundation of America
Export Hotline
(800) 244-7232

Finally, write for a controlled-circulation subscription to:

Export Today Magazine
733 15th Steet NW #1100
Washington, DC 20005

DISTRIBUTION

The best way to crack foreign markets is through shareware, simply because the costs are so low. Once your product finds its way outside the United States and you begin to pick up some users, you'll have the chance to respond to their needs and modify your product to better fit their market. If your product has any success, someone will approach you to act as your agent or publisher in the foreign country.

I suggest that you find foreign agents to handle registrations for your shareware first and then foreign publishers to handle your product in all channels. I also suggest that you move carefully; communications will be difficult, and it's almost impossible to enforce a contract outside of your national borders.

Probably the best place to start is with the ASP vendor list (included in the Software Publisher's Kit) if you are not an ASP member. If you are a member, the ASP CD offers significant savings in mailing to foreign vendors (since it's free) and seems to add significant credibility. ASP membership also seems to have more impact on customers' package selection abroad.

When I need to send a single diskette internationally, I send a single 3.5-inch 720Kb diskette in a #6 (3⅝ x 6½-inch) envelope with a note on a half sheet (5.5 x 8.5-inch) of paper. It weighs just under an ounce, and none has been reported damaged in the mail yet.

Getting overseas distribution through other channels really requires an agent already in the country.

GETTING PAID

Beside the usual problem of getting paid for your work, there are additional problems in convincing foreign users to send money to you in another country:

- It is *difficult* for them. If you are asking for a check drawn on a U.S. bank, chances are that they will have to spend a great deal of time trying to be honest. Ask yourself: If someone wanted me to pay for something I'd already received and asked that payment be made in francs, drawn on a French bank, what would I do?
- They don't know *how much* to send. Can you quote the foreign exchange rate for Australian dollars off the top of your head?
- They are concerned about *your honesty.* If something goes wrong and you don't live up to your end of the bargain, they really have no recourse.
- They know that you are *hardly in a position* to pursue them if they don't pay.
- Your *promises of support* ring hollow. They can hardly just pick up the phone.

• They are concerned about *customs hassles* and fees. Depending on how you send the registration package and what documentation is in it, they may have to pay more than your registration fee to receive the package.

A perfect solution to these problems doesn't exist, but there are some things you can do to help. *Allow for a variety of payment options.* After using a publisher or registration service, the easiest methods for foreign customers seem to be:

• *Sending a check.* I haven't found a reasonable way to accept checks from anywhere but Canada. Try to find a bank that will accept Canadian checks written on Canadian banks without charging an extra premium. Canada is currently levying a "getting a package from the U.S." tax on anything that arrives, so current sales are low, but you can normally expect about 10 percent of your shareware sales to come from Canada. Other sales will come from Canada as well, depending on the spillover effect.

• *Using a credit card.* If you accept credit cards, be sure to include a signature line on your invoice. Currency conversion is fast and fair for both parties, and the customer has the right to protest the charge if you do not fill the order promptly. Be aware, however, that business credit cards are not a universal concept. In some countries (even Germany), credit cards are relatively rare; always offer a second choice. If you use this method, consider installing a fax machine: A signed order could be faxed and processed in the same day.

• *Mailing some of their domestic currency to you.* The U.S. Postal Service is scrupulously honest if not entirely accurate. The cost of certified or registered mail really isn't justified, so I encourage people to take the risk and simply mail the cash. If they want the security of special services, encourage them to use certified rather than registered mail; it is generally cheaper. *BusinessWeek* magazine publishes exchange rate tables for the Japanese yen, German mark, British pound, French franc, Canadian dollar, Swiss franc, and the Mexican peso in each issue. If you limit yourself to this list, you will have no trouble converting the funds at almost any national bank in the United States. Since I have to live with prices given in foreign currencies for long periods, I use the worst conversion rate in the last five years. I then add a percentage to the total to deal with the hassle of converting the currency at a local bank.

- *Mailing some U.S. currency to you.* Most foreign banks have U.S. currency readily available. You might notice that I don't add any additional service charge to foreign addresses that pay in U.S. currency. I figure that if they're willing to go through the hassle of obtaining U.S. dollars, I'll pick up the tab and the hassle of airmailing the package to them.

- *Obtaining an American Express money order payable in U.S. currency.* American Express offices are all over the world, and their money orders also are commonly available in foreign commercial banks. These instruments have the US MICR code across the bottom and, if you look at the very fine print, are payable through a Denver, Colorado, bank. You simply deposit them like any other check.

- *Sending American Express Travelers Cheques.* Obviously, you will have to price your product (with handling charge) equal to the denomination of the cheques ($10, $20, or $50). An additional problem is that these cheques usually are sold only in packages, so your customers then have to "refund" the balance with their bank. You might check with your bank to see if it will convert Barclay's (or any other) traveler's cheques as well.

- *Obtaining an international postal money order* from their local post office, again written in U.S. dollars. You can cash it at any U.S. post office without a service charge. Typically, this is a minor hassle for them—the clerk has to read the instruction book, since this service isn't used very often.

- *Sending a check drawn on a U.S. bank,* written in U.S. funds. Most large foreign banks have accounts in U.S. banks that they can write checks on as a courtesy to their customers. This is usually a major hassle for your customers, and typically is pretty expensive for them.

Be very specific about how the package will be shipped, so your customer can anticipate the customs charges. The next section discusses some of the details.

REGISTRATION SERVICES

Assuming that you're starting in shareware, set up a relationship with registration services in your likely foreign markets as soon as possible. This will let you accept foreign checks mailed to a foreign address. You will still be responsible for fulfillment and support. Registration services generally make no promotional efforts on your behalf.

Many disk vendors offer registration services at a nominal charge or no charge at all. The advantages to disk vendors are that they can offer convenience to their customers and they can build a list of shareware users, even if users obtained their first diskette from a competing firm. Some of the services currently available include:

PC Independent User Group
87 High Street
TONBRIDGE
Kent, TN9 1RX
ENGLAND

The DP Tool Club
102 rue des fusilles
59650 Villeneuve d'ascq
FRANCE

George Margelis
Budgetware
P.O. Box 496
Newtown, NSW 2042
AUSTRALIA

Garnet Brown
Pearl Agency
W-7845 Buggingen
GERMANY

Phillipe Mercier
Copysoft
Rue du Menuisier 109
1200 Bruxelles
BELGIUM

Michael Ingram
Distant Markets
Box 1149, 194 3803 Calgary Trail S.
Edmonton, Alberta CANADA T6J 5M8

Needless to say, contact these people and come to an agreement before you publish their names as registration points. Since shareware continues to circulate "forever," you also will want to ascertain that any services you use have been in business for a while and are completely reliable.

PUBLISHERS

As soon as your sales begin to grow in a foreign country, I suggest that you begin looking for a publisher in that country. I suggest that companies trying to do business in the United States from outside do the same. Why? Because there's no substitute for a local presence that knows the market. While you will have to pay a significant percentage of your gross receipts to publishers, good ones may increase your sales in their countries by an order of magnitude. Good publishers will do most of the things that you do for your product in your domestic market. They will:

- Be responsible for distribution within their market.
- Send out press releases and generally attempt to get some visibility for your product in their market.
- Accept sales locally (to them) in their name, at their address, then forward a percentage to you.
- Manufacture the product—disks, manuals, and so on.
- Provide support in their own country.
- Provide you with bug reports and suggestions as to how your product can better meet the needs of customers in their country.
- Provide the translation services for a foreign-language edition, if necessary.

There are a number of publishers out there. The trick is to find a good and honest one. Probably the best bet is to find an independent software company that reaches the same market that you do in yours and arrange a swap agreement. The key to making a publishing arrangement seems to be to find a publisher who understands your marketing methods, is willing to take the time to really understand and support the product, and has the experience to promote it successfully.

SHIPPING

Once you've been paid, how do you get the product to your customer?

Back to your local post office. Ask for copies of:

Publication 51 and Poster 51
"International Postal Rates and Fees"

and a sheet of Postal Service forms 2976, the little green customs stickers. Ship the product in a white catalog envelope, laser printed with your return address and the customer's address. Fill out form 2976 in this way:

Diskette $
Book $
Intellectual Property License $

In most cases, only the diskette is taxable to your customer. In some cases, the book (manual) will be. Intellectual property licenses almost never are taxable. By filling out the form in this way, you may have legitimately saved your customer a great deal of customs duty. Let prospective customers know that you are doing this in your documentation—those who hesitate to buy foreign (to them) software for fear of a 100 percent customs levy may be more likely to buy once they learn it won't be that expensive.

I have my laser printer set up (with 7-point type) to preprint the customs forms. I just add the dollar amount as I prepare the package.

Most of the time, this type of package will be treated as nontaxable personal mail. If you do include an invoice, break out the physical items on the invoice the same way as the customs form.

If your package is under a pound, ship it "Printed Matter and Small Packet—Airmail," which generally is cheaper than first-class airmail. If it is a pound or more, ship it "Air Parcel Post," in which case you will need to use a different customs sticker, 2966A, "Parcel Post Customs Declaration (Single form)."

Use the U.S. Postal Service, not Federal Express or UPS. Stuff going through the mail rarely gets hung up in customs, while packages shipped via the other services are assumed to be worth close inspection. Additionally, the customs forms used by these services are much more complicated than the postal service's green sticker.

Especially when you are getting a sale from somewhere outside of Western Europe, you'll sometimes get an address that isn't in the English alphabet—or if it is, you can't begin to figure out what it says. I have a somewhat unique way of dealing with that problem. The first step is to figure out what country the order came from. There are usually enough clues, either because of the form of payment or from the postage stamps. What I do then is to photocopy what was sent to me and tape it to the outgoing package, just putting the English-language version of the country name beneath it. This will get the package out of the United States, where, one hopes, the customer's postal service will be able to make sense of it.

PROGRAM DESIGN

Developing a product for eventual translation is at least twice the work. I know, because I developed a man/machine interface for a high-speed corrugated box folding and glueing machine that eventually had to work in English, French (both Canadian and what they speak in France), Spanish (Mexican, Caribbean, and South American), and German (thank God there's only one of them!). I approached the problem thinking that it was straightforward. Even though I couldn't write in these languages, we had translators, so all I had to do was to externalize the strings, right?

Wrong.

First off, both paper and character-based screen displays are fixed length. French especially seems to take at least twice as many characters to express the same thing as we do in English. Added to that, the French absolutely refused to abbreviate anything. (I'm not sure if this is true of all the French or the translator I was working with.) The result was that on report layouts, half the page was taken up by the header.

The other unanticipated issues had to do with national customs, character sets (collation came as a surprise), and little things such as failing to translate the Y/N and resulting keys when simply looking for a positive or negative response.

If you hope eventually to publish your software internationally, some things you might want to consider in your design include the following:

- For a good *overview* about what people might like to customize, take a close look at Control Panel—International in Windows.

- Have an explicit, published policy about whether all or part of your product may be *translated* by your foreign distributors.

- Both the sequence and the separator vary in *formatting dates.* It's easiest to allow users to choose these separately—that is, mmddyy, yymmdd, ddmmyy as possible sequence and a slash, dash, period, or space as the separator between them. My default date is always dd mmm yy, as in 23 May 92. This is acceptable for almost everyone.

- In general, you'll need to accommodate only am/pm or twenty-four-hour time formats. Again, the separator varies; usually this is a colon or a decimal.

- Both the decimal character and the delimiter character may vary in *formatting numbers.* The decimal is usually a period or a comma; the delimiter may be a period, a comma, an apostrophe, or a space. Remember that the number of decimals may vary tremendously if you are working with money. A good lunch for two in Mexico is a five-figure number; the decimal is hardly necessary. Be prepared to round to the user-defined number of decimal places (including negative 3). Some countries, such as Switzerland, need rounding up/down/truncating to 0.05.

- *Currency symbols* may be up to three characters in length. A space between the currency symbol and the number may or may not be used. The symbols may or may not float. They may be to the right or the left of the number. Many countries like the currency symbol left or right aligned with the number of digits in the amount.

• *Taxes* vary tremendously from one country to another. If you are producing a program that is involved in commerce, leave provision for a VAT (value added tax) at the very least. It may make sense to do some preliminary investigation before you begin the design phases. Legislatures around the world are very imaginative in where they think they can collect another percentage point or two.

• *Addresses* may be up to seven lines.

• *Postal codes* vary in length, in what characters are legitimate, and their position within the address. They are not necessarily between the "state" and the "country."

• *ISO paper sizes* (A1, A4, and so on) vary in the number of characters and lines available. Allow the user to configure the program to change maximum characters per line and lines per page on the printer.

• Don't forget the metric system of measurements.

• *Phone numbers* vary in length and whether international dialing codes are needed. If you can, just give the user a long free-format field.

• If you think there's a chance that you'll ever publish a foreign-language version, start out with *externalized strings*. The best way is probably to have an external table that is read in at runtime.

• Externalize your *response keys* as well. Y/N doesn't translate in many languages. While 1 or 0 seems to be more acceptable in Europe, it is unacceptable in the United States and Australia.

• If you include an *800 number* in your documentation, you also should include a local number. People outside the United States ordinarily cannot dial an 800 number.

• Don't try to have a domestic and an *international version*. You'll nearly double your work, and testing and support will become a nightmare. Software travels—you'll never manage to keep the different versions in their intended neighborhoods, anyway. Instead, use a configuration file to select how the program will run.

• Before committing to a *product name,* test its appropriateness by checking with someone familiar with the major languages. One U.S. consumer product translates to the slang word for "enema" in a common European language. If you doubt the need for this, find out what happened when Chevrolet attempted to sell its NOVA in Mexico. (No va translates to "doesn't go.")

• Do not *restrict input* to the ASCII lower 128. Many character sets use characters above 128.

• Don't make assumptions about the use of the *low ASCII* characters either. For instance, ASCII 20 is the paragraph symbol in the United States; in many countries, ASCII 21 is used for this purpose instead.

• Don't use *high ASCII* codes for graphic purposes. They have totally different shapes (that is, letters) when the KEYB definition changes. If you check the DOS 5 manual, you'll see that even the box codes (ASCII 192 through 218) are used for other things.

• With a non-English keyboard, *scan codes* will not give you the correct information. Use BIOS interrupt 16h or any DOS input function (don't hook BIOS interrupt 09h) for input instead. If the lower byte returned by 16h is zero, it is the extended code (arrow, function keys, and so on); otherwise, it is the ASCII code.

• Read up on DOS *interrupt 21/38h* (get country information; note that the high byte varies by DOS version) and DOS *interrupt 21/65h* (get extended country information), but recognize that your user may want to manipulate the way things work; Americans do work in Europe sometimes, after all. The best bet seems to be to set the initial defaults according to the country code, but then allow the user to change them as necessary. Don't assume that the keyboard corresponds to the country code either.

• If collation is important, allow the user to adjust the collation table. A simple ASCII compare will leave the non-English letters at the end of the collation sequence, instead of where they belong. If DOS interrupt 21/65h is available to you (it's available only in DOS 3.3 or later), you can use the country collating table supplied by it as your default.

• The *default* date, time and currency formats, currency symbol and format, thousands, decimal, date, and time separators, and upper/lower case table are all available through DOS interrupt 21/65h. If you support DOS versions prior to 3.3, you'll have to provide a configuration mechanism instead.

- The *British pound* (£) moves around the ASCII table depending upon what printer you are using. The British seem to be willing to put up with leaving the currency symbol blank or entering the ASCII code that their printer uses. I deal with the problem by having separate definitions for the screen and the printer currency symbols.

- Try to standardize on as small a vocabulary as possible, and avoid synonyms, even if they would make the language less boring. (This is good advice even in your domestic market.) If a single word to be used in a pull-down menu has a list of possible nuances of meaning, it will be troublesome for people not familiar with the language. If possible, choose the word closest to a synonym in other languages.

- Don't use @, #, and & at all. They don't mean the same thing in other countries. Mathematical symbols used in a mathematical context are safe.

- In Windows you have lots of user preferences set by Control Panel, which are worth using at every available opportunity. If you don't use SDK, borrow a copy of the article in the SDK help called "International Applications" under Overviews.

- Simply put, give up on all of your character code editing with the exception of checking numeric (ASCII 48 through 57) and nonnumeric. Anything else goes.

- The DOS and Windows character sets have subtle differences—and since Windows uses the DOS character set for file names, you will need to be prepared to convert from one to the other in Windows applications where file names include upper ASCII characters.

- Unless you really know what you're doing, don't attempt to support languages where they write from right to left or have multibyte characters.

- It depends on the application, of course, but I've found that most northern Europeans are willing to work with a program whose interface is in English, so long as they can use their own language for the actual data.

- The French, Italian, and Spanish seem to insist on an interface in their own language, but represent such a small market that they're not usually worth pursuing. My general conclusion is that, unless you're endowed with great resources and are targeting a very large market, the optimal solution is to externalize your strings, try to internationalize the program otherwise (time, paper sizes, and so on), but delay the actual translation until someone volunteers to fund it.

- In the meantime, try to keep the entire system as terse as possible. This will reduce the amount that needs to be understood by your non-English speaking audience and also translated later.

In any case, I'd certainly crack the problem of who's going to sell and support the Italian version before I even thought of attempting a translation.

If you're intent upon doing a translation anyway:

Chris Bowyer suggests, "Use the standard words for standard things. IBM's CUA Advanced User Interface Design Guide contains lists of useful words like file and cancel in several languages. Give a copy to the translator, and don't let them disagree on linguistic grounds—if it's the word that other applications use, then it's the right word in this context."

- Avoid trying to build messages. If you must, define the variables very precisely (part of speech, and so on) and allow the position of the variable to float. If you must use two variables, try to construct two messages. Then test. A lot.

- The [Alt] key combinations ([Alt]+[f] to bring down the file menu, for example) basically require a table and the ability to dynamically allocate the space. In Windows menus, accented letters don't work unless they occur as a single key on your user's keyboard. (Since users may not have the local national keyboard, they are probably best avoided.) Needless to say, [Ctrl] key shortcuts must follow the same rules.

- Have a plan for how you're going to handle the incremental translations that occur after the initial release. Also decide in advance how you're going to cure bugs in both versions simultaneously.

- Translators have a real love of language. This may be a good thing, but it's likely to be a major support headache if you don't keep them in check. Make sure that they understand computers, and the application they are translating, and make absolutely sure that they're willing to translate at a sixth-grade level—both because it makes the instructions for the program clearer and because the translated version may not be your users' first language.

- Avoid humor, especially puns. It doesn't translate. When you give an example, check to be sure that it translates.

- Icons are dangerous. Trash cans don't look the same the world around, and they're used for different things. As an example, Microsoft used to publish a utility called Shaker to randomly move movable memory; the icon was a picture of a milkshake. Outside of the United States, milkshakes are unknown—and they wouldn't be served in that type of container in any case.

- Direct manipulation of the user interface (such as drag and drop to move a file from one directory to another) avoids linguistic and cultural conventions much more effectively than a command button with a picture of a moving file on it (or is it a locomotive?).

Chris Bowyer also told me much more about collation sequences than I ever imagined existed:

> Lexicographical comparison (what most people call alphabetical order) means treating differences of case and accents as significant only if the word is otherwise the same. In DOS, you need a table of the lexicographical significance of each character depending on the character set in use. Going further, alphabetical order varies according to the user's language; in English O umlaut is an accented variant of O, in German it sorts as Œ, in Swedish it is a separate letter coming after Z. You may decide it's not worth doing this properly for most purposes, but you need to be careful about what you claim about alphabetical order, especially if your application is a dictionary—or maybe an address book. In Windows, the lstrcmp function does the job well enough, and since it's used by other applications, it's probably better to use it than to be picky. The SDK function description is wrong about what this does, but there is a better explanation in the International Applications article. Incidentally, if you're sorting names, there are odd rules for the treatment of apostrophes, spaces, contractions like Mc or St, and these differ in different countries. One source of this information is the local phone book.

- If you can think of the keyboard as a source of characters like a file, rather than an array of switches, you shouldn't have any problems. Keyboards can have different numbers of keys, can produce different scan codes, the Shift, Lock, and Alt keys behave differently, the right Alt key often generates Ctrl+Alt for extra graphics, some punctuation characters may not exist or may require extra keystrokes, even the main letter block has several different arrangements (the French for "qwerty" is "azerty"). Also, don't forget laptops where the cursor and numeric pad keys are sometimes doubled with the main keypad and so require extra keystrokes. If you need physical keystrokes for your application, the best way is to let the user configure them by pressing the keys, like the better games do. For defaults, stick to the main keypad plus up, down, and left and right arrows; avoid punctuation and function keys over 10.

CHAPTER 13

Selling to the United States

◆◆◆ The first and last things I will tell you in this section will be to get a U.S. publisher. The United States is an enormous country (both in size and population) that has historically been isolated from the rest of the world. In the United States there has been very little emphasis on foreign language or cultural skills because:

- of our political and geographic isolation.
- there is intense pressure on immigrants to learn American English and the "American way."
- we are a country that has generally been able to be economically self-sufficient because of our natural and human resources.
- export/import forms a much smaller portion of the American economy than in most other countries in the world.

Most Americans haven't the vaguest idea of how to purchase something from outside our borders, and wonder if it's even legal. If you quote a price in marks, lira, or francs, they'll have no idea how much money you're asking, the huge numbers will scare them, and they'll never trust that they'll ever see their money again.

Having said all this, I hope that the following advice will hold you in good stead while you find a U.S. publisher. Quite honestly, you'll have better luck if you are selling from northern Europe, Australia, or New Zealand. If you are shipping from the European Community and live near a border, check out the postal rates in your neighboring country. They may be different enough to warrant a trip.

PAYMENT METHODS

Having said all that, if you want to persist, your first step will be to quote a price in U.S. dollars, accept Visa and/or MasterCard, and prominently display a promise that buyers can reverse the charge with their bank if they're not completely satisfied. The reason for this is that American consumer protection laws allow buyers to reverse a charge if merchandise ordered through the mail is not delivered. With any other means of payment (such as check or money order), they effectively have no recourse if the product fails to arrive or is defective.

SOFTWARE PUBLISHERS

It isn't as if there are people in the adopt-a-struggling-extra-territorial-software-house business all over the United States Finding a publisher will take some hunting, and making the deal work will take a great deal of effort (on both sides). In all probability, you'll end up with some kind of reciprocal agreement with a U.S.-based publisher that is trying to reach the same market as you, but is not in direct competition. This will allow you to "upsell" the other's products to each other's installed base.

Assuming that you have an English-language version of your product, your best bet is probably to start in the shareware channel. Use a U.S. registration service, so that people will feel comfortable that a million zillion lira won't be charged to their credit card.

Get connected. If at all possible, get a CompuServe account. In the United States, the academic intellectuals inhabit the Internet; the entrepreneurs are on CompuServe. It will be on CompuServe that you'll find the people serving the U.S. market you want to reach. An electronic connection will be essential in transmitting communications, data files, and software.

In Germany, GEnie may be cheaper. You should understand, however, that the American user base for GEnie is a small fraction of CompuServe's.

If you have a decent command of written English, you're way ahead of the game. Most people in the United States take a couple of years of a foreign language in their early teens and never use it again. Most of that training was in learning how to buy tulips in a railroad station—not very useful in discussing software. Most of your communications will be written, either through one of the information services or through the Internet.

Both CompuServe and GEnie have local nodes in Europe and Australia. You can write them at:

CompuServe
P.O. Box 20212
Columbus, OH 43220 USA
(614) 457-8650

GEnie Maketing
General Electric Information Services
401 North Washington Street
P. O. Box 6403
Rockville, MD 20849-6403 USA

Assuming that your product is already in English and that the publisher is taking on duplication, marketing, fufillment, and support, a decent royalty will be in the range of 5 percent to 10 percent of gross revenues. This may not sound like a lot, but that's what you'll have to offer in order to get your prospective partner's full attention.

The optimal price in the United States will probably be much lower than the optimal price in your country. There is tremendous competition here, and consumers' expectations have been permanently changed.

Get a U.S. publisher—or move to the United States. There is no other way you're going to have the presence necessary to do justice to this market.

CHAPTER 14

Packaging Your Product and Shipping It

SETTING UP YOUR WORKSPACE

❖❖❖ If you're lucky, you'll have a room to devote to your new business. My workspace is 7 by 8 feet. I'll confess that I have a real preference for a small space; I find that it both cleans up faster and forces me to throw out things before the mess becomes overwhelming.

Along one of the 7-foot walls, I have two file cabinets, one in each corner. Between them is my "desktop," a surface I fabricated out of pine shelving. The desktop is 25 inches from the floor (a comfortable height for typing, and still high enough for writing). It is 33 inches deep by 48 inches wide. To my left, I have my "development" computer with monitor on top of one of the file cabinets. To my right is my "duplication/testing" computer and a small HP laser printer. Power bars are attached to the underside of the desktop so that I can turn each of the machines on easily. An a/b switch is connected to each of the computers' parallel ports, which then runs through an external tape drive to the printer.

I can use this tape drive to back up either computer. I also find it useful for moving files or directories; I simply back up from one computer and then restore to the other.

I wouldn't want the work area to be any wider; at this width, it is possible to work on one computer while duplicating disks on the other; if it was wider, it would be too much of a stretch (literally).

Directly behind me is my physical storage system; I started out with conventional shelves and discovered that they really didn't work for me because I needed to store a lot of things that don't really fit on a shelf, such as shipping supplies, media, product, cassettes (video, audio, and computer), software packages, laser toner cartridges, odd pieces of paper ripped out of things, magazines, and the like. Instead, I eventually ended up with a system of shelves running the length of the wall, 1 foot deep and 5 levels high (on 14.5-inch centers).

On these shelves go "project boxes," which contain materials that belong together. Staples sells cardboard bins with handles that are 12 inches high, 14 inches deep, and 22 inches wide. I use these boxes for archiving things such as software. In the two years between publication of the *The ShareWare Book* and this volume, everything that might serve as material for the new edition went into one of these boxes: magazine articles, diskettes, direct mail, software packaging, loose pieces of paper, audio and video tapes—it all went into the box. Another large box contains "working" shipping supplies; the large cartons the stuff comes in go onto the highest shelf and replenish the "working" carton. Other boxes hold various products ready for shipping.

I also use a lot of 9 x 12-inch boxes of various heights that serve for storing magazines, catalogs, and other papers, filed by subject area. For the magazines that I archive, each has its own box.

Most periodicals hang around for about five months. I hold them temporarily by having two more Staples boxes (nested one on top of the other) on the floor in a corner. As magazines, junk mail, and other stuff that is a potential resource comes in, it gets looked at, ripped up as necessary (putting stuff I want to save in the project box), and then tossed into the top box. When the top box is full, I swap it with the bottom one and dump the contents of the oldest box. When I see some Email telling me about an article in a magazine that I receive but don't really read, I can usually retrieve it as long as it's still in one of the boxes.

On the wall to my left (about 5 feet off the ground), I have a wall-mounted phone/answering machine with a long cord. This keeps my phone off my desk (I used to look for it frantically under the listings every time it rang) and allows me some mobility while I talk on the phone. I can reach the dial pad from my chair but usually use the auto-dialer built into the integrated software package I use.

Of course, I do have bookshelves anywhere there is a bit of space.

I have two chairs: a desk swivel model and a rocker. I find that the rocker gives my back a rest after long hours at the keyboard; it's also my primary reading chair when it isn't full of unread mail.

If you have a family, you'll have to think long and hard about just how close you really want to be to them while you're working. I'm not very "interruptable," but have found that I really treasure the moments when my four-year-old comes in to show me her latest accomplishment. She has learned to knock when the door is closed.

Telephone

I do suggest you have a separate line for your software business. If nothing else, it's nice to have an answering machine pick up at the other end of the house when distributors from Australia call at two in the morning. A separate line also allows you to deduct your telephone costs much more cleanly on your U.S. income taxes.

The question of whether to have a business or residential line is more complicated. If you are also running another business (such as my consulting business) that needs public visibility, a business line is a must. You can get a yellow pages listing or advertisement only if you have a business line. On the other hand, few start-up software businesses need yellow page ads, advertise their numbers in any significant way, or need public visibility. If you are doing business under your own name, chances are good that you will save some money by putting in a second residential line, especially if the phone company charges for local calls for business lines and not for residential lines. Once you start calling CompuServe, GEnie, and local bulletin boards, the message units will add up quickly.

Your local telephone company will be very aggressive in saying that you must have a business line if you use it for any business, so don't ask.

Assuming you do opt for the business line, you can offer toll-free (800 number) calling, and you won't need an extra telephone line to do it. Call your long-distance carrier and ask about low-volume INWATS telephone service. Typically, you'll pay a base fee of about $20 per month, and then something under $.25 a minute for the actual service. Long-distance carriers that offer this service include:

AT&T	(800) 222-0400
MCI	(800) 888-0800
Metromedia	(800) 275-0833
Sprint	(800) 877-2000

A toll-free number makes sense only if you have a credit card merchant account and someone in the office always ready to accept a credit card registration by phone. Given the costs involved, I would wait until I had a service taking fifty credit card registrations per month before I considered taking it in house.

Keep in mind that this line will be used for support, no matter what you say in your documentation. If you choose to have the toll-free service come in on your regular business telephone, you usually can't tell who (you or the caller) is paying for the call. If you can find a service offering a different ring pattern when the inbound toll-free number is being used, it may be worth a higher fee.

If you sell to business, you'll want to consider a fax line as well, especially if you will accept faxed purchase orders.

SUPPLIES

Prices for *disks* vary tremendously from vendor to vendor. I have found the following vendors to be cheap (currently about $.20 each for 360Kb and $.35 each for 720Kb diskettes), with generally acceptable quality for distribution purposes:

Best Computer Supplies
P.O. Box 1826
Oakdale, CA 95361
(800) 544-3472

MEI/Micro Center
1100 Steelwood Road
Columbus, OH 43212
(800) 634-3478

A good source for preformatted diskettes (about $.04 more) is:

Y. Gean Co.
1930 Junction Avenue
San Jose, CA 95131
(800) 879-9536
(404) 456-8848

If you do buy preformatted diskettes, buy them in advance, let them sit for a few weeks, then spot-check them for viruses. Since these suppliers do check for viruses, any you may discover are almost always new ones not yet included in the virus scanners' tables. Waiting a few weeks before checking your order for viruses gives you an opportunity to hear any official, media, and/or word-of-mouth reports of shipments of infected preformatted diskettes.

A telephone headset can be handy if you'd like both hands on the keyboard and don't want a neck ache. You can buy one from:

Plantronics
345 Encinal Street
P.O. Box 635
Santa Cruz, CA 95061
(800) 544-4660

If you work from your home and can't isolate yourself from household noise, you may want to consider a telephone headset with a noise-canceling microphone and dual earphones. Hello Direct sells this type of headset for $185:

Hello Direct Inc.
140 Great Oaks Boulevard
San Jose, CA 95119-1347
(408) 972-1990
(800) 444-3556

For *disk duplication,* the cheapest (under \$.40 for 360Kb and under \$.65 for 720Kb with your label attached) and most reliable source I have found is Bob Falk. Since disk prices can change dramatically in a short time, you may wish to call him for a quotation:

Falk Data Systems
5322 Rockwood Court
El Paso, Texas 79932-2412
(915) 584-7670

I use *catalog envelopes* for sending disks most of the time. These are white envelopes, 6 × 9 inches, with the opening on the long side. They go through a laser printer easily and reliably. My local discount office supply is Staples, which sells them for \$17 for a box of 500. If you need more or can't find a local source, Business Envelope offers them for about \$40 per 1,000. It can be reached at:

Business Envelope Manufacturers
900 Grand Boulevard
Deer Park, NY 11729
(800) 275-4400

I rarely use *diskette mailers,* but when I buy them I use MailSafe (800-527-0754). Their mailers are marginally lighter than others I've used, saving postage, and cost a little less, about \$140 per 1,000. If you will be using a lot of mailers, the following company offers 6 × 6-inch mailers (weighing less than the 6 × 9-inch ones) at a competitive price once you are buying 2,500 or more:

Pack & Wrap
466 Derby Avenue
West Haven, CT 06516
(800) 541-9782

If you use a laser printer, LaserRun *labels* are comparable to Avery at half the price, if you can find them. Quill labels sell at a comparable price but don't stick very well. Quill offers good prices on toner cartridges and on a cartridge refill service:

Quill Corporation
P.O. Box 94080
Palatine, IL 60094-4080
(708) 634-4800

A second source for *laser supplies* is Lyben. It carries Nashua low-speed laser labels for $14.95 for 100 sheets and toner cartridges at competitive prices:

Lyben Computer Systems
1150 Maplelawn
P.O. Box 1237
Troy, MI 48099
(313) 649-4500

You can *shrink wrap* without owning a machine. Simply buy a roll of shrink wrap from a packaging supplier, then use the highest power hair blow-dryer you can find. This will be more than adequate for low-volume production. Eventually you'll need a shrink-wrap machine. Many authors report that they got their best deal at a trade show. You can get information about inexpensive shrink-wrap machines (low volume, can be put on the kitchen table) from:

Chiswick Trading
33 Union Avenue
Sudbury, MA 01776-2246
(800) 225-8708

AJM
1600 Wyatt Drive, #12
Santa Clara, CA 95054
(408) 980-8631
(800) 858-4131

BrownCor
14101 N.W. 4th Street
Sunrise, FL 33325
(800) 327-2278

Another way to package is to use plastic bags you can buy (low volume) from the grocery store or (high volume) from a local industrial supply firm. You can then heat-seal the end of the bag with a battery-operated "EZ-Sealer 2000" ($12.95) from:

American Family (National Syndications, Inc.)
37 11th Avenue
Box 4175, Dept. TR42-VA
Huntington Station, NY 11746

This company tries to be a *software publisher's supermarket*. It carries everything from disk duplication equipment to license envelopes to packaging:

Mediatechnics Ltd.
1320 Chase Street #3
Algonquin, IL 60102
(708) 658-5080
(800) 227-5080

If you really don't want to do it yourself, this company does soup to nuts design, duplication, and assembly of your software package, and then ships to your customers:

Caroline Web, Ltd.
2402 Caroline
Houston, TX 77004
voice: (713) 659-6470
fax: (713) 659-6429

MANUALS

Don't run right out to a printer with an order for 1,000 manuals supporting version 1.0. You'll end up throwing most of them away. A number of *binding technologies* are available to you. The most commonly used in software are "saddle stitching" and the "perfect" binding method. For a manual less than 64 pages long, saddle stitching probably makes the most sense. This is a simple binding process where the pages are folded at the center of the book, then stapled. You've seen this type of binding in mail order catalogs and modem documentation. The upper limit to a saddle-stitched book varies by the weight of the paper and what you're willing to put up with, but a reasonable limit is usually reached somewhere between 84 and 128 pages. Perfect binding is the type of binding typically used in paperback books—the pages are glued to the cover, resulting in a rectangular spine. The lower limit for perfect binding is usually around 65 pages, the upper limit is typically as high as 800 pages.

Your local quick copy shop can produce saddle-stitched manuals quickly but not cheaply. If you are just releasing version 1.0 and you don't have your first review yet, your local shop is your best bet. Most likely you will be making many changes to this first manual.

If you will be using a local copy shop, the first step is to print a copy of the manual in landscape mode, with the page set at 8.5 inches high and 11 inches wide; the right margin is set to 6 inches. This can result in a lot of wasted paper, but the pages come out straight. Early versions of my documentation printed on 8.5-inch high by 5.5-inch wide paper, printed in portrait mode, had chronic problems with the print running uphill or down. An ideal method is to print one page on the left half of each side of the paper, then cut the paper in half. I use a small (12 by 12-inch) paper cutter originally sold for photo-trimming purposes.

Divide the total number of pages in your manual by 4 (rounding up, not down, if necessary). Gather that many pieces of scrap paper in a neat pile and fold the stack in half vertically. Number the pages of your "dummy" booklet with a pencil. When you're done, each individual page of the dummy, front and back, will indicate the sequence your actual page layout must follow as you assemble it for the printer.

The next step is to join your half-sheet pages in the indicated sequence. You will need transparent tape (not the cheap glossy kind), liquid White-Out, a reasonably sharp pair of scissors, a scrupulously clean working surface, and a clean, dry pair of hands. Place a set of pages (double-check the correct sequence from your dummy page) facedown and side by side to form an 8.5 by 11-inch whole; join the halves snugly with a tiny piece of tape near the top, middle, and bottom.

Now flip the page over so it's face-up again. Cover the center "seam" with a strip of tape at least 9 inches long, so it extends over the edges of the paper. Use the scissors to trim off the excess tape. With a thumbnail, rub the strip of tape with enough pressure to make it "transparent." Use small amounts of the liquid White-Out to hide any stray marks, pieces of lint caught under the tape, the dark line where the two halves join, and anything else you don't want reproduced on your manual page.

You may find it useful in this process to have a nonreproducing light-blue felt-tip marker, available at any decent art supply shop. Assuming you use this pen with a light touch, any notation you make on paper will be invisible to the camera's eye and will not reproduce.

Once you have assembled all your page halves into wholes as just described, you will want to clip the "fronts" to the "backs" so the printer knows how you want your pages printed. Referring again to each side of each page of your dummy, pair the appropriate front and back pages of your manual so that the two pages are back to back. To protect the paper surfaces, I first fold yellow stickybacks over the two edges of the pages at the ends. Then I slide a paper clip over each stickyback to hold the pages together.

Finally, I carry my dummy along to show to the printer just in case he or she still doesn't get it.

All this work for a 8.5 × 5.5-inch manual! Why not just print 8.5 by 11 inches in the first place? There are a number of reasons:

- You will save in printing your covers, since twice as many will fit on the press's plate.
- This allows for much easier shipping. Using the smaller size, the book acts as a good stiffener for the disk and fits in your 6- × 9-inch catalog envelopes without being big and thin enough to present a shipping problem or encourage the mailcarrier to bend it anyway.
- Most shelving systems used for computer documentation have very little space high enough to accommodate a book that tall.
- A book of that size requires larger type, resulting in more paper used and, thus, higher printing and shipping costs for you.
- Unless you are writing a very long manual, the book will be so skinny that it will look strange and won't be thick enough for a title on the binding.

Design your cover (more on that later), take the whole thing to your local quick copy shop, and have it make up a dozen (usually the lowest number at which you get any break for quantity).

A good resource for learning to work effectively with printers is:

Getting It Printed:
How to Work With Printers and Graphic Arts Services . . .
Beach, Shepro & Russon
Coast to Coast Books
2934 Northeast 16th Avenue
Portland, OR 97212

Once you have reached the point where your manual is many pages, or you are ready to commit to larger quantities (at least in the hundreds), perfect binding starts to make economic sense. In large quantities, this method is actually cheaper because, while the setup time for perfect binding is considerable, the unit labor costs are lower than for saddle stitching.

Once you're ready to start thinking in terms of hundreds of manuals, get a price quotation from:

Camelot Book Factory
39-B Coolidge Avenue
Ormond Beach, FL 32174
(904) 672-5672

It specializes in runs of 100 to 300 books and offers either saddle stitching or perfect binding. Turn-around time is three to four weeks, and it will quote a price generally less than half of what local quick copy shops charge. In quantity 300, a 48-page saddle-stitched book will run about $.68 each; and a 96-page, 5.5-by-8.5-inch perfect-bound book will run about $1.95 each, plus shipping. If possible, I'd advise you not to use Camelot for a perfect binding. While I was otherwise satisfied with their work, I received a substantial number of complaints when I used this company for the first run of *The ShareWare Book*. The books looked fine, but the pages fell out.

For book runs in the thousands, contact:

BookMasters
638 Jefferson Street
P.O. Box 159
Ashland, OH 44805
voice: (800) 537-6727
International: (419) 289-6051
fax: (419) 281-1731

Patterson Printing
1550 Territorial Road
Benton Harbor, MI 49022
(616) 925-2177

Whitehall Company
1200 S. Willis Avenue
Wheeling, IL 60090
(312) 541-9290
(800) 321-9290

In quantity 2,000, a 96-page book will cost about $.68 plus shipping.

I used BookMasters for the second printing of *The ShareWare Book*. I felt that it did a very good job of handholding with this novice publisher, and the number of books with noticeable defects was under 1 percent.

If you'd like to get bids from local printers, there is always the yellow pages, of course—but a very effective way of *finding printers* that are likely to be competitive is to look in:

Directory of Short-Run Printers
John Kremer
Ad-Lib Publications
P.O. Box 1102
Fairfield, IA 52556

You'll want to use a commercial artist to *design your cover* when you can afford it. A professionally designed cover makes a better impression when your customers are recommending your product, when reviewers are considering it, and if you plan to use other marketing channels. The person who did the *ASP Shareware Catalog* comes highly recommended. She is:

Suzanne Bilodeau
5709 Pebble Beach
El Paso, TX 79912
(915) 581-9608

Or you may want to consider:

Attic Graphics
908 W. North Street
Muncie, IN 47303
(317) 289-7126

If you use a perfect binding, remember to find out how wide the spine will be. Your printer can tell you that, or you can just measure a paperback book of about the same size. Then provide an image for the spine as well as the front and back covers.

PACKAGING YOUR SOFTWARE

If you really mean to use only direct channels to distribute your product, packaging is a reasonably minor point: The product just needs to survive shipping and not disappoint the purchaser. If you intend to use shelfware channels as well, the visual and marketing appeal of the product will directly affect sales.

One of the trade-offs in packaging is between strength and storage. Boxes that will lie flat for you typically deal less well with the rough handling they may get on a retailer's shelf.

Your choice of package types includes the following:

- *Shrink-wrap* the manual with disks inside. Put the license agreement on the back so that it is visible. This is certainly the cheapest way to package a product, but it doesn't do much for presentation on a retail shelf.

- Plastic vacuum-formed (*clamshell*) cases can give a very professional look at a competitive price for low-volume products, since the case is always the same—you just insert your printed cover under the clear plastic. The case opens up like a book and has preformed areas to hold your disks, manuals, and other items.

Many of the Hewlett-Packard fonts are packaged this way. They run about $25 for 100 plus the cost of printing the paper cover.

• Cardboard *boxes* are widely available. You have a choice of the rigid ones requiring a great deal of space to store or the folding kind that fall apart under rough handling. Generally speaking, this is for high-volume, stable products. Printing the boxes requires a lot of setup time, so they are cheap in high quantities but very expensive in low quantities.

• Using a box and *sleeve,* you can either have just your company name printed on the box or simply buy generic boxes as you need them. You then can have the sleeve printed in colors much cheaper than you could the top and bottom of a box. These sleeves also fold flat, saving storage space. If you use this technique, think about having stickers made up to paste on the ends of the box not covered by the sleeve, since packages are frequently returned to the shelf with the end facing out. If you can order in enough volume and get the printing done cheaply, it's possible to come in under $1 per package using this method.

• The *slipcase* is the method you'll recognize from early IBM products. It uses a ring binder that slips into a box with an open side, then is shrink-wrapped. This is an expensive method and is rarely used anymore, but it does provide a very good "thump factor."

Marshall Magee (of Automenu) puts great emphasis on the thump factor—the size and weight of the package. It's possible to get too heavy and too big; but the larger the package is, the more shelf space it will get. If the package is too light, people will resist paying the same price as those of packages with more "thump." I laughed at first, but I think he's right.

The following company sends a catalog with no prices in it, but (especially for low volumes) it is a good source of software packaging:

DataEnvelope
490 Division Street
Campbell, CA 95008
(408) 374-9720   (800) 544-4417

A very inexpensive printer of full-color inserts (2,500 for $325)
is:

Challenge Graphics, Inc.
18 Connor Lane
Deer Park, NY 11729
(516) 586-0171
(800) 242-5364

Print large quantities of the items requiring full-color printing
(usually the box and the cover of the manual). Leave off these
materials the information that might change, such as menus, new
compatibilities, special awards, or perhaps even price. Stickers
(especially under shrink wrap) usually can serve to add this
information (and more color) later. The primary reason for this
strategy is because the setup costs for a four-color press are typically
80 percent to 90 percent of all the costs on runs of under 10,000
copies. For instance, a recent quotation for full-color covers was:

Quantity	Total Price
1,000	$2,260
2,500	$2,630
5,000	$3,120

Because of the tremendous setup costs built into the pricing,
you will save money by printing as many as you can in each run.
To avoid having to reprint or throw out materials, plan to use
preprinted stickers to identify the version number on the package,
and print the number on an inside page of the manual. You also
might consider printing your package sleeves with secondary
benefits featured in a separate area of white space as a kind of a
graphic place holder. Then, should you be chosen "PC Week
Editor's Choice," you can put a foil sticker announcing your award
right over that (expendable) space.

On the other hand, the setup for black ink alone is reasonably low, as is the setup for binding. Bound materials done only in black can be printed more or less as needed.

One of the best ways of getting started in packaging is to browse the shelves at a very large software retailer. Note the packages you really like that are being used by the smaller software houses. Then call their marketing directors, explain who you are, and ask them to refer you to their outside packaging suppliers (design and production). Most people will be pleased at the compliment and, assuming you're not a direct competitor, will be happy to tell you who did the work.

While you roam the larger software stores to research packaging, take an especially careful look at the products in the section where you'd like your product to appear. You may want to use some of the visual cues to fit in, while picking one or two to differentiate yourself. For instance, if the products in this section tend to be printed in blue and white, with horizontal color stripes, you might choose to use either red and white horizontal stripes or a blue and white diagonal motif. The aim is to look as if you belong in the club but have fresher ideas.

You will need a professional for the artwork, but spend some time developing your own ideas before you start paying him or her by the hour. If you can't describe what you're looking for, you may be billed for a lot of false starts. Go to the artist with a couple of very rough designs and some examples of existing packages you like and explain why you like them. Then spend an hour or so kicking ideas around before you leave the artist alone in the studio.

I learned this lesson the hard way with my first business card as a consultant. I needed a conventional design that would assure prospective clients that I wasn't a techno-nerd who was going to stop their factories with half-baked software. The first round of designs were very progressive, avant-garde, and high tech, since that is what the designer assumed a computer consultant would want.

Mock-up your package, take it to your local software super-store, put it on the shelf—try it backward or sideways. Does it look like it belongs? Does it stand out? Take pictures for review. Next take it to your local dog grooming or bridal shop (or wherever else your potential customers shop) and check to see how it looks there.

Here's a list of ideas to consider in designing your packaging:

• *Keep it clean and simple.* Don't clutter your design with loads of fussy details. Avoid mixing and matching multiple typefaces in a single design. A strong and attractive package uses white space wisely to integrate its other elements, such as blocks of color, captions, and areas of text.

• *Include your lead, or motto,* in a noticeable spot. Use color, size, and location to make it the first thing a browser sees. Your motto describes the single benefit the buyer wants most, such as: "Cures Procrastination!"

• *Put your product logo* on all six sides of the box. Use stickers if necessary.

• *List numbers* (that look like stock numbers); they are impressive to some people. It makes you look like a large company.

• *Cite "made in USA"* (assuming this is true) somewhere on the package, both for sales overseas and for the convenience of your customers trying to reenter the country.

• *Include a screen capture* that lets browsers see at a glance what the product does. Make sure this screen is not too busy—that could be perceived as "hard to learn."

• However, avoid (or at least test) using color photography of your screen. Because of the mechanical attributes of four-color printing, it simply won't look the way you expect.

• *Include two reviewer quotes.* You may want to use stickers for these as you get better ones.

• *Print a believable user endorsement* or two. Use a gushy one with slightly awkward language so people will know it wasn't written by a copywriter.

• List *other products* by your company, even if they are not retail. The primary purpose is to make your company look big, stable, and professional. The secondary purpose is to gain name recognition for your other products.

- *Include a green* (recycle) *notice.* Surely the package contains recycled-something! Or could be recycled. . . .

- *List what the product does.* Note the position on this list. The reason this appears on the package at all is to make the benefits claims more believable.

- *Include UPC and ISBN numbers and bar codes.* (More on these later.)

- *State the hardware and system software requirements.*

- If appropriate, *provide information on compatibility.* Will it run under Windows? What printers?

- *State your guarantee*—again, so the customer purchases your product rather than leaves the store merely "thinking about" it.

- *Include your address and phone number,* so stores can order more or ask questions.

- *Print the version number* on a sticker.

- *Name the media size* enclosed in the box.

- If you anticipate selling through channels that are not computer stores, *test your packaging* with a sample of wholesalers and retailers who might carry your product. Each industry has its own idiosyncrasies, and it will serve you well to work with them. Be sure that you have completely described the product and the hardware requirements. These stores won't have clerks who know that PC-DOS and MS-DOS are virtual synonyms, and they won't have a computer handy to demo the package.

If you will be selling through retail channels, you will need a UPC (*Universal Product Code*) symbol on your packaging. It costs $300 (if your sales are still under $2 million) and doesn't take very long to get. On the other hand, the information (location and printing specifications, for instance) provided as a part of the acceptance process is something you will need in designing your packaging, so getting one should be an early step in the process of entering the retail marketplace. If you don't have one, you will be making life difficult for both your wholesalers and retailers. Some will charge you a 5 percent fee to make one up and attach it to the package. You can get information about acquiring a UPC symbol and the necessary forms from:

Uniform Code Council
8163 Old Yankee Road, Suite J
Dayton, OH 45458
(513) 435-3870

On the other hand, bookstores (this includes Software Etc.) have a totally different method of product identification, the *ISBN* (international standard book number). Getting a number typically takes a couple of months and costs $100. You can get more information about getting an ISBN from:

R. R. Bowker—ISBN Agency
121 Chanlon Road
New Providence, NJ 07974
(908) 665-2849

To keep things more interesting, many articles sold through bookstores use the *Bookland EAN* (European Article Number), which uses a UPC code based on the ISBN. You can obtain more information about this from:

Book Industry Systems Advisory Committe (BISAC)
160 Fifth Avenue
New York, NY 10010
(212) 929-1379

If you are going to distribute your product through retail channels, you're likely to need both product identifiers. If you have existing packaging, labels can be printed and affixed later to take care of this problem.

It is almost certainly cheaper to include both disk sizes in shelfware versions of your software than to stock two items. If you ship only one size (many software houses now ship only 3.5-inch diskettes), include an option to swap the disks for the other size. A postage-paid mailer that doubles as a registration card is a good way to do this. Remember that using a single-size disk does deny "immediate gratification" to some part of your market. Sales may increase enough to justify wasting the 5.25-inch diskettes.

Getting people to send in their registration cards is very important—this is your mailing list for offering upgrades. You might want to pay the postage on the card as well as offer some sort of bonus when the card is received.

SHIPPING

If your customer is willing to pay the extra cost of overnight delivery, you'll need one of these numbers:

Airborne Express	(800) 426-2323
DHL Worldwide Express	(800) 225-5345
Emery Worldwide	(800) 443-6379
Federal Express	(800) 238-5355
United Parcel Service (UPS)	(800) 346-0106
U.S. Postal Service	(800) 222-1811

Most of these carriers will come to your home and accept your credit card for payment.

United Parcel Service charges a monthly fee for pickups. Unless you are shipping large numbers of packages, or they are very heavy, the convenience of the U.S. Postal Service is probably worth the extra cost, if there is one. Additionally, the post office has a special "book rate" that can be used for your packages (assuming you're sending a book), which is generally cheaper than any other method.

The U.S. Postal Service (USPS)

The U.S. Postal Service (USPS) is a government-owned service. By law, it has a monopoly on individual written communications. This is called first-class mail; a postcard is $.19 and a sealed letter of up to 1 ounce in weight is $.29.

Second-class mail is a class reserved for periodicals where identical pieces go to thousands of different addresses. Magazines and newspapers fit into this category.

Third-class mail is a class reserved for mailings where identical pieces go to thousands of different addresses. "Junk" (direct advertising) mail fits into this category. The mail rates are much cheaper, but the regulations on how it is to be prepared are more stringent. This type of mail could be used for upgrade offers when an author has many users. The basic rate allows an author to mail a minimum of 500 pieces of up to 3 ounces for $.19 each.

Fourth-class mail is also called parcel post. The Postal Service has much competition in this area, primarily from the United Parcel Service (UPS), an independent company. Since the Postal Service has a monopoly on written communications, fourth-class mail may be used only for "packages"; a registration packet (book and disk) fits this description.

For companies that send many heavy things, UPS is generally cheaper. It is always more reliable, but cannot (by law) deliver to a post office box. On the other hand, all UPS packages are automatically insured.

In order to encourage literacy, the government subsidizes a special USPS "book" rate; I can mail a 1-pound "book" anywhere in the country for $1.05; this is considerably cheaper than UPS. Alternatively, I can use first-class "priority mail" to mail a 2-pound package of anything for $2.90. Priority mail is supposed to get anywhere in the country in two days (usually takes three). On the other hand, third-class mail is supposed to take up to ten days and usually takes three to five days.

Since the replacement cost of my materials is low, and because many of my customers supply a post office box as their only address, I use USPS book rate exclusively for domestic fulfillment. In general, the U.S. Postal Service is (probably true of all postal services) subject to much less scrutiny in crossing borders than are the other package delivery services and also requires much less paperwork, so I use its "Air Mail Small Packet" service for all international fulfillment.

Buying Postage Stamps Wholesale

You can buy your stamps wholesale at a discount, but there is a wrinkle. Amateur stamp collectors frequently purchase sheets of stamps they "know" will appreciate in value over time. Sometimes they're wrong. When the collector dies, the collection is liquidated. Collections are generally sold as lots—bidders have to bid on all of the stamps as a unit. The company that buys the lot typically acquires a number of twenty-year-old uncollectible stamps with weird face values as a part of the lot. Since the philately house can't sell them to collectors, and big business isn't interested in them because of the strange face values, the stamp company sells them off at a discount, just to recover something for them. It made its profit on the "collectible" stamps.

These stamps are available from any large philately house for about a 10 percent discount from face value. Henry Gitner currently offers stamps in $200 lots (check or money order only) at 90 percent of face value, no charge for shipping. The stamps generally range from $.03 to $.22. Call and ask for current information about discount postage:

Henry Gitner Philatelists
P.O. Box 3077
Middletown, NY 10940
(800) 947-8267

You can buy United Nations stamps from this source for an even better discount. These stamps can be used for postage to anywhere in the United States or the world. The only catch is that you have to mail everything from the UN Building in New York City. (See page 93.)

Bulk Mail

If you are regularly mailing over 500 pieces of mail (your newsletter? upgrade offers? vendor mailings?), you can probably save money with a bulk mail permit. If you wish to let people respond to you without need of a stamp, you'll also want to learn about business reply mail. Using this service, you pay only for the material that is actually returned to you. Depending on which services make sense for you, you will need as many as three post office permits:

- *Bulk Mail Permit,* which lets you mail in quantity at a lower rate.
- *Bulk Mail Indicia,* which lets you "print" your own "stamp" instead of licking thousands of bulk mail stamps.
- *Business Reply Permit,* which lets you use "no postage necessary" return mail.

In order to use many of these services, you'll need to update your mailing list to the ZIP+4 specification. The Postal Service will do the first pass for you for free (and subsequent passes if you can sneak past it). For information call the National Address Information Center, Diskette Processing Service at (800) 238-3150.

The Postal Service publishes a booklet that can help you help it to deliver your mail more quickly and accurately. Available from your local post office, ask for:

**Publication 25
"A Guide to Business Mail Preparation"**

If you need all the facts, the Domestic Mail Manual is almost totally unreadable but is what the post office uses as its Bible. It's available with your credit card ($19); call (202) 783-3238.

Finally, postage meters are worth the money once you are sending out a lot of mail. You'll need another permit from the Postal Service, after which you can rent a unit from:

Pitney Bowes	(800) 672-6937
Friden Alcatel	(800) 624-7892
Ascom Hasler	(800) 243-6275

Unless your (U.S.) customer has requested and paid for special handling, use first-class mail for anything under 8 ounces and fourth-class (book rate) for mail over 8 ounces.

If you decide your package needs additional padding (I find that the manual does a fine job on its own), rolls of bubble wrap and standard envelopes are much cheaper than buying bubble-lined envelopes.

Shipping Materials to Keep on Hand

I have a neat little postal scale that I find very helpful. Because it hangs off one of the studio lamps in my office it can't get misplaced, and it works fine for letters up to 4 ounces (or 80 grams). It is calibrated in 5-gram increments on one side and quarter ounces on the other. Because it works on the principle of leverage (rather than springs), it doesn't wear out or go out of calibration. I have found it to be very useful in making late-night postal runs and in figuring out how much stuff I can send without hitting the next bump in the postage rates. It is available (model MP4000) for $4.75 (postpaid) from:

Metal Products Engineering
3864 Santa Fe Avenue
Los Angeles, CA 90058

I keep a couple of USPS priority mail flat-rate envelopes in my office. I live reasonably close to the USPS three-digit sorting center (all 038 mail goes through this center) where there is a special mail drop that has a last pickup at midnight. Anything placed in that box before the last pickup will be in the Postal System's distribution that night. With the flat-rate envelope, you can stuff it as full as you like (no weighing necessary), put $2.90 worth of postage on it, and be pretty sure that it will be delivered the next day or shortly afterward. The envelopes are free at your local post office. You may have to investigate to determine the location of the midnight box; most mail sorting centers have one.

FULFILLMENT

It is important for your reputation and the reputation of shareware that you acknowledge all registrations promptly. At the very least, be sure to send a thank-you postcard. A key to success in this business is repeat sales, either of your products or selling other products using your mailing list. You want to keep your customers' enthusiasm.

One of the questions frequently asked by people registering *The ShareWare Book* is how to set up registration tracking. One method is to use one of the prepackaged systems. My own system evolved before simple and inexpensive tracking systems were available.

First off, the simpler the better. Even a small number of registrations can consume a large amount of time if you try to be too sophisticated. (I think most shareware authors start out this way.)

I use Microsoft Works for Windows for virtually all my word processing, spreadsheet, and database needs—including writing this book, as well as tracking registrations and printing distribution and registration envelopes.

Database elements in my Customer.wdb file are:

Contact: The name of the customer. May be blank if the sale was to a company.

Line1: Generally, a company name, and usually blank if a company name is not present. Exception is when I have a multiline address that can't be accommodated otherwise.

Line2: Generally, the street address.

Town: What you'd expect. For German addresses, this also includes the postal code, since it comes before the town.

State: Or province, or whatever makes sense for non-U.S. addresses.

ZIP: Or postal code. For countries where the postal code belongs in a different position, this is blank.

Country: Blank if the United States, otherwise the country as the U.S. Postal Service recognizes it (England/Scotland/Wales/ Great Britain become "UK" for mailing and reporting purposes).

Phone: I don't ask for this, but it often appears on checks, or people write it down. Occasionally I use it to try out ideas with "real" users.

Email: I don't ask for this, but it often appears in notes people write, or when I receive electronic registrations through Compu-Serve's SWREG.

PaidDate: For people who register with me directly, this is the date I receive their registration. For the registration services, this is the date I actually get paid (blank until then); together with the field "Agent," this serves as a crude accounts receivable system.

Paid$: The actual amount I receive (or am due). This number varies according to the registration service and because of currency fluctuations. In the case of complimentary copies to reviewers, this is 0.

Generation: I get this from my "sales code." While not infallible, it gives me some indication of the pass-along effect, since the program does tend to be run, then rearchived as it passes from hand to hand.

Invokes: From the "sales code." This tells me which registration encouragement techniques (if any) triggered this registration.

UniqueDays: Again, from the "sales code." The number of different days this customer used the product before registering.

Source: From the "sales code"; the distribution channel to which I originally sent this copy of the product.

Agent: If the customer used a registration service, its name appears here.

Shipped: The date the product was actually shipped to the customer. Usually the same as the "paid date," but useful when an agent is used.

Notes: Used for whatever doesn't fit elsewhere.

Since Works uses variable length fields, field lengths are not very meaningful for my purposes. When I have additional versions and products for this market, I'll have to add those fields.

When I receive a registration, I enter this information into the database, then I use a word processing (mailmerge) file called Ship_env.wps to print out the shipping envelopes.

Additional Resources

 I've tried to include resource information together with the other information for a subject. In a number of instances, however, resources cross so many lines that I felt it best to have a section just for them.

PUBLICATIONS

This magazine, which is *absolutely essential,* is oriented toward software and electrical engineers who are trying to bring out products on a shoestring budget. It contains good articles on the basics of business, accounting, marketing, advertising, product development, and the like:

> **Midnight Engineering**
> 111 E. Drake Road, Suite 7041
> Fort Collins, CO 80525-9828
> (303) 225-1410
> $19.95 year (6 issues)

This *very useful* magazine specializes in the issues facing software publishers. It does tend to focus on the problems faced by larger operations:

> **Software Publisher Magazine**
> Webcom Communications Corporation
> 4255 S. Buckley Road, #314
> Aurora, CO 80013
> (303) 766-1687
> $39 year (12 issues; "limited-time offer")

Billing itself as a "provocative, insightful magazine that delivers an unflinchingly honest perspective on the people and companies creating the digital revolution," this magazine is probably the best gossip column about the people in both hardware and software. If you're into hearing about the *personalities in the industry*, you'll find this interesting:

Upside Magazine
Upside Publications
P.O. Box 469023
Escondido, CA 92046
$48 year (12 issues)

Useful, especially if you are a beginner at being in business for yourself, this magazine deals well with the *nitty-gritty of running a small business*, particularly those run from the home:

Home Office Computing
P.O. Box 51344
Boulder, CO 80321-1344
(800) 288-7812
$16.97 year (12 issues)

For the best *gossip in the PC industry*, analysis of market trends and hard news, request a controlled-circulation subscription from:

PC Week
Customer Service Department
P.O. Box 1770
Riverton, NJ 08077-7370
(609) 461-2100

For those targeting the DOS/Windows/MacIntosh markets, this newsletter deals with marketing hints and trends. It tends to focus on those who sell through retail channels and will send a free issue:

Micro Software Marketing
P.O. Box 380
Congers, NY 10920
$87.00 year (12 issues)

Publications oriented to software developers include:

Software Marketing News
130 North Broadway, #300
Shawnee, OK 74801
toll free: (800) 456-0864
voice: (405) 275-3100
fax: (405) 275-3101
$29.95 year (6 8-page issues)

Software Success
11300 Rockville Pike # 1100
Rockville, MD 20852
voice: (800) 929-4824
fax: (301) 816-8945
$197 year (24 8-page issues)

Soft·Letter
17 Main Street
Watertown, MA 02274
voice: (617) 924-3944
fax: (617) 924-7299
$345 year (24 issues)

This is a start-up that is aimed at shareware authors. I'd suggest that you make sure that it got off the ground before sending any money:

Shareware Spotlights
P.O. Box 9
North Andover, MA 01845
$18 year (6 issues)

TOOLS

For general-purpose shelfware, I use PC Connection, primarily because of its excellent service and near-bottom prices. You can reach the company at:

PC Connection
6 Mill Street
Marlow, NH 03456
(603) 446-7721
(800) 800-0004

While I use shareware when I can, the right tool isn't always available. For programmer's tools, I have found good advice, service, and prices at:

The Programmer's Shop
90 Industrial Park Road
Hingham, MA 02043
(617) 740-0235
(800) 447-8041

Programmer's Connection
7249 Whipple Avenue NW
North Canton, OH 44720-7143
(216) 494-8715
(800) 336-1166

FREQUENTLY ASKED QUESTIONS

1.   Can I make a living as a shareware author?

Probably not—but you can make a living as a small software publisher who uses shareware as one marketing channel.

2.   What's the ratio of disks mailed out to shareware registrations? The ratio of downloads to registrations?

This is the classic beginning shareware author question. The answer is that there isn't any real correlation between disks sent out, uploads performed, people downloading shareware, and registrations. The reason is that there are too many other variables to consider. First, people download shareware for all sorts of reasons. Your program description may sound like it will solve an existing problem, but doesn't after they examine it. Vendors download programs as a part of maintaining their libraries. Some people will download anything in order to maintain their download/upload ratio on their local bulletin board. None of these translates into immediate registrations, but they might produce registrations later.

3.   I took a look at some of your other products, and you don't always follow your own advice. Why?

The reason I did them the way I did was because I didn't have my own advice to follow at the time.

4.   If you're so smart, why ain't you rich?

That's what my wife wants to know.

5.   Why isn't this book shareware?

Ultimately, the answer is money. I did well with *The ShareWare Book,* and it was nice keeping all the money; the average cash receipt was above $22; my costs of fulfillment were a book that cost $2.00 to print (quantity 1,000), a $.39 diskette, $1.05 in postage, and some direct labor. My royalty from this book will be less than a tenth of that. On the other hand, I fully expect Wiley to distribute many more copies of the book, I expect about a third of the buyers of the book to purchase my Software Publisher's Kit, and I expect that the added legitimacy of "being published" (as opposed to self-published) will open new doors for my career.

6. *I just want to write good code and get rich. How can I do that without all this business and marketing stuff?*

Get a publisher. Really. That's what publishers are all about.

7. *Will you act as my publisher?*

I am interested in representing products that are needed by software publishing companies, since that is the market I target already; programmer's libraries, installers, text editors, and the like come to mind immediately. I'm especially interested in representing non-U.S. products for Windows, OS/2, and UNIX here in the United States.

8. *Are you available for consulting?*

;-)

Index

Abbot, George, 18
accountant, xiii, 2, 22, 194, 209, 227, 230, 232, 233, 238
Advertise, 4, 6, 17, 18, 33, 34, 39, 40, 51, 53, 64, 94, 97, 98, 106, 108, 112, 115, 120, 121, 123, 125, 126, 148, 149, 167, 171, 178, 180, 184, 188–191, 217, 223, 224, 233, 269, 286, 293
Afghanistan, 244
agents, 125, 160, 161, 174, 238, 247, 248, 291, 292
Airborne Express, 286
airmail, 250, 253, 298
ALADDIN, 61
Albania, 244
Ami Pro, 128
Amiga, 8
APCUG (Association of PC User Groups), 57
Apple, 8
arcade, 64, 95, 154, 214
archive, 18, 28, 51–54, 58–60, 62, 63, 65, 78, 90, 94, 240, 241, 268, 291
ARJ, 63
arthritis, 114
As-Easy-As, 64
ASAD, 237
Ascom Hasler, 289
ASP (Association of Shareware Professionals), 4, 48, 49, 53, 54, 55, 59, 61, 66, 67, 74–77, 81, 87, 93, 95, 99, 186, 196, 202, 207, 234–237, 248, 278, 298
ASQ.EXE, 118
associations
　APCUG, 55
　ASAD, 237
　ASP, 4, 48, 49, 53, 54, 55, 59, 61, 66, 67, 74–77, 81, 87, 93, 95, 99, 186, 196, 202, 207, 234–237, 248, 278, 298
　EAN, 285
　ISO, 256
　Ombudsman, 236, 237
　STAR, 236, 237
　UCC, 285
AT&T, 270
ato, 60, 61, 111
Attard, Janet, 80
attorneys, 2, 212, 220
autoexec.bat, 18, 24
automatic unregistration, 108
Automenu, 280
Avery, 272

bannerware, 37, 38, 40, 108, 118, 245
BBS, ix, 7, 40, 45, 47, 49, 51–53, 55, 57–59, 62, 63, 72, 74–80, 82–86, 88, 90, 93, 98, 106, 112, 121, 159, 176, 193, 213, 234, 235, 237, 241, 242, 269, 296, 298
Be Real, 101
Begware, 235
bookkeeping, 174, 231

Bookland, 285
BookMasters, 278
bootstrap, viii, ix, xiv, 44, 205
Borland, 108, 167, 221, 222
bounties, 113
Bowker, R. R., 3, 183, 285
Bowyer, Chris, viii, 259, 260
Boxer, 298
Branding, 75, 90, 94, 103, 107, 117, 203
BrownCor, 273
Budgetware, 174, 251
bug, 19, 25, 26, 48, 72, 99, 109, 117, 118, 235, 252, 259
Bulgaria, 244
bulletin boards, ix, 7, 40, 45, 47, 49, 51–53, 55, 57–59, 62, 63, 72, 74–80, 82–86, 88, 90, 93, 98, 106, 112, 121, 159, 176, 193, 213, 234, 235, 237, 241, 242, 269, 296, 298
bundled, 33, 37, 159, 160
BusinessWeek, 249
Buttonware, 165
BXA (Bureau of Export Administration), 242–244, 246
Byte Magazine, 174

Cambodia, 244
Camelot, 277
Campbell, Tim, viii, 176
cash (flow), ix, 26, 36, 43, 49, 88, 108, 135, 159, 161, 162, 194, 199, 205, 230–233, 249, 250, 297
catalogs, 1, 3–5, 33, 37, 40, 41, 43, 46, 49–53, 55, 64, 65, 73, 97, 124, 137, 149, 161–164, 167, 169, 170, 180, 184, 216, 221, 253, 268, 272, 274, 276, 278, 280, 298
CD, 40, 55, 65, 66, 181, 234, 235, 248
channel, xi, xiv, 2, 3, 5, 13, 31–39, 44–46, 49, 64, 72, 73, 98, 104, 108, 115, 117, 119–122, 154, 165–167, 170, 178, 184, 191, 193, 221, 248, 264, 278, 279, 284, 285, 292, 294, 296
China, 244
Chromatic Communications, 167, 168, 183
CIS, viii, xii, 23, 25, 43, 46, 48, 52, 55, 60, 61, 63, 78, 88, 92, 110–112, 193, 201, 202, 218, 231, 235, 237, 264, 265, 269, 291, 298
classified ad, 119–121, 123, 125, 189, 241
COMDEX, 184, 186
Commander Keen, 97
communications
　telephone, 45, 85, 87, 113, 131, 135, 138, 145, 187–189, 193, 196, 203, 205, 210, 228, 245, 269–271
　television, 107, 131, 140, 179, 188
Compass / New England, 28, 29, 54, 55, 83, 209
complaints, 26, 55, 97, 98, 108, 114, 196, 200, 222, 224, 236, 277
compliance, 54, 105, 210, 222, 223, 243, 244
compression, 17, 23, 29, 40, 58, 62, 74, 106

THE SOFTWARE PUBLISHER'S KIT

As mentioned earlier in this book, a Software Publisher's Kit is offered separately. The contents of the kit are updated monthly so that it will be current when it arrives. The kit is made up of two parts:

1. Coupons for a whole bunch of services and products you are likely to need, including $35 off on an introductory CompuServe membership, and special deals on VendInfo, Boxer Text Editor, Shareware Tracker, and Andrew Saucci's upload service.

2. A 1.44 Mb DOS formatted diskette with:
   - An *updates file* that contains corrections for this book (they do change a lot), plus new and interesting new ideas, facts, and contacts that have been uncovered since publication of the book.
   - An *ASP product catalog* for finding both competitors and cooperators.
   - ASP vendor and bulletin board *lists* in ASCII format.
   - An *SDN kit* that will let you send to 13,000 FidoNet bulletin boards.
   - A copy of LHA, the *freeware installation program.*
   - A *text file of letters* using the sources in this book: everything from requesting forms for directory listings to subscribing to magazines. Just pull into your word processor and use them.
   - A copy of *Unzip,* a small (30Kb) freeware unzipper.
   - *Lots more stuff* that wouldn't fit on this page (really!).

Please send just $10 and the coupon below to receive your kit by first-class mail (free shipping anywhere, including free airmail overseas).

Name: ....

Address: ....

....

....

City, State, ZIP: ....

Country: ....

Alternative means of contact (phone, CompuServe, or Internet) in case the mailcarrier can't deliver:

Please print clearly; this is your shipping label (photocopy if you don't want to cut the book).

I can accept a $10 bill (picture of Hamilton) or U.S. checks (MICR code on bottom) International Money Orders for $10 (U.S.). At a 25% premium over the exchange rate (I have a greedy bank), I can take Canadian checks in Canadian dollars, and major currencies (Pounds, Marks, Francs, Yen). I can't process credit cards, purchase orders, or EuroCheques at this price.

Mail to: Bob Schenot (Boot v. 2.0)
             P.O. Box 117
             Portsmouth, New Hampshire 03802-0117 USA

Products may have to be substituted according to current license terms and availability. If you want to check on current contents or have any other questions, contact me at 70511.720@CompuServe.com